Decisions and Diplomacy

Decision-making and diplomacy are key elements of twentieth-century international history. Focusing particularly on the origins and aftermath of the Second World War, but expanding the scope broadly, this volume includes original papers on: the management of British foreign policy between 1914 and 1945; the League of Nations and its impact on national and international diplomacy in the 1930s; the response of key powers to international crises and events such as the Manchurian crisis, the Abyssinian crisis, the Spanish Civil War and the Korean War; the intricacies and significance of conference diplomacy, such as the Geneva Disarmament Conference of 1932–34 and the Anglo-American Bermuda and Washington conferences of 1957. Of contemporary interest, there is an important and intriguing essay on the attempt by the Holy See to negotiate a concordat with Belgrade to consolidate the unity of Yugoslavia in the late 1930s.

This collection commemorates two gifted historians and teachers of the International History Department of the London School of Economics: George Grün and Esmonde Robertson. Each piece has been specially commissioned to cover an important aspect of decision-making and diplomacy in the twentieth century.

Dick Richardson is Senior Lecturer in International Relations and Green Politics, University of Teesside. He is the author of *The Evolution of British Disarmament Policy in the 1920s* (1989) and co-editor of *The Green Challenge* (1994). **Glyn Stone** is Assistant Dean of the Faculty of Humanities at the University of the West of England, Bristol. He is the author of *The Oldest Ally: Britain and the Portuguese Connection 1936–1941* (1994) and several articles on Anglo-French and Anglo-Portuguese relations.

Books published under the joint imprint of LSE/Routledge are works of high academic merit approved by the Publications Committee of the London School of Economics and Political Science. These publications are drawn from the wide range of academic studies in the social sciences for which the LSE has an international reputation.

1895–1995
An LSE Centenary Publication

Decisions and Diplomacy
Essays in Twentieth-Century International History

In memory of George Grün and Esmonde Robertson

Edited by Dick Richardson and Glyn Stone

LONDON AND NEW YORK

First published 1995 by Routledge

2 Park Square, Milton Park, Abingdon, Oxon OX14 4RN
711 Third Avenue, New York, NY 10017, USA

Routledge is an imprint of the Taylor & Francis Group, an informa business

First issued in paperback 2016

Transferred to Digital Printing 2006

Copyright © 1995 Dick Richardson and Glyn Stone
Individual contributions © 1995 individual contributors

Typeset in Times by Intype, London

All rights reserved. No part of this book may be reprinted or reproduced or utilised in any form or by any electronic, mechanical, or other means, now known or hereafter invented, including photocopying and recording, or in any information storage or retrieval system, without permission in writing from the publishers.

Notice:
Product or corporate names may be trademarks or registered trademarks, and are used only for identification and explanation without intent to infringe.

British Library Cataloguing in Publication Data
A catalogue record for this book is available from the British Library

Library of Congress Cataloging in Publication Data
A catalog record for this book has been requested

ISBN 978-0-415-09795-6 (hbk)
ISBN 978-1-138-96728-1 (pbk)

Publisher's Note
The publisher has gone to great lengths to ensure the quality of this reprint but points out that some imperfections in the original may be apparent

Contents

Notes on contributors   vii
Foreword by Donald Cameron Watt   x
Acknowledgements   xv

Introduction   1

1 Economics and the crisis of British foreign policy management 1914–45   9
Robert Boyce

2 Intelligence and the Lytton Commission, 1931–33   42
Ian Nish

3 The Geneva Disarmament Conference, 1932–34   60
Dick Richardson

4 The Chiefs of Staff, the 'men on the spot' and the Italo-Abyssinian emergency, 1935–36   83
Steven Morewood

5 The 'proferred gift': the Vatican and the abortive Yugoslav concordat of 1935–37   108
Peter C. Kent

6 Britain, France and the Spanish problem, 1936–39   129
Glyn Stone

7 Britain and appeasement in the late 1930s: was there a League of Nations' alternative?   153
Peter J. Beck

8 The atomic bomb and the Korean War, 1950–53   174
Callum MacDonald

9 **Restoring the 'special relationship': the Bermuda and Washington conferences, 1957** 205
Michael Dockrill

Index 224

Notes on contributors

Peter J. Beck is Professor of International History at the University of Kingston. As an undergraduate student at the London School of Economics and Political Science he was tutored by George Grün, with whom he later collaborated, along with Esmonde Robertson, in supervising higher degree students at Teesside and Kingston Polytechnics. He is the author of five books, including *The Falkland Islands as an International Problem* (1988) and *The International Politics of Antarctica* (1986). He has written numerous essays and articles on international history and edited *British Documents on Foreign Affairs: Reports and Papers from the Foreign Office Confidential Prints*, League of Nations vols 1–10.

Robert Boyce is Senior Lecturer in International History at the London School of Economics and Political Science. A former colleague of both George Grün and Esmonde Robertson, he is the author of *British Capitalism at the Crossroads 1919–1932: A Study in Politics, Economics and International Relations* (1987) and joint editor with Esmonde Robertson of *Paths to War: New Essays on the Origins of the Second World War* (1989).

Michael Dockrill is Reader in War Studies at King's College London and a former colleague of George Grün and Esmonde Robertson. He is the author of several books, including *The Cold War 1945–63* (1988), *British Defence since 1945* (1989) and, with C.J. Lowe, *The Mirage of Power: British Foreign Policy 1902–1922* (2 vols, 1972). In addition he has written numerous essays and articles on international history and is co-editor with J.W. Young of *British Foreign Policy 1945–1956* (1988). He is also Chairman of the British International History Group.

Peter C. Kent is Professor of History at the University of New Brunswick. He obtained his PhD from the London School of Economics and Political Science under the supervision of Esmonde Robertson, having previously completed a Master's dissertation under the supervision of George Grün. He is the author of *Pope and the Duce: International Impact of the Lateran Agreements* (1981) and co-editor with John F. Pollard of *Papal Diplomacy in the Modern Age* (1994). He has written several other essays and articles on Vatican relations.

Callum MacDonald is Professor of History at the University of Warwick and a former colleague of George Grün and Esmonde Robertson. He is the author of a number of books including *The United States, Britain and Appeasement 1936–1939* (1981), *Korea: The War before Vietnam* (1986), *Britain and the Korean War* (1990) and *Last Battle: Crete 1941* (1993) and he has written several essays and articles on American and British foreign policy both before and after the Second World War.

Steven Morewood is Lecturer in Social and Economic History at the University of Leicester. He received his PhD from Bristol University in 1985 with Esmonde Robertson as his external examiner. He published his *Pioneers and Inheritors: Top Management in the Motor Car Industry 1890-1972* in 1990, and his second book, co-written with D.H. Aldrcoft, *Economic Change in Eastern Europe*, is scheduled for publication in 1994.

Ian Nish was Professor of International History at the London School of Economics and Political Science where, until his recent retirement, he worked with George Grün and Esmonde Robertson for many years as colleague and friend. He is a leading authority on Japanese foreign policy before 1945 and the author of many books, including *Japanese Foreign Policy 1869–1942: Kasumigaseki to Miyakezaka* (1977), *Origins of the Russo-Japanese War* (1985) and *Japan's Struggle with Internationalism: Japan, China and the League of Nations 1931–1933* (1993). He is also editor of *The Anglo-Japanese Alienation 1919–1952* (1982).

Dick Richardson is Senior Lecturer in International Relations and Green Politics at the University of Teesside. He is a graduate of the London School of Economics and Political Science where he also obtained his PhD under the supervision of George Grün. He is the author of *The Evolution of British Disarmament Policy in the 1920s* (1989) and co-editor with Chris Rootes of *The Green Challenge: The Development of Green Parties in Europe* (1994). He has written several articles and essays on disarmament and arms control, on which subject he is currently writing another book, scheduled for publication in 1995. Since 1988 he has been Treasurer of the British International History Group.

Glyn Stone is Assistant Dean of the Faculty of Humanities at the University of the West of England, Bristol. He obtained his PhD from the London School of Economics and Political Science under the supervision of Esmonde Robertson. He is the author of *The Oldest Ally: Britain and the Portuguese Connection 1936–1941* (1994) and has written several articles and essays on Anglo-French and Anglo-Portuguese relations. He is currently writing a book on the great powers and the Iberian peninsula between 1931 and 1941. Since 1988 he has been Secretary of the British International History Group.

Donald Cameron Watt recently retired as the Stevenson Professor of International History at the London School of Economics and Political Science where he was for many years a colleague of George Grün and Esmonde Robertson. He has written very extensively on a range of subjects within International History and is the author of the acclaimed *How War Came: The Immediate Origins of the Second World War 1938–1939* (1989) and also *Personalities and Policies: Studies in the Formulation of British Foreign Policy in the 20th Century* (1965), *Too Serious a Business: European Armed Forces and the Approach to the Second World War* (1975) and *Succeeding John Bull: America in Britain's Place* (1984).

Foreword

Donald Cameron Watt

This book is dedicated to the memory of two members of the Department of International History at the London School of Economics and Political Science, George Grün and Esmonde Robertson, by some of their former graduate students and academic colleagues. I have been asked to write an introduction, on the general grounds that I was closely associated with them for all the time they were on the staff of the LSE and shared with them in the development of the graduate side of the department, especially where the study of twentieth-century history was concerned. The development of the department and the specialisation in the history of international relations undertaken by two successive tenants of the Sir Daniel Stevenson Chair, Professors W. Norton Medlicott and James Joll, into one of the three or four most important and significant in the world, owed a good deal to their work, their presence and their inspiration.

They shared their dedication to and absorption in their subject, as they shared in the admiration and affection of their students. They were also alike, in that neither achieved promotion beyond the rank of senior lecturer, a rank too often regarded as the graveyard for old workhorses rather than a reward for scholarship. They differed in that Esmonde wrote by choice; George, equally by choice, did not. Esmonde was a scion of the old Anglo-Irish aristocracy, and from the more personally eccentric wing of that much ignored group. George, though thoroughly anglicised by Winchester and Cambridge, remained recognisably Viennese, *sympathisch, Stimmungsvoll*, a man who lit up every room he entered by his sheer *joie de vivre*. As scholars, both read voraciously. It was my constant experience that any book which covered our common fields of interest I wished to consult from the LSE Library was almost certainly already 'out' to one or the other of them.

Foreword xi

Esmonde I first met when he was acting as research assistant to the later Chichele Professor of the History of War at Oxford, Norman Gibbs, when he was working for the Cabinet Office Historical Section on what was to be the first volume of the Grand Strategy Series in the official History of the Second World War. With his excellent German, Esmonde was screening the German military archives which fell into Allied hands at the end of the war, so that Gibbs could take these materials into consideration for his volume. It was this work that formed the basis for Esmonde's first book, *Hitler's Pre-War Policy and Military Planning, 1933–39* (London, 1963), a book whose arguments have stood up well to the flood of research and monographs that have been produced since that date. By the time it appeared, Esmonde had left the Cabinet Office Historical Section for the university world, first at the Queen's University of Belfast, and then for Edinburgh. He came to LSE in 1968 as an applicant for a job which had been intended for someone much younger than himself, conquering the selection committee by his verve, his enthusiasm and the sheer quality of his scholarship. In the right mood he could charm the hind leg off a donkey, and he awoke affection among all who dealt with him. He was, even by the standard of some of his colleagues, not the most organised of persons. Organisation and the methodical side of life was provided by his German wife, Olive, whom he encountered while he was working at the Institut für Zeitgeschichte in Munich with its substantial archive of private papers and testimonies.

He was a slow worker and it was to be some time before his next major work appeared. Before that he had produced one of the most useful collections of reprinted articles to cross the university teacher's desk, *The Origins of the Second World War* (London, 1971), which brought together nearly all the significant articles and printed lectures on the theme from Alan Bullock's Raleigh Lecture to the British Academy on the controversy provoked by his friend Alan Taylor onwards. The introduction which Esmonde contributed to this collection was an admirable summary of the previous decade's research.

His own interest, however, was turning from Hitler to his Italian partner, Mussolini. The link was provided in part by his interest in the German ambassador to Rome in the 1930s, Ulrich von Hassell, into whose family he had married. But Esmonde's interest was furthered by the immediate entry he secured into the Italian records through the link he established with the great scholar and biographer of Mussolini, Professor Renzo di Felice, one of whose pupils,

Rosario Quartararo, spent a considerable period in London under Esmonde's benign supervision, collecting materials for her own massive study of Anglo-Italian relations in the 1930s, *Roma tra Londra e Berlino; Politica Estero Fascista dal 1930 al 1940* (Rome, 1980).

Mussolini as Empire Builder (London, 1977), the outcome of this change in direction, told the full story of the Italo-Ethiopian conflict in its international context for the first time since the opening of the British archives for the 1930s. It was typical of Esmonde's concern for true scholarly balance that his book was written from the point of view of the Axis that was the outcome of the conflict, rather than from the much more marketable point of view of Britain's wavering between Wilsonian devotion to the Covenant of the League of Nations and *Realpolitik*. It is still the standard work on the subject in English.

As his retirement approached, Esmonde was engaged to put out a new version of his *Origins of the Second World War*. The enterprise was not to be a simple reissue, with the authors given the opportunity to revise their contributions in the light of subsequent research. It was to be a wholly new work. But before it could take shape, Esmonde was dead. On his last day at LSE before his retirement, he called in to collect some books and materials to take home. He died in the cab which was taking him to Charing Cross station to catch a train back to his home in Sevenoaks, from a massive heart attack. The book was completed by his colleague and close friend, Dr Robert Boyce, who is a contributor to this volume. It appeared in 1989 under the title, *Paths to War. New Essays on the Origins of the Second World War* (London, 1989).

George Grün was appointed to LSE in 1950 by the then Stevenson Professor of International History, Sir Charles Webster. At that time the only teaching in International History at LSE was given to specialists in International Relations. Webster had few graduate students, gave few lectures and indeed conducted such teaching as he did from his home rather than from the School's premises. It was only as a recognition of the increasing number of students coming to LSE, in the great postwar rush of wartime veterans taking advantage of the Further Education Grants then made available as part of the demobilisation package to those whose school performance had rendered them eligible for university entrance, that Sir Charles obtained the LSE's permission to replace Philip Reynolds, his assistant, by two junior lecturers, of whom George was one.

Webster was replaced in 1953 by W. Norton Medlicott, then

Professor of History at the University College of the South-West, which was some years later to become the University of Exeter. The appointment was widely criticised as indicative of the LSE's alleged preference for inconspicuous mediocrity to genius, when it become known that the other two scholars interviewed for the Chair were A.J.P. Taylor and E.H. Carr. It was only later that it became clear that the LSE had made the correct choice. Medlicott's scholarship was considerable. He was also an excellent judge of young scholars. The growth of the LSE's Department of International History to its present eminence as a centre of research and a graduate school of international reputation was very largely effected under his direction.

Much of this growth followed traditional lines, with the emphasis at the undergraduate level being placed on the development of special subject papers which required the students to demonstrate a knowledge of set documentary sources. George began by teaching a special subject on the negotiations after the First World War for an Anglo-French entente, this being one of the very few areas in the inter-war years on which the British government had published a Blue Book of diplomatic correspondence. This was replaced later by a special subject on the Manchurian crisis of 1931, which George took charge of until the appointment of the to-be-distinguished scholar of Japanese foreign policy, Ian Nish. With Ian's arrival George developed a new special subject, first at the undergraduate level, and then from the mid-1960s onwards, with the development of the taught Master's degree in twentieth-century international history, at the Master's level, on the negotiation of the Treaty of Versailles.

With the revision of the 1958 Public Records Act (which had set a limit of fifty years before government archives were released to the Public Record Office) in 1967, when the closed period was cut to thirty years, the whole thrust of new graduate research changed to the twentieth century. George and Esmonde both played their parts in supervising theses in this new field. Applicants for the taught Masters programmes flooded away from the nineteenth and eighteenth centuries into the twentieth-century programme. George played a major part in that.

In the much advertised year of troubles at LSE, 1968, it was noticeable that even when the governors closed the LSE's premises for much of the Lent Term, the International History staff insisted on continuing to teach wherever they could find accessible premises, and that the students in the department turned out almost unanimously for those classes. It was not surprising that a survey of student attitudes to their teachers, somewhat to the surprise of those who undertook it, revealed that 80 per cent of the students in the International History Department (classified as authoritarian) expressed strong satisfaction with the quality of their teachers and teaching. Indeed the undergraduates sitting their finals that summer, despite all the disruption, achieved one of the best overall records of class-marks in the department's history. One of the current editors (Dick Richardson) was a member of that cohort.*

This collection of essays is intended as a homage to the memories of two of the best-loved teachers and supervisors in the LSE's Department of International History. To the outside world George Grün and Esmonde Robertson may appear as minor figures in a department whose mere existence in a School of the Social Sciences may strike many as anomalous. Their strength and commitment to the subject and the affection with which they are remembered should show how strong a hold the subject, originally lodged at LSE with the foundation of the Stevenson Chair in the early 1930s, has had on the loyalties of its students, and raise eyebrows not at the presence of the subject in a school of the social sciences, but at the narrowness of the pretensions of those who would deny the relevance of a subject whose themes include the causes, course and consequences of two world wars, examined from their source materials, to any School which claims to study aspects of social organisation and social conflict. Those who were colleagues or students with George and Esmonde count themselves, ourselves, fortunate to have known them and to have worked with them.

EDITOR'S NOTE

* As first student representative in the International History Department and founder of the International History Society, I can confirm that the department was both authoritarian *and* an excellent teaching department!

DR

Acknowledgements

The editors gratefully acknowledge the assistance of the following during successive stages of the project: the LSE Graduate School, for its help in tracing former students of George Grün and Esmonde Robertson; Dr Patrick Davis and Deborah Spring, LSE Publications Officers, for their material support in negotiating with the publishers; Professor Ian Nish, in his role as chairman of the LSE Publications Committee; and Professor Donald Cameron Watt, for his continuing interest and support and for writing the Foreword. And last, but by no means least, Jean Connell and Beryl Wilkinson of the University of Teesside, for word-processing the manuscript and generally keeping the editors sane.

Introduction

The genesis of this collection of essays was a conversation on the beach at Aberystwyth in December 1987, between sessions of the annual conference of the British International Studies Association (BISA) which, incidentally, was also the occasion for the discussions which led to the establishment of the British International History Group. The conversation on the beach elicited a mutual feeling that the editors' respective PhD supervisors, George Grün and Esmonde Robertson, should be honoured in some way for their dedicated support of their postgraduate students. A collection of essays in which contributions would be made by ex-students and colleagues seemed to be the most appropriate way to honour them. Tragically, in the case of Esmonde Robertson, who had died in 1986, this would have to be posthumously. As tragic was the sudden death of George Grün, who passed away shortly before Christmas 1993. Consequently, these essays are now dedicated to the memory of two gifted people who touched and influenced the lives of their authors in so many beneficial ways.

In deciding upon contributions it was clear that it would not be possible to concentrate upon just one particular theme in international history, but it was agreed that the temporal aspect should concentrate on the period both before and after the Second World War to provide some cohesion and focus. The outcome has been a collection which will contribute to several areas of debate in international history, for example institutional perspectives, such as the management of British foreign policy during the period of the two world wars and the League of Nations as an alternative to appeasement in the late 1930s; specific critical events such as the Manchurian crisis, the Abyssinian crisis, the Spanish Civil War and the Korean War; and conference diplomacy concerning disarmament at Geneva in the early 1930s and the restoration of the Anglo-American relationship at the Bermuda and Washington conferences of 1957. For ease of reference, the essays are arranged chronologically.

In the first essay, Robert Boyce seeks to develop the debate surrounding the failures of British foreign policy after 1914 by focusing upon the lack of foreign policy co-ordination within Whitehall, especially the failure to co-ordinate economic and political policy. He does not seek to lay retrospective blame at the door of the Foreign Office or the Treasury but rather to explain that interdepartmental friction transcended personalities or specific policy issues and arose mainly from 'the failure to adapt institutions exercising prerogatives defined in an era of economic liberalism, to meet the requirements of an age of advancing state intervention in economic affairs'. In detail he shows how the Foreign Office recognised the need for institutional change and made three attempts to implement reforms between the outbreak of the First World War and the beginning of the Second. The role and influence of Victor Wellesley, godson of Queen Victoria, Controller of Commercial and Consular Affairs at the Foreign Office and later Deputy Under-Secretary, is highlighted in this connection. Despite the laudable endeavour to reform, the decline of Foreign Office authority over external policy continued and Boyce concludes that this was probably inevitable in view of 'the massive growth of state intervention in domestic economic affairs, the abandonment of free trade and the adoption of a managed currency and overseas lending controls, the increasingly sophisticated techniques of economic analysis and the decline in Britain's formal commitments overseas'.

It is generally agreed, in Ian Nish's words, that the Lytton Commission Report of 1932 was 'a remarkably shrewd document' and that even if no international solution to the Manchurian crisis was forthcoming it could not be said that 'the judgements of Lytton and the League were not based on sound information and analysis'. That the Lytton Report reached such balanced and realistic conclusions is surprising in view of the advanced age of the commissioners, their complete ignorance of China, the absence of Chinese or Japanese linguists, and above all the deliberate smokescreen generated around the proceedings by the Japanese and Manchukuo authorities. In his essay, Professor Nish reveals for the first time the existence of 'a sort of intelligence network' which grew up around the Commission and which consisted of more junior members of staff who were less inhibited than the commissioners and who managed to probe beneath the surface. Two individuals amongst this intelligence network receive particular attention. First,

Introduction 3

William Waldorf Astor, who was just 24 years old and had travelled widely in Japan, Manchuria and China during 1929 and 1930. Lord Lytton himself conceded that Astor could do things he could not do because of his youth which 'enabled him to get away with them!' Second, George Moss, who was a fluent Chinese speaker with recent experience in the British consular service in China. According to Nish, the Lytton Commission was well served by Moss, who performed 'the essential role of conducting covert conversations with a wide range of Chinese leaders'.

At the height of the Manchurian crisis in February 1932, when Japanese forces threatened the international settlement at Shanghai, the World Disarmament Conference which had been in preparation since 1926 opened in Geneva. Dick Richardson in his essay draws attention to the paucity of historical studies on the subject of disarmament and states his intention to shed 'further light on the disarmament problem' and to explain the importance of the Geneva conference in the 'shift of international power relationships in the early 1930s'. The various positions adopted by the leading powers are analysed in some depth both from the political/diplomatic standpoint and their responses to the technical difficulties inherent in detailed disarmament negotiations. Richardson argues that since Japan was in direct confrontation with the League it was improbable that she would sign a disarmament agreement at Geneva. In practice, therefore, the quest for general disarmament was replaced by the search for a regional convention covering western and central Europe, which required a solution to the problem of the French demand for security and the German demand for equality of rights. Certainly, the search for such an agreement was the essential feature of the Geneva negotiations. In this connection, Richardson argues that a number of powers played almost maverick roles at the conference, with the United States deliberately refusing to play a leading part, Italy vainly seeking to secure her military equality with the other leading European states and the Soviet Union presenting herself as an unknown quantity who might side with either Germany or the western powers. He argues that the contradiction between French security and German equality was capable of solution provided Great Britain mediated effectively, and that this she failed to do, preferring instead to pursue her own interests. Britain wanted power without responsibility on the European continent. In reaching this conclusion, Richardson's essay, based on research in the British archives, confirms the work of Maurice Vaïsse, who has based his conclusions on work in the French archives.

4   *Introduction*

Unlike the Geneva disarmament talks, the Abyssinian crisis has been the subject of considerable study by historians. Steven Morewood deliberately avoids a retread of familiar territory. His essay focuses upon four main themes 'pivoted around the question of whether military action could and should have been taken': the limited and ineffectual measures which were instigated against Italy to prevent her conquest of Abyssinia; the underlying reasons for this lukewarm response; the views of 'the men-on-the-spot'; and the ramifications of the débâcle for international peacekeeping and British grand strategy. The limited nature of the British response, already well known to historians, is brought into even sharper relief by Morewood's revelation of 'the extent to which [Stanley] Baldwin's government went to minimise incidents in the Mediterranean and Red Sea as a vital element of its caution-tinged strategy' which can be explained by the deep-seated reluctance of the Admiralty to become involved in sanctions enforcement. In explaining why there was an ineffectual response, he rehearses several well-known reasons such as the French reluctance to alienate Italy as a potential ally against Germany and the risk to British and empire security, especially the defence of the Far East, but he also stresses the less well-known consideration, namely the fear that an Abyssinian defeat of Italy, a fellow imperial power, could prove disastrous to western interests by encouraging national movements for independence within the French and British colonial empires. In emphasising the views of the 'men-on-the-spot', Morewood effectively challenges Rosario Quartararo's judgement that if an Anglo-Italian war had broken out in 1935 the outcome of 1940–41 would have been reversed. He stresses that throughout the crisis the 'men-on-the-spot' in the Mediterranean and Egypt remained ultra-confident of dealing with the Italians. In assessing the ramifications for peacekeeping by the League, he emphasises the missed opportunity for reining in the dictator powers and the impact of Italy's growing confidence which contributed towards scuppering the long-standing Admiralty policy of reinforcing Singapore with the so-called 'Main Fleet'.

The current problems of those at Geneva who are searching for a mediated peace between the warring factions of the former Yugoslavia remind us of deep-seated divisions that have existed for decades, if not centuries, within that troubled area of the world. In December 1937, on recognising the demise of the proposed concordat between the Holy See and Yugoslavia, Pope Pius XI predicted that the rejection of his 'proffered gift' by the parliament in

Belgrade would come to be regretted by many – and not only from religious reasons but from political and social considerations too. Peter C. Kent in his essay rejects the idea that the concordat, signed in July 1935, would, if ratified, have formed the basis for reconciliation and prevented much subsequent bloodshed during the Second World War and later. There was no missed opportunity for national integration because examination of the evidence, Kent argues, demonstrates exactly the opposite. The concordat had been negotiated between King Alexander of Yugoslavia and the Holy See with little reference to Yugoslav religious or ethnic sensibilities. It represented an attempt by the king to use religious institutions to force his country's political integration, to which end he was prepared to deal with a foreign power, the Holy See, in the expectation that Yugoslav Catholics would do his bidding. When it came to ratification it was naturally opposed by Orthodox Serbs, but it also elicited little enthusiasm among Roman Catholics. The only basis for agreement between domestic factions was opposition to the concordat and, in particular, opposition to the royal dictatorship of Alexander which produced it. Indeed, after the king's death, at the hands of an assassin in Marseilles in October 1934, his successors merely went through the motions of concluding negotiations and quickly realised that the concordat was a domestic political liability. Kent concludes that the non-ratification of the concordat signified 'the rejection by Yugoslavs of the centralised direction given by Alexander's royal dictatorship' while at the same time indicating 'the rejection by Yugoslav Catholics of political tutelage by the Vatican.'

Unlike the current situation in Yugoslavia, the civil war in Spain between 1936 and 1939 became an international battleground in which the European great powers sought to enhance their ideological, strategic, military and economic interests with varying degrees of success. Since the end of the conflict historians have compared the effective assistance given by Nazi Germany and fascist Italy to the Nationalist forces in Spain with the inadequate support provided to the democratic Spanish Republic by the western democracies, Britain and France. The blame for the demise of the Republic has been laid at the door of these two powers, but in apportioning blame most historians persist in vigorously prosecuting the British whilst almost excusing the French. In his essay, Glyn Stone seeks to place France firmly in the dock alongside Britain with no opportunity to escape conviction. Stone argues that the degree of convergence in British and French policy, both during and after the Spanish

6 *Introduction*

conflict, was far greater than that of divergence, for example in creating and maintaining the non-intervention policy, in cancelling action which might be seen as contravening non-intervention, such as the closing of the Pyrenees frontier, and in seeking a *modus vivendi* with the Franco regime after the civil war. That French policy converged with Britain most of the time does not, however, provide proof that France merely hung on to the coat tails of her only potential major ally. On the contrary, successive French governments were quite capable of making up their own minds in the Spanish context and settling on policies which best served their country's interests. Sympathy for the cause of the Spanish Republic was never permitted to override political and strategic realities.

The marginalisation of the League of Nations following the end of the Abyssinian crisis and the outbreak of the Spanish Civil War in 1936 continued through to the outbreak of war in September 1939. During the last years of peace, both the British and French governments preferred to actively appease the dictator powers, especially Nazi Germany, rather than to pursue the alternative of containing fascist ambitions by means of a viable and effective collective security policy. As Peter J. Beck shows in his essay, there was widespread support within Britain for such a policy. Apart from members of the League of Nations Union, a wide and diverse group of anti-appeasers (including the Labour, Liberal and Communist parties and sections of the Conservative Party) supported collective security. Winston Churchill's 'Arms and the Covenant' campaign closely paralleled the Labour Party's efforts to persuade Neville Chamberlain's government 'to make support of the League the whole basis of its policy'. Although this 'relatively wide spectrum of support' for the League failed to turn Chamberlain and his Cabinet away from appeasement, it succeeded in forcing them onto the defensive and compelled them to defend their position by using rhetoric which conceded the desirability of League ideals. In emphasising the collective security alternative, Beck also provides an alternative interpretation to the general consensus among historians that Chamberlain was correct in dismissing the League option as a feasible policy option.

After the Second World War, which appeasement manifestly failed to prevent, great power diplomacy had to take into account the existence of atomic and then nuclear weapons. In retrospect, it appears to be a truism that the nuclear reality made general war impossible and the concept of 'limited warfare' inevitable after 1945. However, Callum MacDonald in his essay on the Korean War reminds us that although the Americans, Russians and Chinese kept the war limited rather than risk a wider global conflict – which even at that early stage of nuclear development would have been hugely destructive – it was a close run thing. There were voices close to the US government who urged the use of atomic weapons in the conflict, including Dwight D. Eisenhower shortly after his retirement as Chief of Staff of the US army in June 1950. While the Truman administration rejected this advice, MacDonald emphasises that atomic weapons played a key role in the diplomacy of the Korean War and that the circumstances in which they might actually be employed were also kept under continuous review, to the obvious discomfort of the British government. Moreover, in April 1951 complete atomic bombs were deployed in the Far East as a last resort to ensure that the Americans did not suffer a humiliating defeat. From the perspective of a global nuclear threat, the Korean War was undoubtedly the most dangerous episode in the Cold War before the Cuban Missile Crisis of October 1962, but MacDonald again reminds us of the tremendous destructive effects of conventional warfare by pointing to the deaths of over 2 million North Korean civilians, around a quarter of the population, in a bombing campaign 'that went far beyond anything done in Vietnam in a conscious programme of using air power to destroy a society'.

If the British were concerned to restrain the atomic diplomacy of the USA during the Korean War, it was the Americans who constrained British actions at Suez in 1956, thereby creating a crisis in the so-called Anglo-American 'special relationship'. Michael Dockrill reveals in his essay how the British government, encouraged by President Eisenhower and his Secretary of State, John Foster Dulles, sought to quickly repair the rift and to re-establish the relationship on firmer foundations. The means of achieving this were the Bermuda and Washington conferences held in March and October 1957 respectively. The detailed preparations for these conferences by the British were impressive and appeared to have paid dividends with the restoration of the relationship. Certainly, the Prime Minister, Harold Macmillan, thought the Washington conference was a great success in building on the foundations laid at Bermuda and in creating an intricate machinery for close future co-operation. Indeed, the Washington conference seemed to have given Britain precisely what she had been striving to achieve for most of the 1950s: almost wholehearted American support for her atomic and thermo-nuclear programmes, and close collaboration at working levels between Whitehall and Washington on joint policies across

8 *Introduction*

the globe. In the short term, a new Anglo-American partnership based on equality rather than subordination seemed to have been forged in 1957, but despite Eisenhower's encouraging words Britain could not escape the predicament of her continuing decline. The failure to stabilise the British economy and its consequent impact on British defence and overseas policies made subordination inevitable and this was highlighted by Macmillan's deal with John F. Kennedy over Polaris in 1962. As Dockrill concludes: 'Britain's subordinate status, which had become glaringly apparent by the events of 1956, was, in the end, and despite Macmillan's optimism, confirmed by the Bermuda and Washington conferences'.

These nine essays, covering important areas of twentieth-century international history, are presented here as a tribute to two gifted historians and teachers who left their mark not only on generations of grateful students, but also on their academic colleagues.

Dick Richardson
University of Teesside

Glyn Stone
University of the West of England, Bristol

February 1994

1 Economics and the crisis of British foreign policy management, 1914–45

Robert Boyce

In June 1941, with the war in its grimmest phase, Anthony Eden, the British Foreign Secretary, outlined in Parliament his scheme for reforming the management of Britain's external relations.[1] The Consular and Commercial Diplomatic Services were to be amalgamated with the Foreign Office and Diplomatic Service, the Foreign Office was to be divorced from the Home Civil Service, and new priorities were defined for the Foreign Office particularly in the area of external economic affairs.[2] Britain's pre-war foreign policy, summed up in one word 'appeasement', was commonly held to have failed disastrously, and the Foreign Office was now temporarily marginalised still further by the priorities of military strategy. The Eden reforms were intended to restore confidence in the Foreign Office by increasing its independence and authority within Whitehall. Just how sensitive Foreign Office officials were at this time to charges of failure in the pre-war period became apparent shortly after Eden spoke, when bitter controversy erupted over the part played by Sir Warren Fisher between 1919 and 1939 as the former Permanent Secretary of the Treasury and the first formally designated head of the Civil Service.

According to several prominent retired diplomats, Fisher had exploited his dual position at the Treasury and as head of the Civil Service to cripple the Foreign Office in its management of external relations. Among other things, he had withheld Foreign Office papers from circulation to the Cabinet and interfered in internal appointments.[3] Meanwhile the Treasury and other economic ministries had asserted their influence on issues far beyond their competence, with the result that British foreign policy had lost its coherence and the framework of security had been allowed to collapse. Thus the failure of foreign policy was due not to the Foreign Office but to the decline of the Office's authority within Whitehall.

These charges were officially denied, and after the war several historians entered the lists on Fisher's side.[4] In the first place, they pointed out, some of the Foreign Office officials who made allegations against Fisher had been abroad for much of the period in question, and so could scarcely be sure of what had taken place in London. By the same token, other former officials in a position to judge Fisher had lent no support to the charges against him. Second, the suggestion that Fisher had contributed to a policy of appeasement could not have been further from the truth. Not only had Fisher been a zealous opponent of appeasing Germany and a champion of rearmament, but also his Foreign Office critics had been advocates of the very appeasement policy with which he was identified.

Archival evidence now available does little to enhance the reputation of either side in the dispute. There are few grounds for regarding Foreign Office officials as the unheeded patriots of the inter-war period.[5] At the same time it is also clear that Fisher did compromise Foreign Office efforts to manage external relations, and other ministries also contributed to the problem of policy co-ordination. Even those Foreign Office officials who eschewed criticism of Fisher had cause to deplore the lack of foreign policy co-ordination during the inter-war years, the problem the Eden reforms were designed to remove.[6] Yet clearly the source of inter-departmental friction transcended personalities or specific policy issues. Simply put, it arose mainly from the failure to adapt institutions exercising prerogatives defined in an era of economic liberalism, to meet the requirements of an age of advancing state intervention in economic affairs. The Foreign Office to its credit recognised the need for institutional change and made no fewer than three attempts to implement reforms between the outbreak of the First World War and the start of the Second. Its efforts were severely constrained, both by opposition from elsewhere in Whitehall and divisions within the Foreign Office itself. Whether this goes far in explaining Britain's policy failures seems more than a little implausible. But there is at least room for supposing that the failure to co-ordinate economic and political foreign policy made a bad situation worse.

Until 1914 the Foreign Office contributed to the management of external economic relations only at one remove, by maintaining the framework of international relations in which British trade and commerce could thrive. The Office, it is true, took responsibility for the Consular and Commercial Attaché Services, and occasionally intervened directly in such matters as the negotiation of most-

Crisis of British foreign policy management 11

favoured-nation treaties and the competition for foreign banking or railway monopolies. But, as Consular officials bitterly attested, the Office gave little regard to the actual business of promoting or facilitating commerce,[7] and contemporary accounts amply attest to the fact that diplomats regarded economic affairs as scarcely worthy of their attention. As the former Commercial Attaché, Sir Francis Oppenheimer, recalled, 'Lord Hardinge ... in the spirit of the Old Diplomacy saw in trade and commerce something sordid.'[8] Merchants and industrialists had long sought greater assistance from the Foreign Office in their pursuit of overseas markets, and much of the criticism of the Foreign Service as a preserve of the aristocracy arose from frustration at the lack of support abroad.[9]

In 1907 the Foreign Secretary, Sir Edward Grey, responded to complaints by calling upon overseas missions to delegate one member each to advise and assist British merchants, manufacturers and shipowners.[10] But dissatisfaction with the Foreign Office among businessmen continued to mount when the Foreign Office resisted further involvement in this undignified activity. By this time some inroads had been made on the influence of *laissez-faire*, the doctrine that the state could promote prosperity best by interfering least in private commerce. But if the Foreign Office took little interest in economic aspects of foreign relations before the war, it was as Sir Eyre Crowe, a senior official, said, because it was still widely thought to be 'wrong in principle to interfere in such matters',[11] and since British economic policy was characterised by free trade, unrestricted capital movements and the gold standard, there was little occasion for inter-departmental conflicts over economic and political priorities in the management of external policy.

The first attempt by the Foreign Office to implement reforms arose out of the profoundly altered conditions of the war. By 1916 Whitehall and the business community had turned away from *laissez-faire* in reaction to the evidence of Britain's military and economic unpreparedness at the outset of the war, the contemporary experience of massive state intervention in economic affairs, and the anticipation of intensified rivalry for raw materials and markets in the postwar world.[12] Discussions had already begun within the Foreign Office on the need to adapt to the altered postwar environment when the Board of Trade took the initiative in proposing the reorganisation of Britain's commercial representation overseas. The Board proposed replacing the Commercial Attaché Service, now under Foreign Office control, by an expanded Trade Commissioner Service, now operating under the Board's direction in the

Dominions, and subordinating the Consular Service (also under Foreign Office control) to the same organisation.[13] Ostensibly, this proposal offered a solution to the much criticised dual control of commercial intelligence, whereby the Consular and Commercial Attaché services under Foreign Office direction collected information on firms and markets abroad, while the Board's Commercial Intelligence Department performed the analysis and dissemination to the commercial community in Britain. However, Victor Wellesley, the new Controller of Commercial and Consular Affairs at the Foreign Office, and Crowe, strenuously objected. For one thing it raised the spectre of divided control over British representation abroad, something the Foreign Office had always resisted. Second, it threatened to eclipse Foreign Office authority in Whitehall in the post-war era, when diplomatists anticipated that foreign relations would be dominated by economic considerations.

Wellesley, like Crowe, was profoundly influenced by his intimate knowledge of German affairs. Having grown up in Germany and observed German commercial expansion at first hand as a commercial attaché, he had become convinced that Germany's 'really scientific economic organisation', its rationalised industry and its state-supported commercial expansion overseas, had been the mainspring of its military aggression, and that Britain's failure to understand these developments had been responsible for its own lack of preparedness in 1914.[14] The lesson for Wellesley was clear. Henceforth the Foreign Office must reach beyond the confines of conventional diplomatic circles into the world of commercial affairs to locate the sources of power and comprehend the nature of national ambitions. In itself, he reasoned, the collection of commercial intelligence was a routine activity which could happily be left to the Board of Trade. In the aggregate, however, the management of commercial intelligence was vital to foreign policy making.

> The point to be borne in mind is that economic investigation of foreign countries is in its ultimate aim highly political in character for it prepares the material necessary for the shaping of policy for war as well as peace purposes.

If this was true before the war, it would become even more so afterwards when all the powers would follow the German example and harness their financial, industrial and commercial resources of *raisons d'état*.

> A new epoch of economic life lies before us and all the signs of

the time point to the economic factor becoming the dominant one in our future foreign relations.[15]

Since Britain would compete in a world of aggressive trade relations, it was inevitable that the department of state which controlled foreign commercial intelligence would also control foreign policy.

To Lord Grey, a thoroughgoing economic liberal and personal friend of Walter Runciman, President of the Board of Trade, and to most Foreign Office officials, the Board's readiness to assume responsibility for promoting overseas trade was probably welcomed.[16] As Grey's successor at the Foreign Office, Lord Balfour, wrote in 1917, 'it is certainly not the business of this Office to deal with international economics, nor is it qualified to do so'.[17] But the Foreign Office was not prepared to abandon the principle of unity of foreign representation or the presumption that the Diplomatic Service alone possessed the requisite skills to do the job effectively. Spurred on by Wellesley, the Foreign Office therefore forced the issue by instituting a committee, chaired by Crowe and comprising representatives of industry and commerce as well as Wellesley and other officials, to formulate a scheme for managing post-war commercial intelligence.

The businessmen, as they were to do again in the inquiries that followed, strongly endorsed the Foreign Office claim to control a unified and expanded commercial intelligence service. It was perhaps true that the Office had shown regrettably little interest in commercial affairs before the war. But with the recent strengthening of the Commercial Attaché Service and the Office's unique prestige and diplomatic skills, businessmen continued to regard it as the most potent defender of British interests overseas.[18]

Runciman was stung by this challenge and refused to back down. Having already received the Treasury's assurance of substantial funds for his own plans, he refused to contemplate the implied diminution of the Board of Trade's role.[19] Further negotiations took place between the two departments and a second official inquiry was held in 1917. The result was a compromise, with the creation of the Department of Overseas Trade (Development and Intelligence) incorporating relevant components of the Foreign Office and Board of Trade, and placed under the direction of a parliamentary under-secretary who was responsible to both ministries.[20]

The Department of Overseas Trade (DOT) satisfied no one. Funded at the Treasury's insistence by a separate parliamentary vote,[21] and aggressively directed by Sir Arthur Steel-Maitland, MP, the DOT immediately staked out broad claims to executive authority for 'Development' as well as 'Intelligence'.[22] The Foreign Office soon complained of its intervention in the question of consortium lending to China. The Board of Trade similarly took exception to its unannounced decision to negotiate directly with foreign governments on trade finance. Both the Board and the Foreign Office also complained that the redirection of correspondence to the new department disrupted their mutual relations as well as their respective activities.[23] Dissatisfaction came to a head in April 1919 when the Minister for Reconstruction, Sir Auckland Geddes, denounced the DOT as an administrative disaster and, on the grounds that domestic and foreign commerce must be treated together, urged Cabinet colleagues to agree to its absorption into the Board of Trade.[24] The Cabinet, reflecting its business before politics outlook, sympathised with Geddes's solution. But in view of the complexity of the issue, it elected to institute another inquiry, known as the Committee to Examine the Question of Government Machinery for Dealing with Trade and Commerce, and chaired by the Lord Chancellor, Lord Cave.

In June 1919 Geddes, now President of the Board of Trade, repeated his argument for total control of commercial intelligence before the Cave Committee. Wellesley hoped that Lord Curzon, the acting Foreign Secretary, would personally respond, and was dismayed to find that he disdained to endorse even a written brief. Crowe, in Paris at the peace conference, was therefore forced to return to speak for the Foreign Office.[25] Fortunately for the Office, it was supported by nearly all the merchants and manufacturers who appeared before the committee. The Board saw no alternative but to advise the continuation of the DOT within more restricted terms of reference, which the committee accepted.[26] Defending the committee's report in Cabinet on 23 July 1919, Lord Cave acknowledged his own initial preference for Board control, but pointed to the 'very strong feeling amongst commercial men against the proposal that the Department of Overseas Trade should be abolished or absorbed into the Board of Trade.'[27]

The Cabinet reluctantly adopted the report for lack of an acceptable alternative. Geddes nevertheless persisted in his efforts to extend the Board of Trade's role, and with support from Cabinet colleagues he soon secured the relocation of the main DOT offices to a building shared by the Board of Trade in the City.[28] Wellesley was infuriated when this was decided without reference to the

Foreign Office and thoroughly depressed by the outcome of the bureaucratic struggle. The Consular and Commercial Attaché Services were now responsible to the Foreign Office only through the intermediary of the DOT, and the DOT was now physically remote from the Foreign Office and represented in Parliament by a minister of state with divided loyalties. This left little prospect of increased foreign service competence in analysing commercial intelligence or effective co-ordination of politico-economic policy. The opportunity for appropriate reforms had however passed. Not only was the Foreign Secretary unenthusiastic about any initiative that appeared merely to involve promoting trade, but also with the demand for drastic public sector retrenchment and return to the spirit of *laissez-faire*, the principal motive for widened interest in reforms was now virtually gone.

As Wellesley had foreseen, Britain's post-war foreign relations became thoroughly bound up with economic issues: the persistence of massive reparations and war debt demands, and the currency chaos, trade protection and other consequences of the war remained throughout the 1920s not only important but often crucial elements in international affairs. This led the Treasury, the Board of Trade and the Bank of England to play major roles in British external relations. But because of the persistence of *laissez-faire* or liberal attitudes within Britain, they adopted an essentially *ad hoc* approach to external affairs, treating them as problems to be disposed of in order to return to 'normal' conditions such as had prevailed before the war; and they persisted in regarding themselves as agencies of technical expertise uninfluenced by 'political' considerations.[29] This led to regular friction with the Foreign Office, particularly in the immediate post-war period. In February 1919, for instance, Curzon and the Foreign Office found themselves opposed by the Treasury over aid to the Baltic states to resist revolutionary threats.[30] Later the same year similar friction occurred over aid to Austria.[31] Subsequently, severe friction arose over reparations policy, which went to the heart of Anglo-German relations but which the Treasury insisted upon regarding as a financial matter and therefore solely its responsibility.

The issue became acute in the spring of 1921, when plans were made for a conference in London to settle the amount of reparations to be levied on Germany and other central powers. Foreign Office officials found themselves virtually excluded from arrangements and complained to Curzon.[32] Despite his sympathy, however, the Treasury refused to share authority over the issue. At the urging of senior advisers, Curzon formally complained to the Chancellor of the Exchequer, Sir Robert Horne, in November. It was unacceptable, he wrote, that the Foreign Office should be excluded from reparations policy-making when clearly 'it possesses a political importance of which the Foreign Office must inevitably bear the brunt'. More generally, he complained, decisions taken without regard for the views of all interested departments contradicted 'sound principles of administrative organisation', and 'the present case does not unhappily stand alone'.[33] Curzon's efforts brought no result. Sir Warren Fisher, the Permanent Secretary to the Treasury, had vigorously promoted teamwork within Whitehall since his additional appointment as head of the Civil Service. He dismissed the Foreign Office complaints as evidence of empire-building, and left his Treasury colleagues to continue their sway over external economic relations.

The predicament that confronted the Foreign Office is well illustrated by the dispute over capital exports which arose in 1927. The Office, anxious for increased foreign investment, particularly in Latin America where dollar loans were threatening to eliminate British influence altogether, and mindful of the strategic importance of foreign assets during the recent world war, approached the Treasury that year to propose the removal of the 2 per cent stamp duty on bearer bonds, the usual form of foreign loans.[34] The Treasury pointed to the weakness of Britain's balance of payments and refused to act. For the time being the Foreign Office accepted this decision.[35] But the following year the Foreign Office received reports that a French or Franco-American banking syndicate, benefiting from strong diplomatic support, had defeated its British rivals in the competition for several large European state loans, and that the proceeds of the loans would be earmarked for exports from the lending countries.[36] The Bank of England seemed unconcerned and made no effort to keep the Foreign Office informed of its own loan promotion activity. This led Wellesley to comment, 'A good instance of the disastrous individualistic spirit which still pervades finance and industry in this country while collective effort is becoming more and more the order of the day everywhere else'.[37] The Treasury continued to inveigh against state 'interference' in financial-industrial affairs on the traditional *laissez-faire* grounds that it could only reduce the efficiency of markets.[38] Yet with British financial houses clamouring for official support and British industry desperate for export orders, some co-ordination of effort seemed essential. Accordingly, the Foreign Office drafted a proposal for linking foreign loans with exports and removing the stamp tax, which it justified on the grounds that the strain on the balance of payments from increased lending would be offset by merchandise exports, and the direct loss to the Exchequer from the removal of the tax would be offset by increased taxes from corporate profits.[39]

The DOT initially responded to the Foreign Office proposal with enthusiasm, and suggested that in addition a transfer tax might be imposed on the sale of British overseas firms in order to retain this source of export orders.[40] Soon, however, Sir Edward Crowe, Comptroller-General of the DOT, wrote to the Foreign Office to say that although the banking advisers to the Export Credit Guarantee Department had recently affirmed the City's willingness to drop its long-standing opposition to tied lending, he could not take sides on matters of policy. As he pointed out, the DOT was a subsidiary department and must also defer to the Board of Trade.[41] In the event, Treasury opposition abruptly halted the Foreign Office initiative. A Foreign Office memorandum for circulation to the Cabinet had already received the endorsement of Sir Austen Chamberlain, the Foreign Secretary, when Fisher intervened to insist upon its withdrawal.[42] The Foreign Office had to be content with a private interview with Montagu Norman, the Governor of the Bank of England. As an intensely secretive man, and head of what was formally a private institution under the gold standard, Norman's views were predictable. He charged that the French had thrown their weight around quite improperly in order to obtain control of certain recent loans, and he regretted the necessity of Britain's stamp duty on bearer bonds which undoubtedly handicapped British lending institutions. However, he admitted that for British lenders to offer foreign loans in return for the promise of commercial markets was merely to subsidise British industry, which would be unnecessary if industry were efficient enough to compete in world markets. Since the effect of selling uncompetitive goods must be to reduce the security on the loan, he would recommend that City firms should tie loans to exports only if the government were prepared to accept liability for the loans. Chamberlain, as Norman doubtless anticipated, immediately ruled this out.[43]

As late as 1927, when the Foreign Office again protested against its exclusion from policy-making on reparations, the Treasury had made no reply to Curzon's complaint of five years before.[44] Departmental relations were therefore already strained when preparations were begun for another major reparations conference at the Hague in the summer of 1929, and at this point Treasury–Foreign Office differences were fully exposed.

To Arthur Henderson, the Foreign Secretary in the new Labour government, and to the Foreign Office, a new reparations settlement was imperative. They were principally concerned for the success of the impending Anglo-American naval conversations, but Owen Young and several other prominent Americans had helped to draft the new reparations plan and American goodwill was now bound up with its adoption.[45] Sir Josiah Stamp, Britain's expert on the committee of experts responsible for producing the plan, claimed that, despite appearances, it would cost Britain only nominal losses and could not be further modified without certain repudiation by other interested states.[46] Hence, British demands for an increased share of reparation receipts would not only cause deadlock at the forthcoming conference and trigger a serious financial crisis, but also jeopardise the naval conversations. Another of the Labour government's objectives was to secure an immediate withdrawal of all Allied troops from the Rhineland in the interests of appeasing Germany. The ambassador in Paris, Lord Tyrrell, reported that France would agree to an early withdrawal of her troops if, but only if, the committee's plan were accepted without modification.[47] Thus a second major foreign policy objective also depended upon acceptance of the plan as it stood.

Fisher reluctantly and Sir Richard Hopkins, the Treasury's Controller of Finance, more readily shared the Foreign Office view that the reparation plan should be endorsed unchanged.[48] However, Sir Frederick Leith Ross, Deputy Controller of Finance and the Treasury's most experienced international negotiator, dismissed the plan on the grounds that Germany could not sustain a heavy burden of reparations much longer, and therefore Britain should make no permanent concessions on her claims for the sake of securing a purely temporary solution.[49] The Chancellor of the Exchequer, Philip Snowden, had devoted much of the recent election campaign to attacks upon the Tories for their profligacy in the Anglo-French war debt agreement.[50] He readily endorsed the viewpoint expressed by Leith Ross and left him to prepare his brief for Cabinet.

Available records make it impossible to tell what the Cabinet took into account on 17 July 1929 when it settled policy for the forthcoming reparations conference.[51] However, it is noteworthy that Snowden's brief was the only one formally presented, and the result was a clear victory for his policy of dealing separately with the economic and political issues at the conference while demanding modification of the experts' plan. The Hague conference soon ran into difficulties as a result of Snowden's demands and sterling weakened in the foreign exchanges, but heedless of appeals from Ramsay MacDonald, the Prime Minister, and Henderson, Snowden held fast until he had secured concessions from the other participating countries. Returning to London, Snowden was hailed as the stoutest defender of British interests since Palmerston. His tactics had proved successful. Yet the fact remained that he had jeopardised the government's principal foreign policy objectives and even the stability of sterling for strictly limited, even trivial, financial ends.[52] Through failure to analyse the costs and benefits in a comprehensive way, Snowden had been allowed to pursue the worst sort of brinkmanship.

Events the following year led to further conflict between the Foreign Office and the Treasury. The Treasury had long taken the view that the Bank of England, as the agency responsible for safeguarding the value of sterling, must be protected from political pressure, and insisted that all communication between Whitehall and the Bank must go through the Treasury. In conformity with this policy, the Treasury in March 1930 refused the Foreign Office's request to approach the Bank of England on the matter of appointments to the new Bank for International Settlements (BIS). The Treasury's policy was consistent, but in a world where liberal principles seldom prevailed over nationalism, it also appeared dogmatic and increasingly unrealistic. According to E.H. Carr of the Foreign Office, the Treasury went to 'absurd lengths' to safeguard the independence of the Bank of England. As for the BIS, it was responsible for reparation transfers and hence had 'more to do with international politics than international lending', and the Bank of England had been 'deplorably weak' in asserting British interests during its establishment.[53] In the autumn of 1930 another source of friction between the Foreign Office and the Treasury occurred over the question of compensation for British holders of depreciated wartime franc loans. Snowden, without consulting the Foreign Office, issued a *démarche* in support of the loan holders.[54] The Foreign Office regarded this as wholly futile and calculated only to annoy the French government.[55] At the year end Treasury officials engaged in conversations with their French counterparts without explaining their objectives to the Foreign Office or enabling it to temper the nervous but largely unfounded rumours of large-scale political bargaining that the conversations provoked throughout Europe.[56]

In March 1931 the Treasury reversed its position and supported the Foreign Office in a renewed effort to link British foreign lending to export orders.[57] Worsening British payments problems rather than a willingness to fuse the economic and political dimension of foreign policy had brought the Treasury to accept this further intervention into private sector affairs. But the Bank, which the Treasury had for so long shielded from political influence, remained opposed to such interference and succeeded in burying the proposal.[58] One reason why the Bank prevailed was that Treasury knights as well as central bankers regarded foreign lending controls as at best a regrettable departure from the still valid principle of free trade in capital. Another reason, one may surmise, derives from the fact that after the war most of the Treasury's authorities on international finance migrated to the Bank, leaving the Treasury ill-equipped to argue its case.[59] By this time the Foreign Office had come into conflict with the Board of Trade and Dominions Office over commercial policy. Here, too, the Foreign Office sought to gain leverage in its dealings with foreign powers by developing an integrated approach to external relations, only to find the other departments unprepared to concede authority over their respective spheres of executive responsibility.

From the autumn of 1929 the search for a solution to the economic crisis was dominated by two conflicting approaches. One championed by William Graham, President of the Board of Trade in the British Labour government and a zealous free trader, sought to reverse the trend towards trade protectionism by means of multilateral negotiations; in 1929 Graham had actively promoted 'economic disarmament' starting with a multilateral tariff truce to be arranged under the auspices of the League of Nations.[60] The other approach, popular in many quarters on the Continent, was for regional agreements, drawing together countries prepared to make mutual concessions while leaving out of account others that were unwilling to co-operate on the same basis. The latter approach appeared to find practical expression in a proposal put forward almost simultaneously with Graham's at the Tenth League of Nations Assembly in September 1929 by Aristide Briand, the French Premier and Foreign Minister, when he announced his intention to promote a plan for the federation of Europe.[61]

Senior officials of the Board of Trade, whose economic ideas had been formed around the turn of the century, strongly favoured free trade as the appropriate policy for Britain in view of her dependence upon world trade. They disliked foreign protectionism, but they disliked discriminatory trade barriers even more, for in face of protectionism alone Britain would at least be no worse off than her trade competitors, while in face of discriminatory barriers Britain as a free trade country would have no means of negotiating fair treatment in foreign markets.[62] The Foreign Office, consistent with the memorandum by Sir Eyre Crowe of 1907 setting out the bases of British foreign policy,[63] also favoured free trade for its contribution to international harmony, and the Office's initial reaction to Briand's proposal was a distinctly cool one.[64] But unlike the Board of Trade, the Foreign Office did not favour free trade for its own sake, and, holding that Briand's continued control over French foreign policy was vital to European stability, Foreign Office officials were prepared to offer a cautious but sympathetic response to Briand's plan when it became clear that anything less would endanger his position.[65] The Cabinet insisted upon a cool response to Briand, and at the Eleventh League of Nations Assembly in September 1930 the Board of Trade representative actively discouraged European trade preference proposals.[66] However, the collapse of the second tariff truce conference in November served notice that Graham's approach to trade liberalisation was also impracticable. If capable of resisting the introduction of discriminatory schemes by other countries, Britain lacked the tariffs or quotas with which to bargain for reductions in foreign trade barriers. International efforts to halt the slide into protectionism thus reached an impasse, while the world economic crisis and its political corollary, nationalism, rapidly intensified.

Foreign Office frustration at the necessity to defer to other departments whenever international relations assumed an economic dimension became manifest in December 1930 when Wellesley, now Deputy Under-Secretary, requested his colleagues' support for the creation of a politico-economic intelligence department within the Office.[67] The postwar years had only strengthened Wellesley's conviction that Germany's prewar economic organisation had been the harbinger of a world-wide trend. The Soviet Union's state trading system was now but the most extreme example. Even the United States, albeit with little conscious design, was 'commercially, industrially and financially ... invading every part of the globe [and] acquiring an economic stranglehold, which is gradually tightening and squeezing out all competitors'. And though the United States might be regarded as 'the best example of modern economic imperialism serving, for the present at any rate, purely economic ends', already there was 'a disquieting similarity between present-day conditions in the United States and those of pre-war Germany'. Hence, while the threat of major military conflict may have receded since the war, economic conflict impelled by the universal problem of 'over-production' was rapidly intensifying and threatening to re-create the conditions in which militarism flourished.

The fact was, Wellesley argued, the old calculus of power – of 'armies, navies, annexations, dynasties' – had lost its relevance in an age of large-scale industry and economic inter-penetration. Foreign policy could no longer be divorced from domestic policy, nor could the economic component be divorced from the political. The dissatisfaction of the continental countries with Aristide Briand's belated subordination of the economic aspect of European federation to the political (under British pressure), the League's increasing preoccupation with economic issues, and the fact that 'at least 75 per cent of the work of our missions abroad is economic', illustrated the changed state of affairs. The Foreign Office must anticipate new forms of conflict which, if fought with tariffs, quotas and tied loans rather than armies, were none the less dangerous to Britain. This, Wellesley argued, required better co-ordination of foreign policy-making, and 'a new machinery and a new technique'.

First, Wellesley called for a new department to supervise the flow of economic information to and from overseas missions, to serve the political departments of the Office and as a clearing-house for politico-economic information, to advise the Secretary of State on the foreign policy implications of economic issues and to liaise with other ministries in Whitehall. Here all that was needed was a young, professionally qualified economist to act as adviser. The director and other staff should come from within the Office, since the department's function was essentially political, not economic. Second, Wellesley called for Foreign Office officials to be given a basic training in political economy. Officials might serve an apprenticeship in the new department; new recruits should be required to have some prior formal training. Wellesley reckoned that the total cost of his proposal was only £2,000 per annum, for the salary of the economist. This he regarded as a small amount to pay to enable the Office to provide direction through the tangle of politico-economic problems confronting Britain.

Wellesley's proposal led to a survey of politico-economic co-ordination in the foreign ministries of the other powers and extensive comment from other senior officials in the Office. It was then forwarded to Arthur Henderson, the Foreign Secretary, who on 13 March 1931 passed it on to MacDonald, the Prime Minister, requesting his approval.[68] MacDonald pompously commented that 'I have been urging steps in this direction for some time'. But he

Crisis of British foreign policy management 23

indicated misapprehension of Foreign Office objectives by suggesting that a solution was possible merely by reorganisation of the DOT.[69] The DOT was designed to identify opportunities for foreign trade; the Foreign Office's proposed new department was intended to identify economic issues of importance to national security and to provide a means of co-ordinating policy towards them. Before further steps could be taken, however, the crisis over the Austro-German customs union scheme erupted, bringing pressure for trade preferences in Europe to a head.[70]

The Board of Trade welcomed a complete customs union between Germany and Austria as a step, albeit small, towards European trade liberalisation, but it firmly refused to allow a precedent to be established by countenancing the temporary trade preferences which Austrian industry appeared to require in the first stages of the scheme.[71] Controversy over the scheme, however, went far beyond the question of trade preferences because it pointed towards total *Anschluss*, which was ruled out by the peace treaties, and the Treasury condemned it on account of its evident damage to international financial confidence.[72] Foreign Office officials were hardly less opposed on political grounds, but they recognised that there were also dangers of obstructing a scheme presented as a solution to the economic crisis without coming forward with an alternative, when unemployment and bankruptcy were the common lot of the central European countries.[73] After an initially negative reaction, France too indicated her recognition of the need for a constructive response and approached Britain with a series of proposals, their common features being European industrial cartel arrangements, trade preferences for the benefit primarily of east European cereal producers, and special treatment for Austrian industry.[74]

The Board of Trade's objections were sufficient to rule out support for the first French plan at an inter-departmental meeting on 22 April, and the French were advised of its unsuitability.[75] The French were however not prepared merely to acquiesce in events, and appeals for a more constructive British response now also came from Alexander Loveday, the economist and recently named head of the League of Nations Financial Section, Sir Eric Drummond, Secretary-General of the League, Emile Francqui, the Belgian financier-statesman, and Montagu Norman, Governor of the Bank of England, among others.[76] This led Foreign Office officials to look with sympathy upon a modified French plan, which offered an ostensibly liberal approach to intra-European tariff reductions while ensuring most-favoured-nation treatment for Britain.[77] The officials decided that the Board's economic objections had been removed, and after hurried telephone calls to the Board of Trade and elsewhere in Whitehall, Henderson left for the emergency meeting of the League Council in Geneva carrying a Foreign Office brief endorsing the French plan.[78]

Ironically it was the Dominions Office, anticipating a more aggressive British policy on imperial trade preferences, rather than the Board of Trade on free trade grounds, that first raised objections to the Foreign Office position.[79] With the Foreign Secretary already in Geneva, the Dominions Secretary, J.H. Thomas, was encouraged to call for a complete review of British policy before taking further action. Graham at the Board of Trade added his support, and MacDonald, who knew nothing of recent developments, agreed.[80] Wellesley expressed utter exasperation at this turn of events.

> The real trouble arises from the fact that we have no machinery for dealing with these big politico-economic problems as a whole and in relation to foreign and Dominion affairs. It is this that makes decisions in matters of this kind doubly difficult and at best somewhat haphazard. In fact, without the proper consideration of such problems in all their bearings which can only be done by a Department which can focus all essentials, it is almost impossible to resist the temptation to run with the hares and hunt with the hounds with all the attendant risks of falling between two stools in the end.[81]

Writing to Henderson in 'his struggle with the P.M.', for the creation of 'a politico-economic intelligence Department in this Office', Wellesley pointed to the unhealthy preoccupation of British foreign policy with disarmament, which dealt only with 'a symptom of much deeper underlying causes'. Germany had 'seized upon them with the result that they were greatly jeopardising the success of the Disarmament Conference.... And who is the prominent figure in all this? Dr. Ritter, head of the politico-economic intelligence Department of the German Foreign Office'.[82]

Henderson, who took little interest in economic affairs, was one of the most zealous advocates of disarmament and was soon to become chairman of the League Disarmament Conference. Nevertheless he authorised Sir Robert Vansittart, the Permanent Under-Secretary, to call on the Prime Minister and explain the need for improved machinery for managing 'the economic cross-currents' affecting foreign policy.[83] Noel Baker, a junior minister in the Foreign Office, wrote to MacDonald in support of the request.[84] He assured him that the Office sought merely to establish a 'thinking department', which would not have executive functions and would not 'trespass' on the authority of other ministries. It would not attempt to control economic or even politico-economic policy, but would enable the Office to have 'a larger voice in the joint determination' of policy, which recent events had shown to be absolutely necessary. 'During the past year and a half I have often been shocked at the extent to which our opinions on economic questions, which impinge on foreign policy, are either unsought or ignored'. Crowe of the DOT lent support to the proposed Foreign Office department, which would 'bridge an existing gap between us'. But Henderson, to whom economics was a mystery, personally took no further action, and MacDonald now ruled out 'new and expensive reforms', while warning against any step that would disrupt interdepartmental harmony. Sir Walford Selby, Henderson's private secretary, later asserted that MacDonald's opposition was due to Fisher's intervention, which seems only too plausible in light of Fisher's practice of approaching his political masters in the familiar terms of an equal.[85] Sympathetic historians have pointed out that he zealously pursued Civil Service unity and was hostile to any action that might be construed as evidence of departmental rivalry.[86] But he remained a Treasury man, and seen from other vantage points his defence of unity was all too compatible with Treasury control. Certainly he opposed the Foreign Office initiative: just how strongly is apparent from the archival record, which confirms that he actually demanded the surrender of the Foreign Office memorandum and warned against its circulation to other ministries.[87]

Before reforms could be further considered, the financial crisis brought an end to the economically internationalist Labour government and the advent of a National government dominated by Conservatives bent upon promoting closer imperial economic relations. In September 1931 the decision was taken to abandon the gold standard and allow sterling to float. Two months later, when the worst was over, the Foreign Office renewed its call for an integrated approach to policy-making. A departmental memorandum prepared by Wellesley and circulated to the Cabinet in November argued that all the major problems confronting Britain including German agitation for treaty revision, French opposition to disarmament, and American hostility to war debt reduction were integrally linked. Britain must therefore not allow her newly acquired leverage contained in the threat of introducing trade protection and the option of stabilising sterling to be dissipated in piecemeal initiatives.[88]

Economic policy no less than foreign policy was at stake, for without an 'all-in' solution there could be no restoration of confidence which was a pre-condition of recovery. In retrospect it can be seen that this was thoroughly sound advice. But the recently formed Cabinet was dominated by Conservatives who were determined to break with the past and introduce a policy of imperial protectionism. Britain's new-found freedom of action in monetary, financial and commercial policy thus only further reduced the Foreign Office's role as the co-ordinator of external relations.

The Treasury, assuming executive authority for international monetary policy once the gold standard was abandoned, largely eclipsed the Bank of England in the management of sterling. The Board of Trade similarly gained in executive authority with the institution of emergency duties in 1931, a general tariff in 1932, the negotiation of preferences with the Dominions, and the negotiation of trade agreements with foreign countries. Other ministries, notably the Dominions Office and the Ministry of Agriculture and Fisheries, also shared in the extension of state control over external economic relations. Hitherto the Foreign Office had been frustrated by the reluctance of the economic ministries to treat inroads on *laissez-faire* as opportunities for political bargaining. Now despite abandoning the last vestige of *laissez-faire*, foreign economic policy continued to be treated as wholly separate from foreign policy itself. Co-ordination within Whitehall was not improved. And with the government preoccupied with economic recovery, not only did the Foreign Office become the unwilling agent of the economic ministries, but also the latter increasingly bypassed the Foreign Office by developing their own independent diplomatic channels.

The strain on foreign policy management was nowhere greater than in Anglo-French relations, which the Foreign Office regarded as the key to European tension. In October 1931 the Foreign Office discovered that Sir Frederick Leith Ross was holding private conversations at the Treasury with German representatives on the question of reparations, an issue of intense interest to both Britain and France, without consulting the Foreign Office.[89] At Wellesley's urging, Lord Reading, the Foreign Secretary, complained to the Treasury against this 'highly improper' practice. The Treasury files confirm, however, that Leith Ross continued undeterred.[90] Meanwhile in October the Ministry of Agriculture unilaterally issued an order sharply extending restrictions on potato imports. The order was justified as a sanitary measure, which the Foreign Office did not query. But whereas the benefit was limited to a small section of a single British industry, the effect was to arouse the hostility of the enormously influential farm lobby in France, which in turn constrained French statesmen in their negotiations with Britain on much more important economic and political issues when the Ministry of Agriculture refused to reconsider its decision.[91] In November 1931 the Board of Trade asserted its authority by demanding that the Foreign Office should firmly oppose the French decision to impose a 15 per cent surtax on imports from countries with depreciated currencies.[92] The Foreign Office, stressing the importance of subordinating secondary issues to the pursuit of a general settlement, pleaded for a more flexible approach, but the Board was not prepared to relent in the defence of most-favoured-nation rights for the sake of non-economic objectives.[93] Foreign Office–Treasury relations similarly suffered from mutual incomprehension. While the Foreign Office regarded the Treasury's preoccupation with the cancellation of reparation claims as politically short-sighted, the Treasury privately deprecated the Foreign Office's preference for subordinating international monetary and commercial policy to larger political objectives, and condemned co-operation with France, so long as reparations continued, as 'suicidal'.[94]

Repeated efforts by the Foreign Office to influence economic policy-making proved ineffectual. In September 1931 the Foreign Office had requested a place in the Prime Minister's Economic Advisory Council (EAC).[95] But the EAC, which had not met since the previous spring, was already moribund, and only Leith Ross received an *ex officio* seat on the subordinate Economic Information Committee which continued to function. In October Charles Howard Smith, of the League of Nations and Western department of the Foreign Office, warned Wellesley of the danger that the Foreign Office would become 'merely a post office' for Board of Trade initiatives and foreign protests in the event that Britain abandoned free trade in favour of trade protection.[96]

> The effect upon our general foreign policy of the adoption of tariffs or any other protective measures is obviously so great that it seems to me essential that the Foreign Office should be ... 'in on the ground floor' from the start.

Wellesley fully agreed. But the aura of scientific objectivity that surrounded tariff-making allowed for no such 'political' influence. Despite the obvious impact of tariffs upon Britain's external relations, a Foreign Office request to bring Britain's foreign representations to the notice of the Import Duties Advisory Committee was rejected by the Board of Trade on the grounds that it would 'definitely bring the Committee into the arena of foreign policy'.[97] Nor did the Foreign Office gain a voice in the discretionary control of foreign lending. The advisory committee that was eventually established was comprised of independent members – and a Treasury secretary.[98] Meanwhile the Treasury developed its own diplomatic service with the appointment of three financial attachés to Berlin, Paris and Washington. The financial attachés, like the existing commercial attachés, formally served as advisers to the local head of mission. But much to the annoyance of the Foreign Office, they frequently communicated directly to the Treasury and circumvented the Foreign Office altogether.[99]

British participation at international conferences during 1931–33 illustrated the incapacity of the Foreign Office to manage external relations while the economic dimension of foreign policy was independently defined. Negotiations at the Four Power Conference in London on Danubian reconstruction in April 1932 were handled by the Prime Minister, Chancellor of the Exchequer, and President of the Board of Trade, with the Foreign Secretary, Sir John Simon, little more than an onlooker. The Lausanne conference, held in June 1932 to unravel the tangled web of reparation claims, became another occasion for 'summit diplomacy', with the Prime Minister and Chancellor of the Exchequer in charge of negotiations, and Leith Ross – now bearing the title His Majesty's Chief Economic Adviser and the equivalent rank of a Second Permanent Secretary at the Treasury – their principal assistant. The Ottawa Imperial conference followed in July. Frank Ashton Gwatkin, who had represented the Foreign Office on the inter-departmental preparatory committee during the spring, found Dominions Office and Board of Trade officials unconcerned about evidence of mounting foreign hostility to British plans for intra-imperial trade preferences.[100] In Ottawa for the conference, Gwatkin wrote to Wellesley of his marginal role:

> Our preparation was of an impromptu kind. No lead was given to us, no instructions, and no authority. We have been here as observers. Yet foreign affairs have throughout the conference been an important issue, and at crucial times a dominant one. Before this rather humiliating lesson is forgotten, I hope that serious steps will be taken, so to readjust both the focus of our foreign policy and the machinery of our office, that the next opportunity will not find us unprepared and impotent.[101]

Crisis of British foreign policy management 29

Further humiliations soon followed. In the autumn Sir Warren Fisher opposed Foreign Office representation at the Stresa conference on eastern Europe until the Office, frustrated by this further attempt at marginalisation, called upon the Prime Minister to decide whether the British delegation should comprise two economic experts or just one together with a professional diplomatist.[102] Wellesley was more hopeful about the World Economic Conference, because Sir John Simon, the Foreign Secretary, was president of the Organising Commission.[103] However, despite Wellesley's advice to Simon, the interdepartmental preparatory committee met not at the Foreign Office but at the Treasury. There, Fisher took the chair with two other senior Treasury officials present and the secretary provided by the Board of Trade. The only result of Simon's appeal to the Prime Minister for authority at the planning stage was that the Foreign Office, represented by Wellesley, gained a single seat on the committee along with five other departments.[104]

In December 1931 Foreign Office plans for new internal machinery had been sustained when Vansittart called upon Wellesley to head a politico-economic intelligence section as soon as it could be established. Wellesley readily acceded, but in view of his approaching retirement turned over the practical tasks to Gwatkin.[105] Early in the new year Gwatkin, at Wellesley's suggestion, received authorisation from Vansittart and Simon to compile a handbook on economic issues for the guidance of the foreign service.[106] A small committee of advisers from the Royal Institute of International Affairs and from industry and banking was formed to advise Gwatkin in his task. Progress was slow, for during the year Gwatkin assumed increasing responsibility for the numerous practical tasks the new section was expected to handle, in particular the co-ordination of information necessary for analysing foreign reactions to the international conferences. However, in July 1932 at least one element of the second effort at reform was implemented when economics became a compulsory part of the entry examination for the foreign service.[107] Gwatkin's 'first annual report' in January 1933 highlighted the wide range of issues crossing his desk and led Sir George Mounsey, an Assistant Under-Secretary, to renew the call for an economic intelligence section, and other senior officials to minute their agreement.[108]

Three middle-ranking officials remained sceptical. Owen O'Malley, head of the Dominions information department, deprecated the establishment of a new section on the grounds that it would only incite the Board of Trade and above all the Treasury – 'a more jealous, secretive, and intractable Department' – to 'derision and suspicion', and interfere with the executive functions of the political departments of the Foreign Office itself. Since the other ministries were bound to possess the economic experts, the Foreign Office should concentrate upon improving cooperation with them. G.R. Warner, head of the Treaty department, and Steven Gaselee, the Office librarian, also deprecated the initiative, pointing to the wartime contest with the Board of Trade and recommending that the Office improve co-ordination with the DOT.[109]

Wellesley impatiently accused his critics of 'a complete misapprehension' of the proposal. He dismissed their references to the DOT as irrelevant because he was not concerned with trade promotion, and he denied any intention of creating an 'imperium in imperio': the proposed section would serve a co-ordinating role without executive functions. He also denied that he sought 'to resist the ever growing influence and importance of the other Government Offices in the domain of Foreign Affairs'. In his view it was inevitable that increasing state intervention in economic affairs must profoundly affect the making of foreign policy, and that the economic ministries must remain the repositories of technical expertise. But he also believed that the responsibilities of the Foreign Office would correspondingly increase, for however technical the economic issues became they always remained political in their wider implications, and the Foreign Office alone was equipped to gather the information necessary for evaluating the political dimension. At any rate, economic policy depended for its success upon a suitable political climate, and the danger was that economic decisions would be taken without regard for their effect upon external relations as a whole. Hence a politico-economic co-ordinating centre was vital, and the Foreign Office was the only logical place for it. 'At least 80 per cent of Foreign Office work is now ... economic with its roots deeply imbedded in domestic affairs.' Without new machinery it was bound to degenerate into 'merely a Post Office for other Government Departments, and the Embassies and Legations into pillar boxes, and Heads of Missions into superior Messenger Boys'. Further deliberations followed, and with all five under-secretaries and all but three of the fourteen heads in favour, Gwatkin was authorised to proceed with plans for a system of politico-economic intelligence.

By mid-autumn there was every sign that the third attempt to equip the office with machinery for dealing with external economic affairs would succeed. Without requesting financial support from the Treasury and avoiding premature contact with the economic ministries,[110] Gwatkin had taken a corner of the League of Nations and Western department where he was assisted by Selby until the latter's posting to Vienna; by a second secretary for the duration of the World Economic Conference, and by a typist borrowed on a part-time basis from another department.[111] However, the printing of two circular despatches on economic information required from overseas missions, which had been approved by the Foreign Secretary, alerted the Treasury to Gwatkin's activity. On 21 October Wellesley received a note from Fisher warning that the Treasury was 'far from convinced of the desirability' of such information-gathering plans and requesting a halt to further action until he and Vansittart, now on leave, could meet. 'I am a little surprised', Fisher concluded, 'that the matter should have been taken to so advanced a stage (involving incidentally expenditure on printing) before consultations with the Treasury'.[112]

Wellesley, angry at Fisher's intervention, was infuriated to find it followed by a similar note from Sir Horace Hamilton of the Board of Trade, which he forwarded to the Foreign Secretary with the comment, 'I strongly suspect that this has been prompted by the Treasury'. Wellesley urged Simon to declare this unacceptable interference in the Office's affairs.

> I think it is undesirable in principle that the permanent officials of one Department should interfere in the affairs of another, or seek to dictate to it. The new department in no way interferes with the Treasury or the Board of Trade and may even help them eventually. For other Departments to veto arrangements which we consider necessary for our own efficiency – for I regard Sir W. Fisher's proposal as a side-tracking measure – strikes me as an unjustifiable piece of interference.

Simon preferred to await Vansittart's return, however, and on 13 November the Treasury controller and chief establishments officer, Sir James Rae, called on Charles Howard Smith of the Foreign Office with a further warning.[113] Should the Foreign Office proceed further before Fisher could speak with Vansittart, Rae warned, the Treasury would withhold remuneration for the officials of the new section. Howard Smith did not acknowledge that the section already existed, albeit unofficially, with its staff shown in the Foreign Office list as members of his own department. He asked Rae if he meant that a new section could be created so long as the total Foreign Office staff remained unchanged. No, Rae responded, the Treasury were prepared to suspend the salaries of all existing staff who might be involved. Wellesley renewed his appeal for Simon's intervention the following day. It seemed, he wrote pessimistically, that 'the Secretary of State is not to be master in his own home'. If reforms were to be decided by inter-departmental wrangling, the Foreign Office was almost certain to lose to the Treasury.[114]

Wellesley's and Gwatkin's efforts nevertheless resulted in a modest success. After private conversations with Vansittart in December 1933, Fisher, it appears, agreed to drop his opposition on condition that the economic intelligence function of the new section should be defined by an inter-departmental committee chaired by Leith Ross, to curb, Fisher explained to the Prime Minister, the 'amateurish attempts on the part of the Foreign Office to play the role of "Poobah in the Mikado".'[115] At the first meeting of the 'Leith Ross committee' in March 1934 it became clear that the Foreign Office plan to request lengthy politico-economic analyses from overseas missions, intended in part as an educative measure, was at odds with the economic ministries' preference for up-to-the-minute reports on new developments.[116] At the fourth meeting in April a circular despatch on the interpretation of economic developments, prepared in the Foreign Office, was suppressed at the insistence of His Majesty's Chief Industrial Adviser, Sir Horace Wilson, who had not hitherto participated in the deliberations.[117] In July Gwatkin set aside his draft handbook for diplomatists at Leith Ross's prompting.[118] The Foreign Office, having accepted the Leith Ross committee's right to formulate instructions to its own officers, acquiesced, and Gwatkin spent several months visiting European missions to explain their new reporting obligations.[119]

Creation of the economic section by no means ensured the smooth management of external economic relations. In 1933 liaison had been established between the economic section and the EAC secretariat, and in a separate arrangement the Foreign Office was conceded the right to be informed of pending changes in import restrictions.[120] Thereafter Gwatkin or one of his assistants was usually allowed to attend Cabinet committees engaged in economic policy planning. But as late as 1938, the Foreign Office had to persist in requesting a voice in the deliberations of a new Cabinet committee on agricultural policy, although as it pointed out, the committee's decisions were bound to have an important impact upon Britain's overseas relations.[121] By the same token, City lending activity continued uninfluenced by foreign policy considerations, while the Bank of England, much to the embarrassment and annoyance of the Foreign Office, maintained its studied aloofness.[122] Failure to co-ordinate priorities in the Far East in 1935 again brought the Foreign Office and the Treasury into sharp conflict.[123] And in 1936 the proposal by the Foreign Secretary, Anthony Eden, for the inter-departmental committee merely to consider the merits of various unofficial schemes for European economic recovery, on the grounds that peace and prosperity were inseparable, led Fisher to complain,

> The habit of the Foreign Office of initiating, without consultation, proposals on topics of every kind which are not their business and which they are incapable of understanding is becoming a nuisance. And the time is overdue for disciplining these unorganised, self-satisfied, and most dangerous amateurs.[124]

Despite Fisher's continuing hostility to the Foreign Office's encroachment upon Treasury turf, Gwatkin and his colleagues in the Foreign Office now had less reason for dissatisfaction. Although much of the additional information exchanged between the Office and overseas missions proved superfluous, and under pressure from the approach of war was eliminated, with some experimentation the economic section devised effective systems for identifying reports of special economic importance and expediting their distribution to interested ministries.[125] Meanwhile the Foreign Office participated in overseeing the foreign Industrial Intelligence Centre, a secret organisation housed at the DOT which from 1933 or thereabouts went some way to meet the objectives that Wellesley had identified almost twenty years before, and which moreover brought the main departments of state together in a practical if circumscribed working relationship.[126] More fundamentally, the time of radical departures in foreign monetary, financial and commercial policies was past, and conflicts over the management of external policy therefore diminished. On the one politico-economic issue central to foreign policy in the latter part of the 1930s, that of economic appeasement, most senior Foreign Office officials, including members of the economic section, in fact agreed with the economic ministries: economic concessions should be made to Germany, although only as part of a general settlement.[127] Professional jealousy was naturally aroused when Neville Chamberlain, as Prime Minister, took personal responsibility for foreign policy management in 1937 and used a variety of personal contacts to bypass the Foreign Office in his dealings with foreign states. Chamberlain's closest confidant and agent was Sir Horace Wilson, now a senior Treasury official, whose diplomatic skills had hitherto been limited to labour negotiations.

But if the Office was frustrated by being even more marginalised than before, Chamberlain's and Wilson's involvement scarcely bore upon the problem of politico-economic co-ordination, which receded into the background as the war approached.

The Eden reforms of 1941 endorsed the traditional Foreign Office claim that foreign representation demanded unique skills and expertise. Whereas Fisher had championed unity within Whitehall, the reforms called for the amalgamation of the Foreign Office and Diplomatic Service with the Commercial Diplomatic and Consular Services, and their separation from the Home Civil Service. The amalgamation was intended to provide effective trade promotion in postwar conditions of intensified trade rivalry: senior Foreign Office and diplomatic personnel would be afforded a broader commercial background, consular officials better career prospects. But, together with the separation of Home and Foreign Services, the reforms were also intended to restore Foreign Office authority over external policy. Concern for the diplomat's ability to identify and further the national interest rather than for his value to 'trade' had led a Foreign Office committee to recommend similar reforms in 1938.[128] The (Eden) White Paper might almost have been quoting Wellesley when it stated:

> the conditions which the Diplomatic Service originally grew up to meet no longer exist unchanged in modern international affairs. Economics and finance have become inextricably interwoven with politics.

Separate but equal status, it was hoped, would restore the diplomat to a relevant place in the changed matrix of international affairs and strengthen Foreign Office influence within the policy-making process.

The success of the Eden reforms may be doubted. For one thing, foreign service officers remained reluctant to accept posts involving a primarily commercial rather than a broad advisory function, such as those hitherto staffed by consular officials.[129] For another, the Foreign and Commonwealth Office has probably never regained the role of co-ordinating centre for external policy management. In 1969 the Duncan Committee called upon the Foreign Service to train officials 'for the role of coadjutors of the Government departments which will be conducting a great volume of day to day business directly with the corresponding departments of foreign governments'.[130] But the basic problem proved intractable: since politics became largely a matter of economics, the weakness of the

Foreign Office *vis-à-vis* the economic and economic-related ministries of Whitehall has persisted. Thus, in language reminiscent of Wellesley's appeals over fifty years before, in 1973 an institutional study of the economic aspects of external affairs described the Office as

> not the co-ordinating Department but one extra Department to be coordinated. Its role could decline to that of a post office for specialists of other Departments, with diplomats acting as door openers for the men from London.[131]

Other evidence indicates that this is indeed what has happened.[132]

The relative decline of Foreign Office authority since the First World War was probably inevitable, given the massive growth of state intervention in domestic economic affairs, the abandonment of free trade and the adoption of a managed currency and overseas lending controls, the increasingly sophisticated techniques of economic analysis and the decline in Britain's formal commitments overseas. Yet for the same reasons, machinery for evaluating the politico-strategic costs and benefits of economic decisions has become all the more vital. Members of the Foreign Office were probably not justified in suggesting after the war began that Britain's foreign policy in the 1930s was decisively compromised by Fisher's interference in their activities: appeasement was as much their policy as the Treasury's or the government's. But they were certainly justified in complaining of his interference, which was persistent, destructive and scarcely consistent with his professed commitment to Whitehall teamwork. His Foreign Office opponents and in particular Sir Victor Wellesley, godson of Queen Victoria, in contrast deserve credit for recognising perhaps the most important development in contemporary international relations and persisting in the call for appropriate institutional reform.

NOTES

1 *Hansard Parliamentary Debates*, HC, 5th series, vol. 373, c. 165.
2 *Parliamentary Papers*, 'Proposals for the reform of the Foreign Service', 1943, Cmd. 6420.
3 See statements by Lord Perth, *Hansard Parliamentary Debates*, HL, 5th series, vol. 125, cc. 29–32; vol. 126, c. 939; vol. 131, cc. 816–17; vol. 134, c. 288; Sir Victor Wellesley, letters to *The Times*, 24 June, 3 July, 1 August 1942; Sir Walford Selby, letter to *The Times*, 28 August 1942; Sir W. Selby, 'The Foreign Office', *The Nineteenth Century and After*, vol. 138, 1945, p. 4; Sir W. Selby, *Diplomatic Twilight, 1930–1940*,

London, John Murray, 1953, pp. 4–15, 137–8, 180–6; Lord Murray of Elibank, *Reflections on Some Aspects of British Foreign Policy between the Two World Wars*, London, Oliver & Boyd, 1946, p. 46; F.T. Ashton-Gwatkin, *The British Foreign Service*, New York, Syracuse University Press, 1951, pp. 26–7. The charges in their most explicit and comprehensive form are set out in H. Legge-Bourke, *Master of the Offices*, London, Falcon Press, 1950.

4 D.C. Watt, *Personalities and Policies*, London, Longman, 1965, pp. 100–2; W.N. Medlicott, *Britain and Germany: The Search for Agreement, 1930–37*, London, Athlone, 1969, p. 4, n. 2 and passim.

5 See e.g. the minutes by Gladwyn Jebb, 17 March 1937, and Eden, 21 March 1937, FO371/21215, W6363/5/50.

6 Statements by Lord Tyrrell, Viscount Davidson, Viscount Cranbourne, Lord Rennell, Viscount Cecil and Lord Hutchison, *Hansard Parliamentary Debates*, HL, 5th series, vol. 126, cc. 970–2, 998, 1019; vol. 128, cc. 735–6; vol. 131, cc. 636–7, 652; and vol. 134, c. 301; Lord Hankey, 'The control of external affairs', *International Affairs*, vol. 22, no. 2, 1946, p. 166.

7 According to the retired consul-general, Sir Roger Casement, in evidence to the MacDonnell Commission, 'The Foreign Office entirely controls the Consular Service, but nobody in the Foreign Office has ever been a consul, or knows anything about the duties of a consul', *Parliamentary Papers*, 'Fifth Report of the Royal Commission on the Civil Service', Minutes of Evidence, 29 April 1914–16 July 1914, Cd. 7749.

8 Sir F. Oppenheimer, *Stranger Within*, London, Faber, 1960, p. 305. The economic aspects of foreign relations receive virtually no mention even in later accounts such as H. Nicolson, *Diplomacy*, London, Cambridge University Press, 1941, and Lord Strang, *The Foreign Office*, London, Allen & Unwin, 1959.

9 See e.g. *Parliamentary Papers*, 1914 Cd. 7749, evidence to the MacDonnell Commission from the secretary of the London Chamber of Commerce, Mr C.E. Musgrave, QQ 38,862, 38,877; Sir Francis Hirst, editor of *The Economist*, QQ 40,579, 40,595, 40,658, 40,665; Sir Edwin Peers, appendix lxxxix, p. 321; Association of Chambers of Commerce, appendix xc, p. 326.

10 'Foreign Office statement of Existing Instructions with regard to Economic Reporting and an Outline of the General Requirements', 3 March 1934, FO371/18587, W3982/293/50.

11 Crowe minute, undated, FO368/1855, 175055/f2049.

12 Algernon Law minute, 1 April 1916, FO369/912, 63184/f63184; *Parliamentary Papers*, 'Final report of the Committee on Commercial and Industrial Policy after the War', 1918, Cd. 9035.

13 Hilda Runciman letter with enclosure to Grey, 8 June 1916, and Drummond letter to Runciman, 4 September 1916, FO800/89.

14 Wellesley memorandum, 28 June 1917, FO368/1855, 141670/f2049; Wellesley evidence to the Cave Committee, 28 May 1919, CAB27/57, MTC 3rd minutes.

15 Wellesley memorandum, 9 March 1918, FO368/2036, 62458/f14578.

16 G.M. Trevelyan, *Grey of Fallodon*, London, Longman, 1948, pp. 158, 359.
17 Balfour to Walter Long, 2 August 1917, FO800/207. According to Frank Ashton-Gwatkin, who later collaborated with Wellesley, 'The Foreign Office did not understand or support him', Ashton-Gwatkin, op. cit., p. 20.
18 *Parliamentary Papers*, 'Memorandum by the Board of Trade and the Foreign Office with respect to the Future Organisation of Commercial Intelligence', 1917, Cd. 8715, Foreign Office Committee Report, 10 August 1917, pp. 17–30.
19 Runciman letter to Grey, 29 August 1916, FO800/89.
20 Runciman letter to Grey, 10 September 1916, FO800/89; Crowe minute, 11 March 1918, FO368/2036, 63458/f14578; *Parliamentary Papers*, 'Memorandum by the Board of Trade and the Foreign Office with respect to the Future Organisation of Commercial Intelligence', Cd. 8715, pp. 5–16; Wellesley minute, 26 April 1917, FO368/1855, 83820/f2049, CAB23/3, WC216(10); Wellesley memorandum, 9 March 1918, FO368/2036, 62458/f14578.
21 Llewellyn Smith to Cave Committee, 18 June 1919, CAB27/57, MTC 6th minutes.
22 Steel-Maitland minute, to Hardinge and Balfour, 17 June 1918, FO368/2036, 112207/f14578.
23 Crowe minute, 25 January 1918, FO368/2036, 14578/f14578, Sir Auckland Geddes to Cave Committee, 22 May 1919, CAB27/57, MTC 1st minutes.
24 Statement by Sir A. Geddes, 3 April 1919, CAB23/10, WC553(4).
25 Wellesley letter to Crowe, 14 June 1919, FO368/2253, 93602/f79699.
26 Wellesley letter to Crowe, 7 June 1919, ibid.
27 *Parliamentary Papers*, 'Report of the Committee to Examine the Question of Government Machinery for Dealing with Trade and Commerce', Cmd. 319, 10 July 1919, CAB23/11, WC598(6).
28 Wellesley minute, undated (?16 September 1919), FO368/2253, 134076/f79699.
29 Thus Sir Thomas Heath, the former Joint Permanent Secretary of the Treasury, as late as 1927 omitted from his description of the Treasury all reference to reparations, war debts and international payments questions, despite the fact that they had been preoccupations of the key financial section since the war: Heath, *The Treasury*, London, Putnam, 1927, p. 1.
30 Sir John Bradbury (Treasury) to Under-Secretary, Foreign Office, FO371/3971, N24350/855; E.H. Carr to V. Cavendish-Bentinck, 10 March 1919, FO371/3971, N39120/855; Walford Selby memorandum, 25 July 1919, FO371/3973, N106762/855.
31 Curzon memorandum for the War Cabinet, 15 August 1919, FO371/3535, C146249/5445; P.M.S. Blackett (Treasury) to Foreign Office, FO371/3531, C153772/5445; G.S. Spencer to Treasury, 12 November 1919, FO371/3531, C150052/5445.
32 Sir Robert Vansittart to Curzon, 30 March 1921, Curzon Papers, House of Lords, F112/221B; Wigram, Tyrrell minutes, initialled by Curzon, 21 April 1921, FO371/6024, C8103/2740/18. See also C8331/2740/18. Tyrrell

minute, 30 April 1921, FO371/6027, C9289/2740/18; see also C9290/2740/18; see also FO371/6032, C13392/2740/18, FO371/6036, C18209/2740/18, FO371/6036, C18621/2740/18, C20464/2740/18, FO371/6037, C20573/2740/18, FO371/5978, C21403/416/18, C21572/416/18.
33 Curzon to Horne, 19 November 1921, T160/122, F4566. His brief was prepared by Sir William Tyrrell, see memorandum, 18 November 1921, FO371/5978, C21972/416/18 (reprinted in *Documents on British Foreign Policy, 1919-1939*, 1st series, vol. XVI, p. 812).
34 Vansittart to Secretary of the Treasury, 14 March 1927, FO371/12018, A1458/351/35.
35 Foreign Office memorandum, 12 October 1927, Vansittart letter to Sir Edward Crowe (DOT), 25 October 1927, FO371/11957, P998/150.
36 Sargent letter to Waley (Treasury), 6 March 1928, FO371/12962, C1836/29/37; Crewe to Chamberlain, 7 May 1928, FO371/12962, C3504/29/37; Bateman minute, 3 April 1928, FO371/12853, C2598/12/17.
37 Wellesley minute, 18 January 1929, FO371/13705, C520/47/92.
38 Upcott (Treasury) to Foreign Office, 15 January 1929, FO371/13705, C416/47/92.
39 Hadow memorandum, 24 August 1928, FO371/12728, A5499/108/51.
40 Picton-Bagge (DOT) to Craigie, 21 December 1928, FO371/12728, A8809/108/51.
41 Crowe to Sargent, 4 February 1929, FO371/14094, W1847/1846/50.
42 Foreign Office memorandum, 16 February 1929 and Sargent minute, 18 March 1929, FO371/14094, W1846/1846/50; Leith Ross minute, 1 March 1929, T175/34.
43 Lindsay memorandum to Hopkins, 22 March 1929, T175/34.
44 Gaselee to the Treasury, 12 November 1927, T160/122, F4566.
45 Sargent memorandum, 17 June 1929, and Henderson to Tyrrell, 24 June 1929, FO800/280.
46 Stamp memorandum, 4 July 1929, PREM1/83.
47 Tyrrell to Henderson, 18 July 1929, T160/392, F11300/03/3.
48 Fisher to Snowden enclosing Hopkins memorandum, 19 June 1929, T160/388, F11300/3.
49 Leith Ross to Grigg, 11 July 1929, T172/1694.
50 See e.g. *Hansard Parliamentary Debates*, 5th series, vol. 227, cc. 119–20, 313; *Daily Herald*, 18, 28 May 1929.
51 Cabinet conclusions, CAB23/61, CM27(29)6.
52 R.W.D. Boyce, *British Capitalism at the Crossroads, 1919–1932: A Study in Politics, Economics and International Relations*, Cambridge, Cambridge University Press, 1987, pp. 202–12.
53 Carr minute, 23 May 1930, FO371/14346, C3974/658/2.
54 Snowden minute, undated (?6 June 1930), T160/372, F2321/03/1.
55 Howard Smith (for Henderson) to Treasury, 5 December 1930, T160/372, F2321/03/2.
56 Howard Smith minute, 8 December 1930, FO371/14901, W13122/37/17; Howard Smith to Leith Ross, 13 January 1931, FO371/15640, W240/56/17.
57 Vansittart to Leith Ross, 10 April 1931, T160/394, F11324.
58 Harvey (Bank of England) to Leith Ross, 16 April 1931; Leith Ross

to Harvey, 20 April 1931; Leith Ross minutes to Hopkins, 21, 25 April 1931, T160/394, F11324.
59 With Sir John (later Lord) Bradbury, Sir Basil Blackett, H.A. Siepmann and Sir Otto Niemeyer lost to the Bank, the Treasury at this time had only two officers experienced in international finance: Leith Ross and David Waley. See Sir F.W. Leith Ross, *Money Talks*, London, Hutchinson, 1968, p. 107, and H. Roseveare, *The Treasury*, London, Allen Lane, 1969, p. 254.
60 League of Nations, *Official Journal*, 1929, Plenary meetings, pp. 79–81.
61 ibid., p. 52.
62 Board of Trade memorandum, 5 April 1930, BT11/234, CRT7094.
63 G.P. Gooch and H. Temperley (eds) *British Documents on the Origins of the War, 1898–1914*, vol. 3, London, HMSO, 1928, p. 403.
64 Craigie, Lindsay, Wellesley minutes, 12 July 1929, FO371/13537, A4956/139/45; Minute of Henderson-Briand conversation, 10 May 1930, FO371/14980, W4922/451/98. For a more comprehensive account see R. Boyce, 'Britain's first "No" to Europe: Britain and the Briand Plan, 1929–30', *European Studies Review*, vol. 10, 1980, pp. 17–45.
65 A.W.A. Leeper memorandum, 30 May 1930, FO371/14981, W5585/451/98.
66 League of Nations, *Official Journal*, 1930, Minutes of the Second Committee, pp. 54–5, 87–8.
67 Wellesley memorandum, 1 December 1930, FO371/15671, W3206/441/50. Wellesley's promotion, following the death of Sir Eyre Crowe in April 1925, was opposed by Fisher and effected only after Sir Austen Chamberlain rejected Fisher's right to interfere in Office appointments. It seems at least possible that Fisher's opposition was due to Wellesley's well-known dissatisfaction with the management of foreign politico-economic affairs. See Sir H. Legge-Bourke, op. cit., p. 15.
68 Henderson to MacDonald, 13 March 1931, FO371/15671, W-/441/50 (unregistered).
69 MacDonald to Henderson, 17 March 1931, FO371/15671, W-/441/50 (unregistered).
70 For a more comprehensive account of the crisis from the British point of view, including the frustrations created for the Foreign Office, see M.D. Newman, 'Britain and the German-Austrian customs union proposal of 1931', *European Studies Review*, vol. 6, 1976, pp. 449–72; also Boyce, *British Capitalism at the Crossroads*, ch. 10.
71 Fountain memorandum, 24 March 1931, FO371/15159, C2149/673/3.
72 Leith Ross minute, 23 April 1931, FO371/15160, C2790/673/3.
73 Sargent memorandum, 14 April 1931, FO371/15160, C2462/673/3.
74 Sargent memorandum, 22 April 1931, FO371/15160, C2703/673/3.
75 Sargent memorandum, 23 April 1931, FO371/15160, C2790/673/3.
76 Waley to Sargent, 27 April 1931, FO371/15676, W4802/3191/50; Sargent minute, 30 April 1931, FO371/1516, C2982/673/3; Drummond to Cadogan, 30 April 1931, FO371/1561, C2969/673/3.
77 de Fleuriau memorandum, 4 May 1931, FO371/15161, C2966/673/3.
78 Vansittart to MacDonald, 20 May 1931, PREM1/106.
79 Thomas to MacDonald, 16 May 1931, PREM1/105.
80 Vansittart to Selby, 19 May 1931, PREM1/106.

81 Wellesley minute, 12 May 1931, FO371/15730, W5383/4884/98.
82 Wellesley to Selby, 8 May 1931, FO800/283.
83 Vansittart minute, 23 April 1931, FO371/15671, W-/441/50 (unregistered).
84 Vansittart to MacDonald, 4 May 1931, ibid.
85 Selby, *Diplomatic Twilight*, p. 4.
86 Watt, op. cit., p. 104; Sir H. Hamilton, 'Sir W. Fisher and the Public Service', *Public Administration*, vol. 29, pp. 3–38.
87 Norton to Fisher, 9 April 1931, FO371/15671, W-/441/50 (unregistered).
88 CP301(31), 26 November 1931, CAB24/225.
89 Wellesley, Reading minutes, 3 November 1931, FO371/15198, C8097/172/62.
90 Leith Ross minute, 10 November 1931, T160/437, F12360/02/1.
91 Vansittart minute, 8 October 1931, FO371/15646, W11703/689/17. A detailed account of this strange affair is given in R.W.D. Boyce, 'Insects and international relations: Canada, France, and British agricultural "sanitary" restrictions between the wars', *International History Review*, vol. 9, 1987, pp. 1–27.
92 Fountain to Howard Smith, 19 November 1931, FO371/15643, W13324/137/17.
93 Simon to Runciman, 23 December 1931, FO371/15643, W14308/137/17; Simon to Runciman, 3 February 1932, FO371/16360, W970/16/17; Howard Smith to Board of Trade, 7 March 1932, FO371/16371, W2544/659/17.
94 Wellesley to Simon, 4 December 1931, FO371/15682, W14032/10755/50; Leith Ross minute, 1 December 1931 and Eden to Simon, 8 December 1931, FO371/15200, C8945/172/62.
95 Norton minute, 30 September 1931, FO371/15671, W12197/441/50.
96 Howard Smith to Wellesley, Wellesley to Simon, 30 October 1931, FO371/15683, W12622/11082/50; Kelly memorandum, 3 March 1932, FO371/16382, W3248/20/50.
97 Howard Smith to Jenkins (Board of Trade), 19 July 1932, FO371/16391, W7258/63/50; Jenkins to Howard Smith, 16 August 1932, FO371/16392, W9358/63/50.
98 Craigie minute, undated (?8 January 1932), FO371/15868, A241/187/45.
99 Wigram minute, 28 March 1933, FO371/17318, W3986/278/50, Mounsey minute, 27 April 1933, FO371/16604, A2972/59/45.
100 Foreign Office minute, 17 March 1932, FO371/16406, W3498/1167/50.
101 Gwatkin to Wellesley, 19 August 1932, FO371/16409, W9649/1167/50.
102 Simon to Butler, 28 July 1932, FO800/287.
103 Wellesley to Simon, 25 July 1932, FO371/16418, W8647/8034/50.
104 Simon to MacDonald, 26 July 1932. FO800/287.
105 Wellesley to Vansittart, undated, FO371/15671, W-/441/50 (unregistered). For another account of the creation of the section, see D.G. Boadle, 'The formation of the Foreign Office Economic Relations Section, 1930–1937', *Historical Journal*, vol. 20, 1977, pp. 919–36.
106 Gwatkin memorandum, 5 January 1933, FO371/17318, W278/278/50.
107 Weekes (Civil Service Commission) to Montgomery, 24 July 1932, FO371/905, X4442/37/504.
108 Gwatkin memorandum, 5 January 1933, FO371/17318, W278/278/50.

Crisis of British foreign policy management 41

109 O'Malley, Warner, Gaselee, Wellesley minutes, 5–16 May 1933, FO371/17218, W3986/278/50.
110 Gwatkin minute, undated (June 1933), FO371/17318, W9851/293/50.
111 Gwatkin memorandum, 5 January 1934, FO371/18487, W293/293/50.
112 Fisher to Wellesley, 21 October 1933, Wellesley to Simon, 24 October 1933, FO371/17318, W12966/278/50.
113 Howard Smith to Wellesley, 13 November 1933, FO371/17318, W12966/278/50.
114 Wellesley minute, 15 November 1933, FO371/17318, W12966/278/50.
115 Fisher to Chamberlain, Baldwin and MacDonald, 25 January 1934, T160/742, F13701/1.
116 Gwatkin minute, 8 March 1934, FO371/18487, W3928/293/50.
117 Mounsey minute, 4 May 1934, FO371/18487, W4907/293/50.
118 Leith Ross to Gwatkin, 31 July 1934, T160/574, F13701/01/3.
119 Gwatkin memorandum, 11 February 1935, FO371/19597, W1264/23/50.
120 Gwatkin memorandum, 5 January 1934, FO371/18487, W293/293/50.
121 Halifax to Chamberlain, 8 March 1938, FO371/22487, W3123/41/50.
122 Sargent, Vansittart minutes, 2 February 1934, FO371/17676, C749/1/18; Vansittart minute, 7 July 1934, FO371/18451, R3922/3922/37; Vansittart to Fisher, 15 August 1934, T175/86.
123 Vansittart to Simon, 29 October 1935, FO371/19245, F6729/6/10.
124 Fisher to Fergusson, 25 July 1936, T160/633, F12777/1.
125 Edgcumbe to Gwatkin, 31 October 1935, FO371/19599, W10155/23/50; Halifax circular despatch, 19 April 1938, FO371/21799, W4351/107/50; Cadogan circular despatch, 11 January 1940, FO371/23947, W17882/15128/40.
126 J. Young, 'Spokesmen for economic warfare: the Industrial Intelligence Centre in the 1930s', *European Studies Review*, vol. 6, 1976, pp. 473–89.
127 B.J. Wendt, *Economic Appeasement: Handel und Finanz in der britischen Deutschland-Politik 1933–1939*, Düsseldorf, 1971, pp. 60, 321–30. Wendt properly notes that the case for economic appeasement advanced by Gwatkin, Lord Cranborne and others in the Office did not go unchallenged: Vansittart argued the opposite case. Ibid., p. 329.
128 Majority report, January 1939, FO366/781.
129 D.C.M. Platt, *The Cinderella Service, British Consuls since 1825*, London, Longman, 1971, p. 238. A more favourable view of Foreign Service export promotion efforts is given in D.C. Watt, 'Britain's representation abroad', *The World Today*, vol. 25, 1969, p. 328, and A. Schonfield, 'The Duncan Report and its critics', *International Affairs*, vol. 46, 1970, p. 263.
130 *Parliamentary Papers*, 'Report of the Review Committee on Overseas Representation, 1968–1969', Cmnd. 4107, July 1969, p. 66; cf. Schonfield, op. cit., p. 256.
131 P. Byrd, 'Trade and commerce in external relations', in R. Boardman and A.J.R. Groom (eds) *The Management of Britain's External Relations*, London, Macmillan, 1973, p. 193.
132 See the report on the Think Tank in *The Times*, 14 January 1977.

2 Intelligence and the Lytton Commission, 1931–33

Ian Nish

On 18 September 1931 the Japanese army in Manchuria felt provoked by the anti-Japanese activities on the Japanese-owned South Manchurian Railway line. They moved into townships and occupied arterial highways in the south and centre of Manchuria. They encountered little opposition and in the following six weeks drove the Chinese armies out of southern Manchuria. This came to be known to the Japanese as 'the Manchurian incident', to the foreign community as 'the Manchurian crisis' and to some Chinese as 'the North-eastern War'.[1]

The Chinese appealed to the world powers for their intervention. But, weakened by the effects of the world depression, the latter had no desire to get involved, either individually or collectively, and were content to leave the matter to the League of Nations to which China had made an appeal on 19 September.[2] The League found it impossible to take effective steps to control military activities in Manchuria and could only come up in December with the solution of appointing a commission of inquiry to investigate China's complaint. The Commission, which was headed by Lord Lytton, the British nominee, and became known as the Lytton Commission, assembled in Geneva on 21 January 1932 and received briefings from Sugimura Yotaro, the Japanese under-secretary on the League secretariat.[3] Immediately, trouble broke out at Shanghai and China again appealed to the League. It seemed likely that Lytton's party would proceed direct to Shanghai by the shortest route, the Trans-Siberian Railway. But this proposal lapsed when the Japanese argued that the line was not secure.[4]

Instead the Lytton Commission reached Tokyo on 29 February by the Trans-Pacific steamer. Almost simultaneously with this, the Japanese army in Manchuria encouraged the setting up of the new state of Manchukuo. It was to be a state governed by a council of

Intelligence and the Lytton Commission 43

ministers who were to be mainly Manchu Chinese but who were to be guided by a group of Japanese independent of the control of Tokyo. The new government was hostile to the involvement of the League Commission and irritated by the resolution passed by the League of Nations Assembly on 11 March which laid down that members of the League should not recognise the new state of Manchukuo.

In China the Commission visited Shanghai, the Yangtse valley and Peking before venturing into China's north-eastern provinces. When its members finally reached Manchuria in April, they were subjected to intense police spying and were hemmed in by the tightest protocol. The Japanese army and the new government of Manchukuo were anxious that the evidence which the Commission heard should not be hostile to Manchukuo and that only petitions from those favourable to the new state should be presented to the commissioners.[5] Documents coming through official channels had the appearance of being censored while evidence offered at public sessions was carefully scrutinised. The commissioners, aware of eavesdroppers, found that the only place safe for conversation was the golf course. Lytton, who described his time in Manchuria as the most unpleasant time of his life, was disheartened at this and had to take steps whereby he as an official could get at the truth which did not emerge from the formal sessions.

The Commission eventually signed its report to the League in Peking on 4 September. It was a remarkably shrewd document. The puzzle is how the commissioners, who were elderly, had no previous knowledge of China and included no Chinese or Japanese linguist, should have managed to penetrate the smokescreen that was generated around the proceedings and reached an assessment of the situation which, if not pleasing to Manchukuo, was at least generally thought to be balanced and realistic. This raises the question: how did the Commission overcome the obstacles placed in its way? There were various ways in which it countered the restraints placed upon it by virtue of its status as the investigator of an international dispute. But in general it could be said that there grew up around it a sort of intelligence network, consisting of the more junior members of staff, who did not feel so inhibited and managed to probe beneath the surface. This essay is an account of some of the ways in which Lytton and his colleagues used 'intelligence' sources in order to build up a more realistic picture of the events of 1931–32.

Lord Lytton as a former governor of Bengal was well aware of the uses of political intelligence and appreciated in advance that his position would involve much protocol which would hamper his investigations. From the start he recognised the need for someone outside the officialdom of the League who could act as the eyes and ears of the Commission away from the scrutiny of the Chinese and Japanese. He agreed to the appointment to his personal staff of William Waldorf Astor, who was then 24 years old. On 15 December Astor had made indirect approaches to the League:

> I have studied the situation [in Manchuria] for some time, twice as secretary to the Institute of Pacific Relations conferences at Honolulu and Kyoto 1927 and 1929. I also travelled in Japan, Manchuria and China in 1929 and 1930. I got to know both sides quite well and have since kept in close touch with the situation.[6]

It appears that he knew particularly Chang Hsueh-liang, the Young Marshal of Manchuria, a central figure in the unfolding events in that territory. Astor, who had been serving on the staff of the Pilgrim's Trust, was appointed as 'secretary of the chairman and enquiry assistant'.[7] Lytton in his later letters was to compliment Astor, conceding that he could do things that Lytton himself could not do and could do so because of his youth which enabled him to get away with them!

USING BRITISH SOURCES

The Commission's first port of call in China was Shanghai, where for the first time it was joined by the Chinese and Japanese assessors. The assessors' function was to serve as a conduit between the Commission and their communities and governments. They assisted the work of the Commission greatly by arranging and presenting much documentary evidence. The first snag with this arrangement was that the evidence they presented had to be shown to the other and an opportunity given for subsequent comment. Because of the confrontational aspects of the dispute, therefore, it was not desirable to use the assessors too much. The second snag was that, while their staffs were not small, they could not cope with the volume of the work. Moreover, it was not possible to expand the staffs because the Commission had in the main to be funded by the parties to the dispute. It would have been unwise for Lytton and his colleagues to have been restricted in their inquiries to what the assessors were able and willing to offer. They had to look for other sources of information and other services. This did not, however, mean that their relations with the Chinese assessor, Dr Wellington Koo, and

Intelligence and the Lytton Commission 45

the Japanese assessor, Yoshida Isaburo, were insignificant. Each was an experienced diplomat, had League of Nations experience and had kept abreast of developments over the Manchurian crisis.[8]

The possibility of using British sources was discussed when Lytton met the British minister to China, Sir Miles Lampson, in Shanghai on 18 March. Lampson noted in his diary:

> I found it very difficult to answer some of his questions – they dealt with things from such an unreal angle. As I told him, it is extraordinarily difficult to give anyone coming fresh to China any coherent expression of one's views: the whole thing is so involved and so inchoate.[9]

None the less, Lampson was sympathetic to Lytton's dilemma. Lytton, to his credit, was well aware of the weak composition of his mission, especially in regard to information-gathering and 'confidential interpretation'. He asked Lampson in a preliminary way whether he could spare someone of experience from the British legation to join the Commission when it went into Manchukuo.

Lampson entered in his diary for 20 March that Bill Astor, whom he had known in China some two years earlier, had called in for a discussion. Astor had asked, first, for the loan of someone to act as interpreter and general factotum for the Commission; and second, for any reports on the Manchurian crisis which would help Lytton to grasp the essentials of the problem. Lampson held out the possibility of deputing someone from his staff, while adding cautiously that he did not have men to spare. On the second point he was more reserved, hesitating to offer Lytton his reports to the Foreign Office which 'he might think showed a bias'. Lampson throughout had strong objections to British consuls in Manchuria giving evidence before the commissioners and was not keen on their reports being widely circulated among the Commission and the League.[10]

Nothing was resolved until Lytton reached Peking on 11 April when he asked 'that all relevant information in the Legation archives regarding Manchurian crisis since September 18th and general survey of events leading up to it in previous years [should] be placed at disposal of the Commission so that they can study it before proceeding to Manchuria in a week's time'. Lampson, who was still on duty in Shanghai, reported to Whitehall that he was prepared to give Lytton personally access to such reports for his confidential information but objected to British reports being quoted in any report the Commission might make to Geneva. The Foreign Office endorsed Lampson's wishes.[11]

Lampson further agreed (with the approval of Whitehall) to second to the Commission a member of the British Consular Service, who had some years' experience, was a fluent Chinese linguist and could be spared from his legation duties. This was George Moss, who was to be loaned for a period of two months or longer and was described in League documents as 'Chinese interpreter and enquiry assistant'. He had been born in Yokohama, the son of an official of the Supreme Court for China and Japan, and educated at King's College, London. Appointed as Student Interpreter in China in 1902, he spent fifteen years studying the Chinese language and literature in various consular posts scattered about China.[12] In 1916 when he was district officer in Weihaiwei, he was seconded from the consular service and served as Chinese secretary and principal assistant to the War Office representative for recruitment to the Chinese Labour Corps until its demobilisation in 1920. This was to be a valuable experience for Moss in so far as that corps was mainly recruited from Shantung province and this was the area from which the bulk of immigrants to Manchuria was drawn.[13] During the 1920s Moss held various consular posts throughout China, apart from a year spent in the Foreign Office from January 1925.

During the early phases of the Manchurian crisis, when the League was frustrated by its inability to influence the situation on the ground, it proposed that the military attachés of the powers in China should visit Manchuria to report on the facts. Britain, the United States, France and Germany took up this invitation. Moss, who was acting consul-general at Nanking at the time, went with Colonel Badham-Thornhill to Chinchow in late November and presented a report on political developments in his capacity as 'consul-observer'.[14] Following this, he returned to Weihaiwei on 8 January 1932 as full consul.

It might be thought that Lampson could have made available as interpreters, translators and inquiry assistants personnel from the staffs of the consulates in Manchuria. But, as we have seen, Lampson and Whitehall considered this to be a sensitive issue and did not want to implicate their officials too deeply in the inquiry. Another point was that the staffs of the British consulates in Manchuria tended to be drawn from the Japanese service rather than the China service and spoke Japanese rather than Mandarin. Lampson had little option, therefore, but to select a representative from a China post who commanded a good knowledge of Mandarin. Moss, who had seen service in Manchuria the previous November, was a natural choice both because of his fluency and his experience

Intelligence and the Lytton Commission 47

on the ground. Now that he had taken over as consul in Weihaiwei, he was, moreover, most conveniently situated for this task.

Moss joined Lytton on 24 April at the British consulate-general in Mukden, which was serving as the headquarters of the Commission in the International Settlement there. He never made an official report on his activities for the League but he was later to draw up an unofficial 'account of my doings in Manchuria' for the amusement of family and friends.[15] While this never found its way (so far as I am aware) into the public domain, it is one of the most authoritative accounts of how the Lytton Commission was able to cope with the problems of gathering information in the hostile environment of Manchukuo and of processing the vast amount of evidence collected within the Commission secretariat. In his capacity as inquiry assistant, Moss found himself discussing issues independently with a wide range of residents in Manchuria, foreign residents, Chinese magistrates, missionaries and Korean nationals.[16] He then had to analyse the material and, where necessary, translate the written submissions.

The itinerary which George Moss gives in his 'account of my doings in Manchuria' is most revealing:

> [Lampson] instructed me by telegram to join Lord Lytton at Mukden to assist him and the Commissioners of the League of Nations Enquiry Commission generally and as confidential Interpreter during their tour of Manchuria. I reported to Lord Lytton on April 24th at Mukden. Finding that only persons introduced by the Japanese authorities and by Japanese advisers to the new Manchurian State (Manchoukuo), which is effectively under Japanese control, were allowed access to the Commission, I arranged to stay at HBM Consulate-General with my friend A.E. Eastes. By not using too often the motor cars placed officially at the disposal of the Commission I was able to get in touch, without being unduly spied upon, with members of the foreign Community, missionaries, Chinese and Manchu ex-officials, bankers, professional men and some of the common people. I was also employed to assist in receiving on behalf of the Commission Deputations of Chinese who called to state views favourable to the Manchoukuo. These generally left written Statements, the gist of which had to be translated at once for the Commissioners. This took a lot of time. I also attended some of the interviews with officials, Japanese and others. However I

found time to play an occasional game of golf with Lord Lytton and with General McCoy (the United States Commissioner).

From Mukden the Commission went to visit Changchun, the new capital and 'among other visits' Moss was present at the Reception of the Commission by 'Regent' Pu Yi:

> We had been told by the Chinese that he was a most unwilling tool of the Japanese and spent his nights weeping and sorrowing. However, I thought he looked remarkably well and cheery. He spoke without trace of nervousness in a loud, resonant voice and made appropriate remarks to the Commissioners, e.g. he talked of India and his former tutor (Sir Reginald Johnston) to Lord Lytton and of Mussolini to Count Aldrovandi.

After Mukden the Commission went on to Kirin in a special non-stop train which took three hours for the journey. According to Moss, it was raining slightly and all along the route were stationed troops and railway guards with Japanese troops on the station platforms. Apparently, the same display of military power awaited them at Changchun, where they had a banquet with Japanese and carefully selected Chinese representing the Manchukuo government. After interviewing the governor, Moss and Astor got away to meet some missionaries from whom they received 'a most interesting account of what had passed in Kirin'. The Commission then went on to Harbin, a semi-Russian city, where Moss stayed at the consulate with C.E. Garstin. According to Moss:

> We had several interesting interviews here, and I was able to do a lot of private interviews although I had to be most circumspect as we were much spied on. There was a good deal of fighting going on in the neighbourhood and we found it impossible to carry out our original intention of visiting the Chinese General Ma Chanshan, who is still opposing the Manchoukuo. The Manchoukuo look on him as a rebel and their officials were very much annoyed by our persistence in endeavouring to see him. But, from the Chinese point of view, they are rebels.[17]

IN SEARCH OF MA CHANSHAN

General Ma, a warlord in northern Manchuria, had originally identified himself with the new state of Manchukuo by joining its Council as defence minister. But he had within a month distanced himself from the Manchukuo government and gone back to his own power-base. Because of his resistance to the Japanese at the battle of Nonni bridge in November 1931, he had become something of a symbol of resistance to Japan and had a considerable following to the north of the Chinese-Eastern Railway. In April he was bold enough to send an open telegram to the League of Nations denouncing the new administration and distributed it widely around the world. It was unlikely that the Japanese Kuantung army could pursue him with any prospect of success. Meanwhile Ma's guerrillas marauded in the vicinity of the Chinese-Eastern Railway and made life difficult for the Japanese defenders.[18]

The Lytton Commission took the view that it wanted to interview people in Manchuria of all shades of opinion and take the oral evidence of General Ma. The Japanese were highly suspicious of this proposal, while the Manchukuo authorities were unwilling to give facilities for contacting Ma in exile as he was regarded as a rebel against whom hostilities were proceeding. In any case they could not guarantee the security of the commissioners on the bandit-infested railway route. It was one of several confrontations between Lytton and the Manchukuo authorities and resulted in a partial climb-down by the commissioners, who decided not to press the issue. Instead they decided to send four deputies to see Ma. Four younger members of the commission, Astor, Biddle, Hiam and von Kotze, together with Moss as interpreter, were to follow a circuitous route: by air to Tsitsihar, then by rail to Blagovestchensk, thence to Ma's hideout at Heiho. In the event this did not materialise because the Soviet authorities declined to give visas.[19] George Moss's presence as interpreter was essential to the success of this adventurous project though he was rather older than the others at 50 years of age.

Moss's own narrative reveals his personal view of Ma's character. He claimed that his own enthusiasm for the journey was 'much abated by hearing of the misdeeds of General Ma', who was 'a typical opium-smoking Chinese General who had formerly sold refugee Russians back to the Soviets who shot women and children on the ice of the Amur River. Ma is a very poor hero'. According to Moss the main body of the Commission returned to Mukden while six of them flew by Japanese aeroplane to Tsitsihar because the railway was considered unsafe. At Tsitsihar the six 'had some unsatisfactory official interviews and some interesting private ones'. At Taonan, on the return journey, they 'had an interesting drive through the Chinese city' and Moss managed 'to get into a car alone with the Chinese magistrate and hear his true views which were very interesting'.[20]

There are grounds for believing that the commissioners were well satisfied merely to have proposed to conduct an interview with the dissident General Ma, even though it did not in the end come off because of Soviet opposition. Apparently, the Japanese did not veto the undertaking. When their officials reported the arrival of 'Astor and party' in Tsitsihar, they observed, so they claimed, 'an attitude of tact (*oshuburi*)'.[21]

The Japanese were determined to prevent not only representatives of the League but also the representatives of the world's press from delving too deeply into Manchurian affairs. In particular they were preoccupied with the movements of the *Journal de Genève* correspondent, Dr August Lindt, who managed to meet Ma Chanshan on June 13. Archibald Steele of the *New York Times* accompanied him. Ma later reported the meeting in a telegram in which he hinted at the connection of Lindt and Steele with Lytton or rather with the League,[22] though because of the position of Switzerland and the United States *vis-à-vis* the League this was basically implausible. At the same time, there is evidence that Ma may have deduced that they were Lytton's envoys. Lindt says that it was the presence of the word 'Geneva' on his business card that created the misunderstanding. The Japanese, who protested to the Commission about this visit, may have been under a similar misapprehension. At all events, the secretary of the Commission, Haas, denied any connection. None the less, Ma treated the interview as a propaganda victory and took full advantage of it by sending messages criticising Japan far and wide. The two journalists published signed articles about their encounter. It was certainly damaging for the Manchukuo authorities and indirectly for those of Japan. They responded by interrogating Lindt in the French consulate in Harbin and Steele in the US consulate.

Neither Lindt nor Steele was detained, but many telegrams which were exchanged at this time show the extent of the undercover operations which were going on below the rather lofty veneer of the League of Nations Commission.[23] It was clearly a matter of even wider importance for the Japanese, who felt that Ma's guerrilla movement could survive only with the aid of outside assistance, by which they implied Soviet assistance from over the River Amur. While this was unlikely in reality, it was a scare which led to vigorous enquiries being pursued, both by the army and the civilians.[24]

TRANSLATION OF WRITTEN EVIDENCE

As the commissioners returned to Peking, they faced the formidable task of writing their report. They had accumulated evidence from an extended programme of interviews and also a mountain of written statements and letters. The official responses to the Commission's questionnaires were the responsibility of the assessors; but the private and often confidential submissions which reached it through consulates and other bodies did not come within that category. Moss, who met Sir Miles Lampson in Dairen on 27 May, had thought his tasks were over but he was asked to continue his services for Lytton a little longer. With the commissioners he stopped for inspections and interviews with Japanese and Chinese authorities at Chinchow, Shanhaikuan and Peit'aiho. But on return to Peking he was asked to address the problem of translation. How were large numbers of letters of a secret nature, which might be critical of the Manchukuo authorities, the Japanese and the former Chinese rulers of Manchuria, to be handled discreetly? How was such an immense volume of documents to be translated in time for absorption in the ultimate report while preserving the confidentiality of their authors?

The Lytton Report itself did not conceal the embarrassing complexity of the problem. The commissioners recorded that in the course of their travels, they had been presented with a great quantity of printed pamphlets, petitions, appeals and letters. So far as letters alone were concerned, they had received in Manchuria 'approximately 1550 letters in Chinese and 400 letters in Russian, without mentioning those written in English, French or Japanese'.[25] The Commission was clearly ill-equipped to cope with translation on that scale. Some emergency steps for making précis of the Chinese letters had to be taken if the commissioners were to obtain any message from them. (The report does not indicate what fate awaited the 400 letters written in Russian or the message they conveyed.)

Moss's own account, which differs in some respects from the statistics of letters shown in the report, reveals the size and composition of the group charged with the task of digesting the multitude of written submissions:

In Manchuria we had collected some 60 Statements in Chinese favouring the Manchoukuo and over 1700 letters in Chinese denouncing it. These letters reached us in all sorts of devious ways, chiefly through foreign Consulates. There was no machinery for translating this mass of documents and Lord Lytton asked me what I could do about it. I went to Mr Wellington Koo, the

Chinese Delegate Assessor, and pointed out that as the majority of these documents were pro-Chinese and as neither his Office nor the Chinese Official of the League of Nations, Dr Woo Sao-fong, were able to cope with the task of translation, I proposed to hire a staff of competent Chinese translators at $15 a day if he would help me by providing an office and putting me in touch with appropriate Professors from the Universities or other qualified English or French scholars. This he promised and I went straight at Peiping to the Waichiaopu (Ministry of Foreign Affairs) where three large and handsomely furnished Salons were put at my disposal with three Chinese diplomats. In a short time I found myself working with Dr Woo Sao-fong, 4 Chinese diplomats, 7 highly qualified Professors (mostly PhDs of US Universities), 2 Chinese Doctors and 2 students, a Russian and 3 typists.

I undertook the supervision of the translations and the writing of the report on the pro-Manchoukuo documents and left Dr Woo to digest the pro-Chinese documents. In the end we signed a joint report and had translated all the important documents and summarised the rest in 12 working days.[26]

Dr Woo, who was a member of the Information Section of the League secretariat, had gone out to China to work with Robert Haas in connection with the National Economic Council and was diverted to the work of the Lytton Commission when Haas became its secretary-general. With his help Moss was responsible for the arrangement, translation and analysis of these documents. He eventually prepared an overview of the attitudes taken towards the new state of Manchukuo by correspondents, both individual and institutional, in which he reported his personal impressions of the feelings of the inhabitants of Manchuria. Those who favoured Manchukuo included the Japanese of mixed careerist origins (political visionaries, adventurers, retired military officers and civil servants, etc.) who held appointments in the new Administration, and Chinese officials who sought revenge or self-aggrandisement. In 'determined and close connection with these' were 'all the 250,000 Japanese residents in the country and all Koreans (900,000) identified with the Japanese and who are not anti-Japanese revolutionaries'. Certain former officials of the Ching dynasty who were working for the restoration of the Imperial House also favoured Manchukuo and some of these, like the Prime Minister, were 'genuinely imbued with the idea that they can form a Government fundamentally Chinese

Intelligence and the Lytton Commission 53

in character, which will later absorb China whilst remaining friendly to foreign Powers'. Associated with these was the small but rapidly increasing Mongol minority who saw in Manchukuo 'a means of saving the Mongols of Inner Mongolia from extrusion and extermination'. These Mongols were trying to resuscitate a feeling of race-consciousness and nationalism among the Manchus. They and the Japanese claimed that the Manchus were with them. The Chinese claimed, however, that the Manchus no longer existed as a separate race and had been merged with the Chinese, which to Moss seemed to be the better opinion. He conceded that 'a line of cleavage may however develop later under the stress of propaganda and self-interest'. Moss concluded:

> The above people are staunch supporters of the New State. Whatever its Genesis, their true interests are bound up with it. They – and particularly the Japanese – will probably seek to control it by supporting the Minorities against the pro-Chinese majority. They will 'Divide et Impera'. The balance of the pro-Manchoukuo factions may be classed as those whose loyalty is to their 'rice-bowl', e.g. officials who cannot get jobs elsewhere, troops, police etc etc.[27]

Moss was clear that the rest of the population, at least 80 per cent of the total of 30 million, was opposed to Manchukuo. The Chinese civilian population was apparently 'overwhelmingly against the Manchoukuo. Their hearts are turned towards China and their deeper loyalties are truly Chinese. They may perforce submit, but they are opposed strongly to any non-Chinese Government'. He believed that the Japanese claim that 'the mass of the Chinese population is passive and grateful to them for having got rid of the oppressive Chinese militaristic Government, whose place has been taken by an efficient Government ruling in accordance with the principles of Morality and Justice', was objectively absurd. Quite apart from the question of deep-seated racial and national loyalties and prejudices 'it would be necessary for the mass of the population to receive many tangible benefits in the way of increased security, considerably reduced taxation, financial control and popular political representation etc, before they could be expected to regard favourably a New State, in whose formation they had no part'. Moss was convinced that Manchukuo was considered to be entirely alien in conception and that 'the Chinese masses appear to be bitterly hostile to the Manchoukuo'.

When the Commission set off for its second visit to Japan, Moss obtained leave to return to his consulate at Weihaiwei. Its members wanted him to assist them while they were compiling their final report, after coming back from Tokyo. Moss, however, argued that he had organised a Translation Bureau for them at Peking with Dr Woo in charge of four picked professors and that it should be possible at Peking to find many more competent translators than himself and all the expert advice on things Chinese they could possibly need. He concluded that it would be needlessly expensive to retain his services, which were required during the summer at Weihaiwei, the station for the British China squadron. He returned to Weihaiwei in HMS *Suffolk* at the end of June, visiting Chinwangtao, Shanhaikuan and Chifu on the way, and was not required to return to Peking again on League business.

AFTER THE LYTTON REPORT

The report of the Lytton Commission was signed in Peking on 4 September, printed in Lausanne and published in Geneva on 1 October 1932. As this essay has suggested, it had to make great use of the less formal activities of the Lytton team. There had been a serious conflict of evidence. Moss had put it to Lytton this way:

> When the statements presented by Delegates, by members of the Japanese Assessor's office or by officials of the Manchoukuo are compared with the letters which reached the Commission from the people in Manchuria through the medium of the post or through foreign consulates or private sources, it is patent that the latter category represent the unconstrained and spontaneous expression of the ideas of citizens of all degrees, whereas the former category represent views which, although in part probably held honestly enough, obviously reflect the orthodox and approved official opinions of the Manchoukuo authorities who almost certainly inspired and reviewed them. It is equally patent that the Statements all strongly support the Manchoukuo, whilst the Letters all strongly condemn it and all its works.[28]

In their report, Lytton and his colleagues included a weighty section on 'the opinions of the inhabitants of Manchuria' which they considered to be of fundamental importance. The written evidence led them to conclude 'that there is no general Chinese support for "the Manchukuo Government" which is regarded by the local Chinese as an instrument of the Japanese'.[29] This led them to condemn Manchukuo, a conclusion which was deeply resented by the

Japanese. It shows how far the report was dependent on the behind-the-scenes activities of Moss and his helpers.

After the report was written, the intelligence needs did not end, though they were needed by the League rather than the Commission. I have written elsewhere of the problems over Japanese translation of the report. So far as Chinese translations were concerned, Moss was able to help, assuring the secretariat that the Chinese version published by Waichiaopu had been well done without omissions, interpolations or glosses.[30]

While translation of the report was necessary for deliberation by the two disputants, China and Japan, the report also required careful steering in Europe, if it was not to land the League in further difficulties. As one Member of Parliament in Britain wrote on 9 October before a speech he was due to make in his constituency: 'I shall only talk about the Manchurian Report which needs handling properly and will, of course, be misunderstood equally by the Tories and the League of Nations Union'.[31] In other words, both the League believers and the League sceptics in Europe were raring to scrutinise the report for any imperfections. There were those who felt that the League had interfered too much and aggravated the situation and those who felt that the League's involvement had been weak and unproductive.

Two issues arose for the secretariat in Geneva: how Lytton's report would be steered through its assemblies; and how the League would devise its own report. It was necessary in November to publish the translators' report on which the League Commission's findings had been based. This was the 'Report on the written or printed statements or declarations, presented in the Chinese language, by Delegates of Associations to the Commission in Manchuria'. It was stated to be written 'under the supervision and responsibility of Mr. Moss, an expert of the Commission'.[32] While some sections are similar to Moss's personal account, on which this essay is based, some are dissimilar and, in any case, the style is much more official. His Chinese colleague, Dr Woo, gave his impressions on the material he had translated separately. There is no evidence that the commissioners had read the translated documents themselves but the joint commentary was comprehensive and shrewd though, from the nature of the evidence on which it was based, the tone was sceptical of Manchukuo as a truly independent state.

The League secretariat needed to keep abreast of developments in Manchuria. One of the problems was that the scene there was a changing one and had radically altered from that in May when the commissioners had made their circuit of the territory. To bring the picture up to date, Adrianus Pelt, an energetic Dutch member of the Information Section deputed to the Commission's secretariat, who had spent ten days investigating in Manchuria in May and July, took time on his return journey to Geneva to stay over for further investigations. He left Peking on 9 September but found the land route via Shanhaikuan too unsafe on account of the raids by Chinese volunteers operating in the Jehol border region. He stopped over in each of the principal Manchurian cities: 'In Changchun, as in all other places I went through, Japanese consuls and Manchukuo authorities showed extreme courtesy and did everything in their power to be helpful, while the military authorities give their cooperation with visible reserve and reluctance'.[33] Before joining the Trans-Siberian Railway, he managed to have some informal discussion with Soviet officials. He returned to Geneva on 2 October and handed over a note concerning the situation in Manchuria in September. Interestingly enough, he was sufficiently optimistic to propose that copies of the Lytton Report which had just appeared should be sent to certain Japanese and Manchukuo officials 'who either are privately in sympathy with the Commission's point of view or are prepared to make a serious attempt to understand this point of view'.[34] He gave no sign of who these officials were; but it is an illuminating new insight into the Manchukuoan scene to know that some of them were at least tolerant of the League's thinking.

Pelt invited subsequent reports from the Netherlands consul in Harbin, L. van der Hoeven. These came in at almost monthly intervals, were translated or paraphrased by Pelt and circulated to the secretariat.[35] It cannot be judged what weight they carried nor whether this was a piece of private diplomacy by Pelt or something authorised from Geneva. But at least the League, when it was taking the agonising steps towards its final report early in 1933, was reflecting the contemporary position in the country.

On 24 February 1933 the Assembly of the League passed its long-awaited report. In general, it adopted many of the recommendations of the League Commission, which had in turn adopted many of the findings of George Moss (and his other colleagues on the panel of experts). Moss, who had been very close to the deliberations of the commissioners while they were in Manchuria, summed up their views as follows:

> I think they realize the predominant military and naval position

of Japan; also that the Japanese are in a state of spiritual excitement and tension in which anything like coercion or threat would be fatal. Japan is in a mood 'to call a bluff', and the plain fact is that no-one wants to tackle her over Manchuria. She has or rather had a fundamentally sound case for a revision of her position with the Nationalists. Although she has flouted all the ideals which the League stands for, it is desired rather to bring her back to the international fold than to outlaw her. It is a great deal to hope for, but the aspiration is to find practical means of satisfying the Moderates on both sides without sacrificing the League ideals.[36]

Such hopes were not to be fulfilled: the League did not resolve the Manchurian problem; and Japan did not stay within the international fold. It could not be said to be a successful diplomatic solution. But it could equally not be said that the judgements of Lytton and the League were not based on sound information and analysis.

This essay has suggested the limits within which international bodies have to operate. The Lytton Commission and later the League itself had difficulty in getting below the surface of the situation on the ground, bearing in mind the formal procedures it had to follow. The Commission had to weigh the evidence it obtained from its interviews against what might be called political intelligence sources. In this respect, it was well served by George Moss, who performed the essential role of conducting covert conversations with a wide range of Chinese leaders. The thrust of Moss's reports was adopted by the Commission, whose report always refers to 'Manchukuo' in inverted commas, thereby suggesting that it was not a genuine state.[37]

ACKNOWLEDGEMENTS

The author expresses his thanks to the International Studies Research Division of the London School of Economics for two research grants, also the Japan Foundation, Tokyo, for assistance over research in Japan.

NOTES

1 See I.H. Nish, *Japan's Struggle with Internationalism: Japan, China and the League of Nations, 1931–1933*, London, Kegan Paul, 1993, for the most recent analysis of the Manchurian crisis from contemporary sources; cf. C. Thorne, *The Limits of Foreign Policy: The League, the*

West and the Far Eastern Crisis of 1931–33, London, Hamish Hamilton, 1972; R. Bassett, Democracy and Foreign Policy, London, Longman, 1952; Sadako N. Ogata, Defiance in Manchuria: The Making of Japanese Foreign Policy 1931–1932, Berkeley, University of California Press, 1964.
2 Nish, op. cit., pp. 30–4.
3 Exposé by Sugimura, 21 January 1932, in League of Nations Archives, R1975 (Salle des Archives de la Société des Nations, Geneva). Hereafter cited as *LNA*. It should be pointed out that Esmonde Robertson acquired much information about Sugimura, who became ambassador to Italy after Japan left the League of Nations in 1933.
4 Drummond to Lytton (at Knebworth), 29 January 1932, *LNA* R1874
5 *Gendaishi Shiryo*, vol. 11, 'Zoku Manshu Jihen', Tokyo, Misuzu Shobo, 1965, pp. 817ff and 834–5.
6 Astor to Robert Cecil, 15 December 1931, *LNA* R1874; D. Wilson, *The Astors, 1762–1992*, London, Weidenfeld & Nicolson, 1993, pp. 261–2.
7 From 'Organization of League Commission', undated, *LNA* R1875.
8 Chu Pao-chin, *V.K. Wellington Koo*, Hong Kong, Chinese University, 1981, ch. 6. On Yoshida, see *Nihon gaiko bunsho*, 'Manshu Jihen', vol. I/iii, pp. 716, 748–9.
9 Diary of Sir Miles Lampson, Britain's Minister to China (in private hands), entry for 18 March 1932.
10 Lampson diary, 20 March 1932; Cadogan to Drummond, 29 April 1932, *LNA* R1875.
11 *Documents on British Foreign Policy, 1919–1939*, 2nd series, vol. X, nos 197, 208, 497 and 521.
12 P.D. Coates, *The China Consuls: British Consular Officers, 1843–1943*, Hong Kong, Oxford University Press, 1988, p. 529; 'Organization of League Commission', *LNA* R1875.
13 A.P. Jones, *Britain's Search for Chinese Cooperation in the First World War*, New York, Garland, 1986.
14 Lampson to Simon, 7 December 1931, FO371, F287/1/10.
15 G.E. Moss to his family, 14 July 1932, in the papers of Sir James Haldane Stewart Lockhart (National Library of Scotland, Edinburgh), 4138/6. A copy was sent to Sir Reginald Johnston, who passed it on to Stewart Lockhart with the request to burn the notes when read. This was not done. R.F. Johnston to Stewart Lockhart, 9 September 1932, ibid. Hereafter cited as *SL*.
16 'Organization of League Commission', *LNA* R1875.
17 Moss to family, 14 July 1932, *SL* 4138/6.
18 Ma Chanshan to League of Nations, etc., 14 April 1932, *Foreign Relations of the United States*, 1932, vol. III, pp. 741–7. *Gendaishi Shiryo*, Tokyo, 1965, vol. 11, pp. 675ff.
19 Nish, op. cit., pp. 142–50.
20 Moss to family, 14 July 1932, *SL* 4138/6.
21 *Nihon gaiko bunsho*, 'Manshu Jihen', II(i), p. 879.
22 A.R. Lindt, *Special Correspondent: With Bandit and General in Manchuria*, London, Cobden-Sanderson, 1933. See also *The Times*, 12 June 1932.
23 *Nihon gaiko bunsho*, 'Manshu Jihen', II(i), pp. 891–939 passim.
24 Nagaoka (acting consul-general, Harbin) to Yoshizawa, 25 May 1932 in

Nihon gaiko bunsho, 'Manshu Jihen', II(i), pp. 881–2. Nagaoka thought wrongly that Moss after thirty years in China could be regarded as pro-Japanese.
25 *Report of the Commission of Enquiry: Appeal by the Chinese Government*, Geneva, League of Nations, 1932, p. 12. Also p. 107: 'All these 1550 letters except two, were bitterly hostile to the new Manchukuo Government'.
26 Moss to family, 14 July 1932, *SL* 4138/6.
27 ibid.
28 ibid.
29 *Report of Commission of Enquiry*, pp. 107–11.
30 Moss to R. Haas, 23 February 1933, *LNA* R1875.
31 Antony Lytton, MP, to Lord Lytton, 9 October 1932, in Victor, Earl of Lytton, *Antony, Viscount Knebworth*, London, Peter Davies, 1935.
32 League of Nations, *Supplementary Documents to the Report of the Commission of Enquiry*, 15 November 1932, Part II, Annex C, pp. 22–6.
33 'Note by Pelt concerning the situation in Manchuria during September', *LNA* P105.
34 Pelt to Avenol, 6 October 1932, *LNA* P105.
35 'Situation in Manchuria: mostly letters in Dutch from the Netherlands Consulate in Harbin and some translations to English and report [by Pelt]', 11 December 1932–11 December 1933, *LNA* P105. These reports are not included in the official collection of Dutch diplomatic documents, *Documenten Betreffende de Buitenlandse Politiek van Nederland, 1919–45*, series B, 1931–40, vols i and ii. But van der Hoeven and Dutch persons connected with the Lytton Commission like Pelt and Dr de Kat Angelino were regularly in contact with the Hague.
36 Moss to family, 14 July 1932, *SL* 4138/6.
37 While the commissioners in their final report placed 'Manchukuo' inside inverted commas, they did not adopt Moss's spelling of Manchoukuo or his quaint usage of putting 'the' in front of it.

3 The Geneva Disarmament Conference 1932–34

Dick Richardson

The problem of international disarmament was one of the most complicated issues left unresolved by the Treaty of Versailles in 1919. Arguably, it is the least researched problem of major significance in twentieth-century international history. With one or two exceptions, notably Maurice Vaïsse, historians have been reluctant to tackle the subject. Considering that the powers represented at Geneva were discussing the momentous question of the distribution of world power and the realignment of the status quo of 1919, it is perhaps surprising that only a modicum of studies have as yet been published.[1] This essay constitutes one of a series of my contributions: I hope not only to throw further light on the disarmament problem but also to explain the importance of the Geneva Disarmament Conference in the shift of international power relationships in the early 1930s.

Under Part V of the Treaty of Versailles, Germany was disarmed to the lowest point consistent with the maintenance of internal order and control of her frontiers. Her army was limited to 100,000 men and she was prohibited from possessing 'aggressive' weapons such as tanks, heavy guns, battleships over 10,000 tons, military aircraft and submarines. By these and other security measures, notably the territorial settlement and the establishment of the League of Nations as an organ of collective security, the victor powers of 1919 hoped to prevent a resumption of German aggression. However, to make the disarmament clauses more palatable to the new Weimar Republic, it was stated in the preamble to Part V of the treaty that the arms reductions required of Germany were also intended 'to render possible the initiation of a general limitation of armaments of all nations'.[2]

It was primarily upon the preamble to Part V of the Versailles Treaty that Germany was to base her claim for equality of rights

The Geneva Disarmament Conference 61

with the other powers in the disarmament negotiations of 1919–34. Her interpretation, which was difficult to deny, was that the other powers had a moral, indeed legal, obligation to disarm in response to her own enforced disarmament; and that if the other powers did not disarm, Germany would be relieved of her obligation to remain disarmed. This interpretation was reinforced by the so-called Clemenceau Letter of 16 June 1919 by which the victor powers of 1919 stated specifically that the reductions required of Germany were 'the first steps towards that general reduction and limitation of armaments which they seek to bring about as one of the most fruitful preventives of war, and which it will be one of the first duties of the League of Nations to promote'.[3]

Not surprisingly, the Allied powers did not put the same interpretation on the preamble to Part V of the Peace Treaty and the Clemenceau Letter. Whilst recognising a certain moral obligation – considering that moral obligations count for little in the realm of international diplomacy – they asserted that their legal obligation to disarmament devolved from Article 8 of the League of Nations Covenant, which stated that the maintenance of peace required 'the reduction of national armaments to the lowest point consistent with national safety and the enforcement by common action of international obligations'.[4]

Even if, in terms of legal obligations, it was from Article 8 of the Covenant that the disarmament negotiations of the 1920s and early 1930s devolved, in practice the impulsion behind the negotiations was the potential threat of Germany to the Versailles security system. As the years progressed, and German power grew in relation to that of Britain and France, more particularly with the political isolation of both the United States and Soviet Union, it became increasingly clear that, if the powers failed to negotiate an international convention acceptable to Germany, Germany would rearm unilaterally. In this sense, the disarmament problem was the problem of European security, and the problem of European security was the problem of German power.

Effectively, negotiations for disarmament did not begin until after the security settlement at Locarno in October 1925. In 1926, the League of Nations established the Preparatory Commission for the Disarmament Conference, and for four and a half years this body involved itself in a series of technical discussions concerning the principles and methods of disarmament. So profound were the discussions that Salvador de Madariaga, head of the League of Nations Disarmament Section, suggested that the only questions that had been overlooked were the influence of monotheism and polytheism on armaments and the beauty of princesses as causes of war.[5] A draft convention was produced in December 1930 as the basis for the Disarmament Conference's discussions, but it contained no figures and was full of so many reservations that as a practical document it was useless.

By the time the Disarmament Conference opened at Geneva on 2 February 1932, the prospects for its success could hardly have been less favourable, at both the technical and political levels. It was clear that the draft convention produced by the Preparatory Commission was an unacceptable basis for agreement. Not only was it opposed outright by Germany and the Soviet Union, but also it was so full of reservations and caveats as to be meaningless. This was hardly surprising. Powers had been putting forward maximalist positions to which they would not necessarily adhere when substantive negotiations opened. Besides, there was the question of whether or not the Disarmament Conference could ever have been successful within its own terms of reference. As the Washington Conference of 1922 had shown, it is often difficult for a handful of nations to reach even a modicum of technical agreement on a restricted number of arms questions. In comparison, some fifty-nine states were represented at the opening of the Disarmament Conference, and yet they were expected to negotiate a convention covering land and air forces as well as naval forces. This fact in itself gives an indication of the difficulties involved in negotiating a convention at the technical level – even if the will to disarmament were there.

At the political level, international relations had deteriorated considerably since the adoption of the Draft Convention. Partly, this was a consequence of the collapse of the international economy following the Wall Street crash of October 1929. The world recession deepened. International trade slumped. Governments followed policies of nationalist economics. Internal difficulties were blamed on external problems. There was a wholesale move to the political right. Variants of fascism gained increasing influence. In many states, the military controlled the strings of power. Hardline governments, opposed in principle to the concept of disarmament, entered office. Amongst the policy-making elites of the various states, belief in disarmament as a catalyst towards solving international problems declined.

The rise of militarism and militant nationalism could be seen world-wide. In South America, Paraguay and Bolivia were embroiled in their dispute over the Chaco. In Germany, democratic

The Geneva Disarmament Conference 63

government broke down after the Reichstag elections of September 1930, in which the National Socialists made significant gains. The right-wing chancellor, Heinrich Brüning, resorted to ruling by decree under Article 48 of the Weimar constitution. In the Far East, Japan embarked upon a policy of military aggression in Manchuria on 18 September 1931, establishing the puppet state of Manchukuo on 1 March 1932. Effectively, the Japanese army was running the government rather than the government the army. The security system erected at Washington in 1922 was breaking down. From December 1931 onwards, successive Japanese governments based their policies on the exigencies of power rather than the search for international agreement.

In the circumstances, it was highly unlikely that Japan would sign a disarmament agreement at Geneva. Yet, if Japan refused to sign, it was doubtful whether the Soviet Union or China, confronted by the Japanese threat on their borders, would sign. And if the Soviet Union refused to sign, it was unlikely that the states on her western border would sign. The Germans, too, might use Soviet nonsignature as a pretext for refusing an agreement. Nevertheless, even if a general convention of all fifty-nine powers represented at the conference proved unattainable, two possibilities remained. First, a convention might be limited to a restricted category of armaments. For example, there might be an extension of the Geneva Gas Protocol of 1925.[6] Second, there was the possibility of regional arms conventions limited to powers in specific geographical areas. For example, one convention might cover western and central Europe. In this particular case, the central problem would be the equation of the French demand for security with the German demand for equality of rights. Perhaps not surprisingly, the search for such an agreement became the essential feature of the Geneva negotiations.

The Franco-German demands were not incompatible. In fact, during the Lausanne conference in June 1932, there were direct talks between Edouard Herriot and Franz von Papen, French Prime Minister and German Chancellor respectively, for a disarmament agreement as part of a wider settlement covering the abolition of reparations, a Franco-German customs union and some kind of alliance against the Soviet Union. The scheme was put forward by Papen. Herriot, while sceptical of the new Chancellor's intentions, saw possibilities in the scheme and decided to follow through the initiative. Eventually, the talks broke down, but, interestingly, one of the principal reasons for the breakdown was the opposition of the British Prime Minister, Ramsay MacDonald, who was haunted by the spectre of a Franco-German alliance which would 'upset the balance of European power'.[7] The talks may well have broken down anyway, as there was much opposition to them within nationalist circles in Germany, and they did not represent the mainstream line of advance towards a settlement at Geneva on the part of either Germany or France. Nevertheless, they illustrate the fact that the two powers were not averse to a disarmament agreement. Rather, they recognised that through such an agreement it might be possible for them to secure their interests. After all, the essence of the disarmament discussions at Geneva was the distribution of world power and the realignment of the existing status quo.

The French objective at the Disarmament Conference was to maintain as great a military superiority over Germany as possible. It was hoped that this might be accomplished by retaining as many heavy weapons as possible, whilst still denying to Germany the weapons denied to her by the Treaty of Versailles. However, in the knowledge that such a scheme would not be looked upon favourably by Germany, the United States or Britain, the French were prepared to make reductions in their heavy weapons and to hand the remainder over, at least nominally, to the League of Nations for use as an international deterrent. In this way, it was hoped that the heaviest weapons would remain under French control while still being denied to the Germans. This was the basis of the Tardieu Plan of 5 February 1932. The plan involved the creation of an international air force, the internationalisation of civil aviation, the prohibition of bombing, rigid verification procedures and the strengthening of the League. Qualitative restrictions would be placed on future armaments construction (to ensure that Germany would not gain access to heavy weapons), but states could retain existing weapons in excess of the dimensions agreed for future construction provided they were used only in self-defence or on orders from the League.[8]

In practice, France was prepared to reduce her existing military superiority over Germany only if she were given adequate compensation in the form of security guarantees. There were a number of possibilities. France could seek new or additional commitments from other major powers, primarily the United States, Britain, Italy or the Soviet Union. She could seek to strengthen the security provisions of the League of Nations. She could press for tight verification procedures in the proposed disarmament convention. She could press for automatic sanctions in cases of violations of the convention. In fact, at various times and through various channels, she sought them

The Geneva Disarmament Conference 65

all. As early as 1931, for example, she made approaches to Italy and the Soviet Union. Whilst not immediately successful, they were to lead to the Rome accords and Franco-Soviet alliance of January and May 1935 respectively. Primarily, though, France sought additional security guarantees from Britain, either directly, through military commitment, or indirectly, through the League of Nations or disarmament convention.[9]

The extent of France's security demands depended on three factors which individually and collectively were to change during the Disarmament Conference: the political persuasion of the French government; the nature and policy of the German government; and the extent to which individual disarmament proposals reduced French military superiority over Germany. The greater the move towards German equality, the greater the demands for enhanced security. Perhaps the most desirable outcome from the French point of view was a system of collective security under the general auspices of the League but with non-League powers, more especially the United States, attached. Paul-Boncour put forward such a plan on 14 November 1932. Security would be maintained through the organisation of states into three concentric 'circles'. The outermost circle would consist of all states represented at the Disarmament Conference, and its members would agree to consult with each other in the event of a breach of the Kellogg Pact. The second would comprise of all members of the League, who would reaffirm the obligations they had assumed under the Covenant (especially Article 16, the sanctions article) and all other treaties, such as Locarno, which had been concluded in conformity with the Covenant. The third and innermost circle would include the nations of continental Europe, who would enter a pact of mutual assistance. To make for equity, each of the powers in the mutual assistance pact would organise their 'permanent defensive forces' on a standardised model based on universal short-term service and limited effectives.[10] Failing such a reorganisation of the international security system, the French would eagerly have accepted either an Anglo-French alliance, or a military back-up to Locarno. Nevertheless, throughout much of the Disarmament Conference, France was willing to accept rather less in the way of compensation than any of these possibilities provided that the procedures for verification in the disarmament convention were stringent enough.[11]

The French were in the unenviable position that they could not be precise about their security demands until they knew the precise nature of Germany's claim for equality. To what extent would the

Germans try to translate equality of rights into equality of armaments? From intelligence sources, they had a clear enough idea of covert German rearmament and the aspirations of the German military, but such information could hardly be released in public. Militarily and economically, Germany was in an extremely weak position in February 1932, but diplomatically she was in a far better position than at any time previously. The occupation forces had been withdrawn, and she had the assurance, implicit in the Locarno treaty, that France would not pursue a policy of coercion such as that followed at the time of the Ruhr crisis. Besides, now that the time had arrived for substantive negotiation rather than discussion of abstract principles, the onus could be put on the other powers, France in particular, to make good the 'promises' of 1919.

As far as Germany was concerned, the Disarmament Conference provided a near-perfect cover for the pursuit of rearmament. A modicum of rearmament had already taken place in the early years of the Weimar Republic, partly as a result of covert military collaboration with the Soviet Union. However, the watershed in German rearmament was the approval by Hermann Müller's grand coalition Cabinet in October 1928 of a four-year programme of arms expansion. Projected for completion by 1 April 1933, the programme envisaged the establishment of a 16-division army compared with the 7-division army organised under the Versailles restrictions. The initiator of the proposal may have been the Minister of Defence, General Gröner, but it is significant that the programme had the backing even of Social Democrat ministers.[12]

Preparations for a second, more substantial armaments expansion programme covering the period 1933–38 proceeded apace during the run-up to the Disarmament Conference. Although not formally approved by the Reichswehr minister until November 1932, they formed the essential milieu of German disarmament policy throughout the first year of the conference's existence. The new programme involved the development of a 21-division army of some 300,000 men equipped with a given number of weapons expressly forbidden to Germany by the terms of the Versailles Treaty, notably heavy artillery, tanks and military aircraft. The period of service in the Reichswehr would be reduced, and a militia would be organised based on three-month service. The idea was that the Disarmament Conference be used to secure international recognition for the expansion programme. It was considered that the demands for rearmament were consistent with a legal claim to parity either with France alone or with Poland and Czechoslovakia combined. How-

The Geneva Disarmament Conference 67

ever, if the demands were not conceded by the other powers, it was thought that Germany should break off negotiations for an international convention and the Reichswehr restructured within the framework of the demands.[13]

At the Disarmament Conference itself, the Germans could afford to follow a reactive rather than proactive policy. It was more advantageous to say 'not enough' to the proposals of other powers than to formulate a defined position. They wanted to be in a position where they could ask for 'more'. It is interesting, therefore, to note that there was only one occasion prior to their final withdrawal from the Disarmament Conference in October 1933 that they put forward a specific proposal for an overall settlement. This was in April 1932, when Brüning endeavoured to gain an agreement at Geneva which would preserve his precarious position at home. The one pitfall which German leaders had to avoid was pressing their case to the extent that they created a united front against Germany and left themselves open to accusations of deliberately breaking up the conference.

Given the circumstances of the time, the objectives and policies pursued by France and Germany were both natural and understandable. In practice, however, the realisation of their objectives depended on the policy pursued by Britain. Effectively, Britain was the only power capable of mediating between the two continental powers, of squaring the circle between French security and German equality. This was hardly a new problem as far as the British were concerned. The same question had underlain the failed discussions for a Treaty of Mutual Assistance in 1923 and the Geneva Protocol in 1924.[14] It was never far from the surface of the discussions in the Preparatory Commission. In the past, successive British governments had tried to ignore the question, or prevaricate, usually successfully. But, once substantive negotiations were opened at the Disarmament Conference, there was no way Britain could avoid taking a stance on the issue. In the final analysis, there was no way either the French or German governments would allow Britain the luxury of standing aside.

The problem was not that the British government failed to recognise the interrelationship of disarmament and security. Not only did the French consistently press the matter, so too did the Foreign Office.[15] In practice, however, the government was unwilling to accept that the exertion of British power through direct participation in the European security system was an essential component in bringing about an agreement acceptable to both France and

Germany. The Cabinet discussed the question on 15 December 1931, and again on 13 and 20 January 1932; but, crucially, it was decided that Britain could not accept commitments in addition to Locarno which might involve European war. The decision effectively sounded the death knell of the conference even before it had started.[16] Britain would not give France the guarantees she needed to make arms reductions in relation to Germany sufficient to bring about a Franco-German agreement.

On the armaments side, the British position was in many respects similar to that of the Germans. The government deliberately set out to use the Disarmament Conference to improve Britain's power position in world affairs. For example, with regard to air armaments, the aim was to elevate Britain from fifth to first place in the ranking of powers. At one point during the conference, Britain in effect asked France to reduce the number of her aircraft from nearly 2,000 to 500 in return for the Commonwealth being allowed to increase its numbers from 1,000 to between 1,200 and 1,400![17] Similarly, with regard to tanks, British policy anticipated the scrapping by the other powers of heavy tanks above an agreed limit of some 16–20 tons (Britain had none over the proposed limit) whilst allowing an increase in British tanks from some 208 to 550.[18] Moreover, when reviewing a proposal by the British delegates at Geneva for presenting a draft convention to the Disarmament Conference, the Ministerial Disarmament Committee decided that the figures envisaged for British effectives represented such an increase over existing levels that the figures should be omitted.[19]

The reality is that the British government did not have a disarmament policy. It had an armaments policy which it hoped to push through in the guise of disarmament. The majority of ministers were sceptical of disarmament, if not actively opposed to it.[20] They felt that Britain had already carried out arms reductions in the 1920s which entitled her to demand further reductions from other powers whilst leaving Britain free to increase her own armaments. They did not believe in the Disarmament Conference or its objectives, rather they felt obliged to take part in it due to the undertakings of 1919 and the fear that Germany would openly renege on her obligations under the Treaty of Versailles if no agreement was reached. As far as the outcome of the conference was concerned, the government hoped that France, somehow, could be induced into drastically reducing her armaments in relation to Germany whilst claiming no additional security guarantees from Britain, with the result that

The Geneva Disarmament Conference 69

German armaments could be kept at levels similar to those imposed at Versailles. This was, indeed, a hope rather than a policy.

The conventional view of British policy at the Disarmament Conference is that Britain actively pursued the role of mediator between France and Germany.[21] But this was not the case. From the outset, the British government deliberately shunned the role of mediator, for to mediate effectively meant deeper British participation in the European security system. Essentially, British policy was to be one of prevarication, equivocation, an avoidance of commitment, best expressed by MacDonald's comment of 6 December 1932 that French and German ministers should 'put their demands in such a way that Britain could say that she supported both sides'.[22] The Disarmament Conference was to be in session for some thirteen months before Britain produced a disarmament plan, the ill-named MacDonald Plan of 16 March 1933. Even then, this plan was produced more to escape responsibility for the projected failure of the conference rather than as a means of resolving the Franco-German dispute.[23]

It would be wrong to suggest that a successful outcome to the Disarmament Conference depended solely on Britain. Other great powers involved in the negotiations were in a position to help promote agreement, in particular the United States. The power potential of the United States was such that the French declared themselves willing to undertake more substantial arms reductions – and the British to reconsider their attitude to French security – if only the US government would bind itself more closely to the European security system. This, however, was not to be. If anything, the world economic crisis reinforced the isolationist tendencies of the Americans and made them even more insular in their attitudes and policies. They were quite unwilling to become involved in the politico-military problems of Europe, even for the sake of bringing about a Franco-German agreement. In any case, the major concern of President Hoover during 1932, apart from the economic crisis, was not the Disarmament Conference, but the forthcoming presidential election. Accordingly, Hoover sought the moral high ground of castigating the European powers for pursuing the old policies of the arms race and competitive alliances. In his inaugural address to the Disarmament Conference, the chief US delegate, Hugh Gibson, suggested that the real problem facing the conference was simply 'how promptly and smoothly mankind will cast aside the weapons and traditions of old'.[24]

In its attempt to divorce the problem of security from that of disarmament, and in its unwillingness to play a leading part in negotiations, the US government was to play almost a maverick role at the Disarmament Conference. The same too could be said of two other major powers, Italy and the Soviet Union. As far as Italy was concerned, there was a dichotomy between the militaristic outpourings of Mussolini for internal consumption and his wish to use the Disarmament Conference as a means of securing military equality for Italy with the other leading states of Europe. Equally, Soviet leaders were in a dilemma. On the one hand, they wished to continue their alignment with Germany, which had proved so successful in the Preparatory Commission, since both powers were dissatisfied with the status quo of 1919. On the other, they wished to court the western powers in order to protect themselves against the resurgence of German nationalism. The Soviets also needed to protect themselves against Japan on their eastern borders. In practice, therefore, they followed the ideological line of championing the cause of total disarmament or, alternatively, drastic proportional disarmament, and withdrew themselves from the mainstream discussions and conversations. Their influence on proceedings at Geneva was therefore negligible.[25]

One of the distinguishing features of the Geneva conference was its lack of political leadership. At Washington, in 1921–22, the Americans had taken the lead, promoting large-scale reductions in capital ships. At the Preparatory Commission France and Britain had given the proceedings a sense of direction by the promulgation of their draft conventions in March 1927. Hoover and MacDonald had been the driving forces in the London Naval Treaty. But no single power or person was willing, or able, to give effective leadership at Geneva. No single power was willing to grasp the nettle of equating German equality with French security. Each power was more concerned with avoiding responsibility for the failure of the conference than with forwarding its success. By default, the Germans assumed a kind of negative leadership, by claiming that the programmes of work presented by other powers did not go far enough to meet their demands for equality. The exception to this came in April 1932, when Brüning put forward a plan to secure equality of rights for Germany. The Nazis had just made considerable gains at provincial elections in Prussia, Bavaria, Anhalt, Württenburg and Hamburg (an area representing some four-fifths of Germany) and the German Chancellor hoped to bolster his fragile internal position by securing a disarmament settlement to Germany's advantage.[26]

The proposals which Brüning put forward were designed to

achieve equality of treatment rather than equality of armaments. On 26 April, in private conversation with MacDonald and the US Secretary of State, Henry L. Stimson, he insisted that he would be satisfied with a reduction in the period of service in the Reichswehr from twelve years to six, and a reduction in the armed forces of France – though not to the German level – through the abolition of 'particularly aggressive' weapons. Equality of rights would be secured through the transfer of Germany's disarmament obligations from Part V of the Treaty of Versailles to the proposed disarmament convention, which might last for ten years. In return, Brüning indicated a willingness to consider the establishment of an international force along the lines of the Tardieu Plan, with the ultimate objective of abolishing the 'more aggressive' weapons under its control. To facilitate the establishment of an international air force, Germany would accept the internationalisation of civil aviation.[27]

In the circumstances of the time, Brüning's plan appeared to be very moderate. It assured France of military superiority in Europe for a period of ten years, whilst satisfying the German demand for equality – temporarily at least. MacDonald and Stimson, while not going so far as to accept the plan, agreed that the discussions of 26 April had helped 'towards immediately clearing away some of the fundamental obstacles towards ultimate agreement'.[28] But any chance of success depended on French acquiescence, and so a further meeting of government representatives was scheduled for 29 April, which would include the French Prime Minister, André Tardieu, and the Italian representative, Dino Grandi, as well as Stimson, Brüning and MacDonald. The meeting, however, did not take place. Tardieu was unable to travel to Geneva because of an attack of laryngitis (real or diplomatic depending on the source) and two days later was defeated in the first round of the French general elections.[29] Despite the fact that he was replaced by the more moderate Herriot, any chance of agreement melted away as Stimson returned to the United States and MacDonald to Britain. Within a month, the Brüning government had been replaced by the more militant nationalist administration of Franz von Papen.

It is an open question as to whether the possibility of agreement existed on the basis of the Brüning plan. Many who were close to the personnel involved, notably A.C. Temperley, the military adviser to the British delegation, and the political commentator John Wheeler-Bennett, a confidant of Brüning, believe the April conversations were a lost opportunity. Both attack Stimson and MacDonald for their failure to press Tardieu to return to Geneva for direct talks with Brüning.[30] Tardieu's position is interesting. A hardline conservative, he was rightly worried that any appearance of concessions to Germany on equality of rights might cause his defeat in the elections of 1 May. Certainly it would have been difficult for him to backtrack on his security plan of 5 February in the middle of the election campaign. At the same time, he was aware of the danger of Brüning being replaced by a more strident nationalist, and from conversations in Geneva in March and April 1932 it seems that, in the event of an electoral victory, he might have reduced his security demands on Britain and the United States to well below those put forward on 5 February.[31]

The British position regarding the Brüning plan is ambiguous. There are no records of the conversations of 26 April in the British archives (which, to say the least, is surprising considering that records were taken of far less important discussions at Geneva). Moreover, MacDonald appeared to regard any subsequent reference to the deliberations as a personal affront.[32] In essence, the 'April episode' should be seen as an early indication that Britain wished to shun the role of mediator between France and Germany. Doubtless MacDonald viewed the conversations as an advance in general terms, but there are indications that he was relieved that Tardieu did not appear at Geneva on 29 April. The British Prime Minister did not relish the possibility of being faced with new French security demands, even if they were pitched at a lower level than in February, since the Cabinet had rejected the possibility of additional continental commitments. In this sense, MacDonald's reluctance to press Tardieu into returning to Geneva becomes understandable. His desire to avoid new security commitments was greater than his desire to promote disarmament.

For the greater part of its proceedings, the Disarmament Conference was bogged down in technical discussions. To a large extent, this reflected the unwillingness of the politicians to take decisions or responsibility regarding the direction of the conference and the promotion of disarmament. Nevertheless, technical factors were an important element in the negotiating process in their own right. At one level, it was essential to secure agreement on technical problems if a disarmament agreement was to be achieved. At a second, the position of the powers on technical matters formed a yardstick by which responsibility for the failure of the conference could be measured. In this respect, Germany had a decided advantage. The fact that Germany was prohibited from possessing certain categories of weapon under Part V of the Versailles Treaty made it possible

The Geneva Disarmament Conference 73

to draw a distinction between 'offensive' and 'defensive' weapons. Those prohibited to Germany could be deemed 'offensive', those not prohibited 'defensive'. In other words, the Germans could claim that the effective technical decisions had been made in 1919. Thus, from a purely technical standpoint, Germany was enabled to direct the agenda of the conference onto the question of equality of rights. If the other powers were to concede the principle of equality, they could not reasonably deny to Germany the weapons they themselves were permitted to retain. Either they must disarm towards the German level, or, alternatively, allow Germany a quota of all armaments not specifically proscribed for all other powers, even those deemed 'offensive' in 1919.[33]

The technical discussions revolved around three key issues: tanks, air disarmament and verification. Because of the existence of the Washington and London treaties, naval problems were of relatively little importance. As regards tanks, there was general support for their complete abolition, partly as a means of disarmament, partly as a means of securing equality for Germany. Of the great powers, Italy and the Soviet Union consistently supported abolition, and the Americans adopted a similar stance in the Hoover Plan of 22 June 1932. As a means of disarmament – as distinct from a means of securing equality for Germany – abolition had two major advantages. It secured the elimination of a whole category of weapons which was regarded as offensive rather than defensive; and it was easier to verify than merely a restriction of numbers. Two major powers were opposed to abolition – Japan and France. The Japanese were open and forthright in their rejection of abolition, but the French, very astutely, advocated the abolition of tanks in 'national armies' but their retention, along with other heavy weapons, in 'specialised contingents' under League of Nations authority. The French objective was to maintain a considerable superiority in *matériel* over Germany, but there was a definite logic in their concept of an international force equipped with heavier weapons than national armies.[34]

Notwithstanding the essential difficulty caused by the attitude of the Japanese delegation, progress on the tank issue seemed possible, at least within a European context, if the British supported the concept of abolition. Such, however, was not the government's intention. Far from wishing to abolish tanks, the government wanted to increase their number. The objective was arms increases for Britain, arms reductions for other powers. In practice, there was no way the other powers would allow this to happen. But this did not stop the government making the attempt. The British line was not to claim increases openly, but to suggest that light and medium tanks of some 16–20 tons were defensive – a euphemism for the fact that the military authorities regarded such tanks as necessary compensation for the manpower constraints of a voluntarist army. Adhesion to this line was inconsistent with British policy regarding the Franco-German problem. If tanks of 16–20 tons were classified as defensive, a given number could hardly be denied to Germany, more especially after the formal concession of equality of rights in the five-power declaration of 11 December 1932. In such a circumstance, the arms increases for Germany would not simply have negated Britain's policy of restricting German rearmament, they would have generated further unwelcome demands by France for security compensations. Moreover, from a technical standpoint, Britain was isolated at Geneva in wanting to retain tanks of 16 tons. Whatever the intrinsic merits (or demerits) of the British case, it was Britain that appeared to be the major stumbling block to disarmament as regards tanks.[35]

A similar situation arose over air disarmament. The great majority of powers favoured the abolition of both bombing aircraft and aerial bombardment, partly as a means of securing equality for Germany, partly as a means of disarmament. From the latter point of view, as with tanks, abolition had two major advantages: it eliminated an entire class of 'aggressive' weapons, and was easier to verify than quantitative restrictions. Of the great powers, Italy, the United States and the Soviet Union, along with Germany, consistently supported abolition. France supported abolition as regards 'national' air forces but advocated the establishment of an international air force under League of Nations authority. Japan opposed abolition, which was hardly surprising given her contemporary bombing campaign in Manchuria.

Again, notwithstanding the essential difficulty caused by Japan, progress towards air disarmament appeared to depend on the attitude taken by Britain. On the surface, it seemed that the abolition proposal was clearly in Britain's interest. The equalisation of bombing forces at the level of zero would improve Britain's ranking in air power from fifth to joint first. However, the government adopted the Air Ministry's line of making Britain the foremost air power through rearmament rather than disarmament. The idea was to use the Disarmament Conference to demand equality with the other great powers in Europe whilst claiming additional aircraft for use in the Empire. Abolition was opposed on two grounds. First, it was claimed that the elimination of bombers would necessitate the internationalisation of civil aviation, in order to prevent civilian aircraft being used as bombers. This was ruled out on the assumption that internationalisation was 'impracticable'. Second, it was claimed that aerial bombardment was cheaper and more effective as a means of policing the remoter parts of the Empire than ground forces. Rather than abolish bombing, therefore, it was suggested that limits be laid down as to where bombing could take place. Again, however, the government's technical and political objectives were inconsistent. Britain's technical policy encouraged German rearmament whereas her political policy was to restrict it. Certainly, if bombers were not abolished, under the principle of equality Germany would have to be accorded the same theoretical rights to aircraft as the other powers, and any German rearmament in the air was likely to give rise to renewed security demands from the French. At the same time, the more immediate problem at Geneva was Britain's refusal to accept the unconditional abolition of bombing. Throughout the conference, Britain wanted to retain bombing 'for police purposes in outlying districts', without specifying which territories were to be accorded the rather dubious distinction of being outlying districts. The 'police bombing' reservation was so patently insincere that Britain became not only diplomatically isolated on the air question but also the laughing stock of Geneva.[36]

The third major technical problem was that of verification. Without a proper verification regime, there was no way of ensuring that the proposed disarmament convention would be adhered to; no way of exposing a party which violated the convention; no way of taking action against a recalcitrant party. The French took the lead on the issue, demanding that a provision for regular, periodic and automatic on-the-spot investigation be built into the convention. Unless they could be satisfied that Germany would fulfil her obligations, the French would not reduce their military superiority over Germany by any significant amount. Initially, among the great powers, the French were alone in demanding stringent control measures. Britain took an especially strong line in opposition, arguing that if states acted in good faith then verification was unnecessary, but that if good faith did not exist then verification would be useless. It was even claimed that verification would be counterproductive in that it would show up weaknesses in states that observed the convention while failing to expose violations in states that infringed the convention. During the summer of 1933, however, events in Germany in the aftermath of Hitler's appointment as Chancellor, together with actual and suspected violations by Germany of the Treaty of Versailles, prompted the Italians and Americans to accept the French position. The Germans adhered to the French line in July 1933, and even the Japanese maintained a studious silence on the issue. So by September 1933, the British delegation found itself isolated at Geneva in opposing automatic and continuous verification.[37]

From a technical standpoint, Britain and Japan must bear prime responsibility for the failure to reach agreement, in that their policies were so much out of line with the policies of the other major powers. Japanese responsibility is clear, and, given the militaristic nature of the Japanese government, hardly surprising. The extent of British responsibility, however, is rather more interesting, more especially given the government's proclaimed support for disarmament. Basically, the problem lay in the mindset of Britain's policy-making elite. The government based its policy on premises which were antipathetic to disarmament at both technical and political levels. Paradoxically, the nearer the technical committees came to success on the key issues of tanks, air disarmament and verification, the greater became the gap between the necessities of an international convention and the politico-military assumptions of the British disarmament programme. This latter fact became increasingly clear as the Disarmament Conference progressed.[38]

Basically, the various plans laid before the Disarmament Conference revolved around the same questions. At the technical level: tanks, air disarmament and verification. At the political level: the Franco-German problem. The policy of the powers was not so much to gain agreement, rather to avoid responsibility for the lack of agreement.[39] From March 1933 onwards, the issues converged in the MacDonald Plan, which was accepted by the powers as the basis of an international convention.

The MacDonald Plan went some way towards meeting the German demand for equality of rights.[40] Equality of rights in tanks under 16 tons would be assured at the end of five years. There would also be a standardisation of continental armies on the basis of short-term service for each of the powers, France and Germany both being accorded standing metropolitan armies of 200,000 men. There would, however, be no equality for Germany in military aircraft, merely an international investigation into the possibility of abolishing all military aviation and internationalising civil aviation. In the interim period, each of the great powers would be allocated 500 military machines with another 25 per cent in immediate reserve. Given that Germany already possessed some 125 fighting machines,

The Geneva Disarmament Conference 77

either fully operational or under construction, there was no possibility that the new Hitler government would accept the British convention in this respect. If military aviation were not abolished immediately for all states, Germany would claim the right to 'samples' of military aircraft while the investigation into abolition was in progress. In analysing the draft convention before its presentation at Geneva, the British Cabinet even considered the possibility that Germany would use the air clauses as an excuse for leaving the Disarmament Conference and lay the blame on Britain.[41]

On the security side, the MacDonald Plan offered little to the French. There would be a consultative pact whereby states would confer with each other in the event of a violation of the convention, but no outright security guarantees or provision for sanctions. Equally, the verification clauses of the MacDonald Plan were weak, and in particular there was no provision for regular, periodic and automatic on-the-spot investigation. Yet without such measures, the French would not accept the military clauses which gave advantages to Germany.

By September 1933, Britain found herself isolated amongst the major international powers even regarding her own convention! On the technical issues, she was supported only by the Dominions and Japan. On the political issues, she was unwilling to give either full equality to Germany or a modicum of security to France. The government's handling of policy was inept, even by its own standards. The British Cabinet had boxed itself into a corner and appeared to be the major obstacle to a disarmament agreement – which indeed it was.

At the last minute, the British government was offered a means of escape from its dilemma by the French. The French, fully aware of increasing violations by Germany of the Versailles Treaty and the radical internal revolution being pursued by Hitler, judged the time was ripe to try to force the Germans into an agreement on better terms than currently on offer. They were conscious that the MacDonald Plan gave them no real security compensation in return for a diminution of power in relation to Germany, and so during the summer of 1933 produced a disarmament plan of their own, disguised as amendments to the MacDonald Plan. In effect, the five-year convention envisaged by MacDonald (after which Germany would assume full equality of rights if no agreement were reached regarding a second convention) would be converted into an eight-year convention divided into two equal parts. The first stage would constitute a 'trial period' during which the agreed verification procedures would be tested for effectiveness. Only after these procedures had been declared acceptable would France, in the second four-year stage, undertake major arms reductions to facilitate equality of rights.[42]

The Americans and Italians accepted the French amendments to the MacDonald Plan in September 1933. The idea was to present a united front to Germany: either accept the agreed plan or assume responsibility for breaking up the Disarmament Conference. For Britain, the French amendments offered a lifeline: a means of escaping from isolation at Geneva. The consequences of accepting the plan, however, were momentous. When presented with the French amendments by the four-power combination on 14 October 1933, the German delegation announced that Germany was withdrawing from both the Disarmament Conference and the League of Nations. They had good reason to do so. The demand for a trial period of four years of international control before securing equality of rights would effectively have put the Germans on probation, with no control over whether or not they had fulfilled their obligations. Full equality of rights after a five-year convention was to be replaced by a vague possibility of equality of rights after eight years. In July 1932, Hitler's conservative predecessors had withdrawn from the conference ostensibly because little or no progress had been achieved in some five months of discussion. In October 1933, Hitler could rightly claim that the western powers, Britain in particular, had gone back on their word regarding equality of rights.

Hitler took a calculated gamble in withdrawing from the Disarmament Conference. There was always the possibility, however vague, that the French might react forcibly against his action. But there was never any likelihood that the British would support such a move. Hitler also took good care to continue negotiations for a convention through diplomatic channels until the French finally broke them off in April 1934. There is, in fact, little doubt that Hitler favoured a disarmament convention if it were possible to negotiate one, if only as a short-term measure. It was far better to achieve German rearmament through international agreement than against international opposition.[43] His instructions to Nadolny, the chief German representative at the Disarmament Conference, make this clear. Less than a month before the final German withdrawal from the conference, he stated that it would be 'desirable to bring about a disarmament agreement even if it does not comply with all our wishes' since it would be wrong to 'demand more than

The Geneva Disarmament Conference 79

we could obtain in the coming years, given the technical, financial and political means at our disposal'.[44]

Even at the very last minute, Hitler was willing to accept a compromise agreement. On 12 October, Mussolini formulated a series of proposals for an eight-year convention which included a system of permanent and automatic verification but allowed Germany progressively to acquire weapons which were not generally prohibited.[45] The underlying principle of the plan was that it was better to concede German rearmament in stages under strict international control rather than to concede nothing for four years and then 'everything' in the ensuing four under the terms of the French amendments to the MacDonald Plan. Hitler accepted Mussolini's proposal on 13 October, and there are indications that both France and the United States were also willing to accept the proposals, at least as a basis for discussion.[46] Britain, however, remained intransigent and refused to consider the Italian proposals even as the basis of discussion.

In assessing responsibility for the breakdown of the Geneva conference, a number of questions must be borne in mind. First, there was the difficulty referred to at the beginning of this essay whereby the consent of some fifty-nine states was necessary if total agreement was to be achieved. Second, there was the omnipresent obstacle of the Japanese military. But the problem must also be considered within the context of European political relations and the distribution of power on the European continent. In this respect, the conclusions of Maurice Vaïsse are extremely interesting. Working from the French archives, he has suggested that prime responsibility for the failure of the Disarmament Conference must lie with the Anglo-Saxon powers and in particular Britain because of her negative attitude towards involvement in the European security system.[47] The evidence in the British archives would support this conclusion – at least as far as Britain is concerned – from both a technical and a political standpoint.

NOTES

1 It is almost sixty years since a full-length study of the Geneva Disarmament Conference was published: J.W. Wheeler-Bennett, *The Pipe Dream of Peace*, New York, Morrow, 1935. P.J. Noel-Baker's semi-autobiographical *The First World Disarmament Conference 1932–33*, Oxford, Pergamon, 1979, is sketchy and can hardly be considered a full-length study.

   On the history of the negotiations which led to the Geneva conference see J.W. Wheeler-Bennett's *Information on the Reduction of Armaments*, London, Allen & Unwin, 1925; *Disarmament and Security since Locarno, 1925–1931*, London, Allen & Unwin, 1932; *The Disarmament Deadlock*, London, Routledge, 1935. The following academic articles should also be noted: D. Richardson, 'Process and progress in disarmament: some lessons of history', in V. Harle and P. Sivonen (eds) *Europe in Transition*, London, Pinter, 1989, pp. 26–44; D. Carlton, 'Disarmament with guarantees: Lord Cecil 1922–1927', *Disarmament and Arms Control*, vol. 3, 1965, pp. 143–61; D.J. Whittaker's biography of Philip Noel-Baker, *Fighter for Peace: Philip Noel-Baker 1889–1982*, York, Sessions, 1989, is both informative and useful. See especially chapters 3 and 4 on the period covering the Geneva Disarmament Conference and the negotiations leading up to it.

There have been few full-length published studies of the policies of individual countries or individual aspects of the disarmament problem. The most significant are R.A. Chaput, *Disarmament in British Foreign Policy*, London, Allen & Unwin, 1935; M. Vaïsse, *Sécurité D'abord*, Paris, Pedone, 1981; D. Richardson, *The Evolution of British Disarmament Policy in the 1920s*, London, Pinter, 1989. C. Hall, *Britain, America and Arms Control 1921–37*, Basingstoke, Macmillan, 1987, constitutes an analysis of naval disarmament rather than the negotiations for general disarmament.

A number of memoir sources are useful, notably A.C. Temperley, *The Whispering Gallery of Europe*, London, Collins, 1938; S. de Madariaga, *Morning without Noon: Memoirs*, Farnborough, Saxon House, 1974. The Eden memoirs (Earl of Avon, *Facing the Dictators*, London, Cassell, 1962) are little more than an amalgam of Foreign Office documents.

2 The Treaty of Peace between the Allied and Associated Powers and Germany, 28 June 1919, *Parliamentary Papers*, 1919, Cmd. 153.
3 Reply of the Allied and Associated Powers to the observations of the German delegation on the conditions of peace [16 June 1919], *Papers relating to the Foreign Relations of the United States, Diplomatic Papers*, 1919, Paris Peace Conference, vol. VI, pp. 954–6. Hereafter *FRUS*.
4 The Treaty of Peace, 28 June 1919, *Parliamentary Papers*, 1919, Cmd. 153.
5 Madariaga, op. cit., p. 81.
6 The Geneva Gas Protocol of 17 June 1925 prohibited the wartime use of chemical and bacteriological weapons. It did not, however, cover the manufacture or deployment of such weapons, and signatories could reserve their rights in respect of non-signatories. For the text, see United States Arms Control and Disarmament Agency, *Arms Control and Disarmament Agreements*, New Brunswick, NJ, Transaction Books, 1984, pp. 9–13.
7 See Notes of an Anglo-French-German conversation, 27 June 1932, *Documents on British Foreign Policy 1919–1939*, 2nd series, vol. III, no. 150. Hereafter *DBFP*. Also E. Herriot, *Jadis*, Paris, Flammarion, 1952, p. 345; F. von Papen, *Memoirs*, New York, Dutton, 1953, pp. 181–2.
8 For a full analysis of the Tardieu Plan, see Vaïsse, op. cit., pp. 193–207; J. Néré, *The Foreign Policy of France from 1914 to 1945*, London, Routledge, 1975, ch. 9.

The Geneva Disarmament Conference 81

9 See. e.g. Néré, op. cit., chs 10, 11; W.E. Scott, *Alliance against Hitler*, Durham, NC, Duke University Press, 1962.
10 For a full analysis of the Paul-Boncour Plan, see Vaïsse, op. cit., pp. 292–318.
11 See e.g. French Cabinet instructions of 2 May 1933, *Documents diplomatiques Français 1932–1939*, 1st series, vol. 3, no. 229. Hereafter *DDF*.
12 On German disarmament policy, see e.g. M. Geyer, 'The dynamics of military revisionism in the inter-war years: military politics between rearmament and diplomacy' in W. Deist (ed.) *The German Military in the Age of Total War*, Oxford, Berg, 1985, also the first two chapters of Deist's *The Wehrmacht and German Rearmament*, Basingstoke, Macmillan, 1981. Further papers of note by Deist are 'Internationale und nationale Aspekte der Abrüstungsfrage 1924–1932', in H. Rössler (ed), *Locarno und die Weltpolitik 1924–1932*, Göttingen, Musterschmidt-Verlag, 1969; 'Brüning, Herriot und die Abrüstungsgesprache von Bessinge 1932', *Vierteljahrshefte für Zeitgeschichte*, vol. 5, 1957, pp. 265–72, and 'Schleicher und die deutsche Abrüstungspolitik im Juni/Juli 1932', ibid., vol. 7, 1959, pp. 163–76. See also E.W. Bennett, *German Rearmament and the West 1932–1933*, Guildford, Princeton University Press, 1979.
13 See Deist, 'Schleicher', p. 167; W. Deist *et al.*, *Germany and the Second World War*, vol. 1, Oxford, Oxford University Press, 1990, pp. 398–9.
14 See Richardson, *Evolution of British Disarmament Policy*, especially chs 2–4.
15 See, e.g. Note by Vansittart, 23 December 1931, Simon Papers, FO 800/285.
16 For an analysis of British policy at the Disarmament Conference, see D. Richardson and C. Kitching, 'Britain and the World Disarmament Conference', in P. Catterall and C.J. Morris (eds) *Britain and the Threat to Stability in Europe 1918–45*, Leicester, Leicester University Press, 1993, pp. 35–56. Chaput, op. cit., is rather out of date, but see also J.J. Underwood, 'The roots and reality of British disarmament policy 1932–34', unpublished Ph.D thesis, University of Leeds, 1977.
17 Memorandum by Leeper, 29 May 1933, *DBFP*, 2nd series, vol. V, no. 179.
18 Minute by Leeper on War Office Memorandum, 30 May 1933, FO371/17360, W6215/40/98.
19 Ministerial Disarmament Committee, 14th and 15th meetings, CAB 27/505.
20 Richardson and Kitching, op. cit.
21 See e.g. P.M.H. Bell, *The Origins of the Second World War in Europe*, London, Longman, 1986, p. 205.
22 Record of a five-power meeting, 6 December 1932, *DBFP*, 2nd series, vol. IV, no. 211.
23 Richardson and Kitching, op. cit., pp. 43–4.
24 Cited in T.N. Dupuy and G. Hammerman, *A Documentary History of Disarmament and Arms Control*, New York, Bowker, 1973, p. 189.
25 The opening of the former Soviet archives supports this line. See V. Zubok and A. Kokoshin, 'Opportunities missed in 1932?', *International Affairs* (Moscow), February 1989, pp. 112–21.

26 J.W. Wheeler-Bennett, *Knaves, Fools and Heroes*, London, Macmillan, 1974, p. 50; Temperley, op. cit., p. 204; Madariaga, op. cit., p. 252; Deist, 'Brüning, Herriot', p. 268.
27 American-British-German conversation, 26 April 1932, *FRUS*, 1932, vol. I, pp. 108–12. It is interesting that no record of this conversation exists in the British archives; cf. the German account: Memorandum by Bülow, 26 April 1932. *Akten zur Deutschen Auswärtigen Politik 1918–1945*, series B, vol. XX, no. 69.
28 Gibson to Acting Secretary of State, 29 April 1932, *FRUS*, 1932, vol. I, pp. 112–14.
29 Temperley, op. cit., p. 202; Wheeler-Bennett, *Knaves, Fools and Heroes*, p. 51; Madariaga, op. cit., p. 252.
30 Temperley, op. cit., p. 204; Wheeler-Bennett, *The Pipe Dream of Peace*, p. 34.
31 See Gibson to Stimson, 17 March 1932 and Gibson to Acting Secretary of State, 21 April 1932, *FRUS*, 1932, vol. I, pp. 54–9, 104–6; Basil Liddell-Hart, *Memoirs*, vol. 1, pp. 194–5; cf. Vaïsse, op. cit., pp. 225–34.
32 Wheeler-Bennett, *Pipe Dream of Peace*, p. 34.
33 See e.g. memorandum by Leeper, 29 May 1933, *DBFP*, 2nd series, vol. V, no. 179. For a general analysis of the political underpinnings of technical questions, from a British perspective, see Richardson and Kitching, op. cit., pp. 44–52. For the question of equality of rights, more particularly the discussions which were to lead to the five-power declaration of 11 December 1932 by which Britain, France, Italy and the United States conceded the principle of German equality 'in a system which would provide security for all nations', see *DBFP*, 2nd series, vol. IV, nos 211–16; *DDF*, 1st series, vol. II, nos 72, 76, 80–2, 88; *FRUS*, 1932, vol. I, pp. 492–501.
34 See Vaïsse, op. cit.
35 Richardson and Kitching, op. cit., pp. 46–7, 49, 52.
36 ibid., pp. 47–9, 52.
37 ibid., pp. 49–51.
38 ibid., p. 52.
39 Vaïsse, op. cit., p. 614.
40 For the text of the British draft convention, see Dupuy and Hammerman, op. cit., pp. 221–38.
41 CAB23/75 CM18(33). See also CAB24/241 CP129(33); CAB24/242 CP184(33).
42 The French Cabinet agreed the proposals on 2 May 1933, *DDF*, 1st series, vol. III, no. 229. They then pressed them in private conversations with the other powers. See e.g. *DDF*, 1st series, vol. IV, nos 160, 177, 213, 224, 233, 237, 241, 260, 261.
43 Nadolny to Neurath, *Documents on German Foreign Policy 1918–1945*, series C, vol. I, no. 94.
44 Memorandum by Neurath, 30 September 1933, ibid., no. 475.
45 Mussolini proposal, ibid., no. 494, enclosure.
46 Minutes of the Conferences of Ministers of 13 and 14 October 1933, ibid., no. 499. See also *DBFP*, 2nd series, vol. V, nos 432, 441, 451, 453.
47 Vaïsse, op. cit., pp. 612–13.

4 The Chiefs of Staff, the 'men on the spot' and the Italo-Abyssinian emergency, 1935–36

Steven Morewood

Imagine the international uproar that would have erupted had the 1990–91 Gulf crisis ended with the massed United Nations forces returning home without firing a shot, leaving Saddam Hussein still in possession of Kuwait. The consequences of scrapping 'Operation Desert Storm' can easily be envisaged: the United Nations would have lost all credibility, its resolutions reduced to meaningless rhetoric; the aggressor could look forward to expanding his fledgling empire. Failure to rescue Kuwait then would almost certainly have ensured a greater conflagration later on.

In the 1935–36 Italo-Abyssinian crisis this scenario was played out for real. The ramifications of the League of Nations' failure to halt Benito Mussolini's empire-building in its tracks at the Abyssinian hurdle were profound. The peacekeeping organisation, what teeth it had now completely extracted, was shunted onto the sidelines; the billowing war clouds built up inexorably as the Italian and German dictatorships became convinced that they could raise the stakes and get away with it. Rightly, the lamentable episode has been identified as a turning point towards a second world war. Memories of the Abyssinian débâcle returned to haunt the debate as to the desirability of military measures against Iraq, when one columnist referred to the 'inadequacy of the [British] naval and military experts at the time'.[1]

In the Gulf crisis the largest military power involved, the United States, was prepared to act resolutely, with its allies playing an active supporting role. The Soviet Union, the other military super power within the United Nations, despite recent close ties with Iraq, also proved willing to support military action, albeit without committing itself militarily. In 1935–36 Britain, the one major military power to move its forces into position, proved unwilling to take the steps necessary to ensure that the League prevailed. Instead, it stood and watched Geneva's authority collapse.

The Italo-Abyssinian crisis has been much studied and it is not the intention to retread familiar territory; rather four main themes will be explored, pivoted around the question of whether military action could and should have been taken. First, the limited and ineffectual measures which were instigated against Italy to prevent her conquest of Abyssinia. Second, the underlying reasons for this lukewarm response on the part of Britain. Third, the views of the 'men on the spot', which have not received detailed analysis up to now. Finally, the ramifications of the débâcle for international peacekeeping and British grand strategy.

SANCTIONS WITH THEIR TEETH DRAWN

Although Italian designs on Abyssinia had been apparent at least since the Wal Wal incident of December 1934, the actual invasion the following October came as a shock. It marked the failure of belated diplomatic efforts to persuade Italy to back down. In response, the League began the process of implementing sanctions. Before their timid nature became apparent, the outward indications suggested they would serve their purpose and defeat the impudent aggressor. For the first time in its history, the League brought out its 'big gun' against an aggressor. Article 16 of the Covenant – the sanctions article – was applied.

Beguiled, Winston Churchill, with his usual eloquence, pronounced that the League, tarnished by its impotency over Manchuria, 'has passed from shadow into substance, from theory into practice, from rhetoric into reality'. Confirmation of this seemed to come when the British Prime Minister, Stanley Baldwin, addressed the Peace Society at the end of October: 'Judgement may lead to action, cautionary action, restraining action, at the extreme to coercive action. We mean nothing by the League if we are not prepared, after trial, to take action to enforce its judgement'.[2] It soon emerged that of these three basic choices, the 'cautionary' path was selected.

Such timidity allowed the Italian leader, Benito Mussolini, rather than the League, to broadly lay down which sanctions were acceptable. The day before the invasion he delivered a speech whose message was that while economic sanctions would be tolerated, military measures meant a European war. He cannily mixed this threat with an assurance that Italy did not want a wider conflagration: 'We shall do everything possible to avoid a colonial conflict assuming the character and bearing of a European conflict'.[3] In making this statement, he was deliberately playing on Whitehall's fears. The dictator was privy to Britain's growing trepidation of Nazi Germany through his intelligence service's access to the safe of the British Embassy in Rome.[4] His sentiments were not lost on the British government. Baldwin admitted as much when he declared in a Chequers radio broadcast that there were 'risks of peace ... in the type of sanctions imposed'.[5]

Although a series of proposed sanctions were quickly agreed, conspicuous by their absence were the two punitive measures which would have forced Mussolini to think seriously about abandoning his adventure: an oil embargo and the closure of the Suez Canal, through which passed all Italian supplies to their forces in East Africa. Neville Chamberlain was alive to the potentially devastating impact of halting these shipments. 'By putting his great army on the other side of the Suez Canal', the Chancellor informed his sister Ida, 'Musso has tied a noose round his own neck and left it dangling for anyone with a navy to pull'.[6] But despite the presence of considerable British naval forces in the vicinity, this measure was never seriously considered. The oil embargo remained on the agenda, but it was kept in the closet lest Mussolini carry out his threat to go to war if it were implemented. When the time came to confront Italian aggression, the western powers preferred the alternative of the cringing climb-down represented by the Hoare-Laval Pact of December 1935.

The diplomatic machinations preceding the failed attempt to buy off Mussolini while leaving a semblance of Abyssinia intact need not be repeated here.[7] What is less well known is the extent to which the Baldwin government went to avoid or minimise incidents in the Mediterranean and Red Sea as a vital element of its caution-tinged strategy.

The implementation of this temperate policy was soon apparent. On 27 October an over-zealous Royal Navy commander, acting on the basis of a British press report that munitions of war intended for Italy had been banned, confined the British ship *El Amin* to port pending instructions as to whether her Massawa-bound cargo of 80,000 gallons of benzine constituted war material. The vessel was released later that day on Admiralty instructions. True, benzine was not on the exclusion list, but in any event the Admiralty preferred the interpretation that, notwithstanding the cargo's destination, it might be utilised for peaceful as well as destructive purposes.[8]

Such leniency reflected the Admiralty's deep-seated reluctance to become embroiled in sanctions enforcement, the reasons for which will be explored later. Throughout the crisis, it was the Admiralty who dissented from the Foreign Office thesis that successful sanctions could be imposed without provoking war.

> If it is decided to put League sanctions into force, and if (as is only too probable) the exercise of sanctions involves war, the strategic position is such that the conduct of the war will be primarily naval. On the other hand, even if we are not actually involved in war, hostilities in which a naval Mediterranean power is one of the belligerents must require immediate naval readiness on our part, and constant preoccupations such as the exercise of belligerent rights and the non-interference with our legitimate trade.

Acting on the supposition that Italy would assume belligerent rights against Abyssinia, and given the importance of averting delays to British merchant shipping, the Admiralty favoured implementing a scheme similar to the 'navicert' one applied during the First World War. All westward-bound British merchant ships should call at Aden or Berbera, eastward-bound at Alexandria, Port Said or Port Sudan. Italian consular authorities would be permitted to examine ships' manifests; if they were satisfied that no contraband for Abyssinia was aboard, passes might be issued freeing the ships from interference from Italian naval patrols. At the same time, the Admiralty made apparent its objections to closing Suez, reminding the Foreign Office that such a step would contravene the 1888 Constantinople Convention which decreed that the international waterway must remain open to all ships, regardless of flag, in peace or war.[9] Again, the Admiralty was rejigging the facts to suit its case. Just as easily it might have stated that when the situation demanded, as it did between 1914 and 1918, the convention could and should be overridden.

The issue of Britain's stance over belligerent rights assumed vital importance as an Italo-Abyssinian war loomed nearer. Three days before hostilities began, the recently formed Committee of Imperial Defence (CID) Sub-Committee on Abyssinia found all three services agreed that Italy should be permitted to exercise belligerent rights unless military sanctions were approved at Geneva.[10] In the event, these deliberations proved academic. Italy did not take up belligerent rights: she failed either to officially declare war or to publish a contraband list, both necessary prerequisites before belligerent status could be assumed.

Rome's propaganda-laden explanation was that to declare war against Abyssinia would be to confer on a 'barbaric' nation an equal status it did not deserve. The reality was rather different. After making informal soundings, Britain's ambassador to Rome concluded that belligerent rights would be foregone to avoid 'serious outside complications which ... Mussolini is particularly anxious to avoid'.[11] Direct supporting evidence for this interpretation came late in October when the dictator raised the thorny topic of the 'military control of economic sanctions'. To stop and search vessels, he warned,

> was likely, indeed bound to lead to war. After all what was the object of sanctions? It was not simply to punish the offending state; it was to bring war to an end. When it was found that economic sanctions would not achieve their object, resort would naturally be had to military sanctions and that definitely meant war.[12]

Mussolini's posturing followed Anthony Eden's gallant, but vain, attempt to inject some meaning into sanctions at Geneva. The British Minister for League of Nations Affairs went beyond his instructions in proposing to forbid all Italian shipping to touch in League ports.[13] However, as early as 22 July 1935 the Admiralty's Naval Plans Division had foreseen that the Red Sea needed to be reinforced commensurate with Italian naval deployments in the area in order to safeguard British neutrality and preclude 'any highhanded or illegal interference on the part of the Italians'. Thus, in September sixteen warships arrived at Aden, a disposition which, together with the substantial Royal Navy units in the Mediterranean, effectively constrained Italy to diplomatic protests over economic sanctions.[14]

At first it appeared as though Britain would use its naval muscle to enforce a rigorous interpretation of the Hague rules of neutrality, which were imposed on 14 October 1935. For example, at Aden no Italian warships were permitted to remain for more than twenty-four hours to replenish their supplies, or take on more fuel than would enable them to reach Massawa, the nearest Italian port. Moreover, a warship's definition was extended to include vessels used as transports, fleet auxiliaries or chartered ships.[15] The Italians took umbrage. On 7 November a written protest 'expressing the fullest reserves' regarding the legality of Britain's action was delivered.[16] Next day the Admiralty drew attention to reports that after Italian vessels at Aden were refused fuel or stores they proceeded to procure them from Djibouti which implied that the French were less stringent. Furthermore, Britain's interpretation of neutrality during this emergency might prejudice her position in a future war when the Admiralty intended to charter all Britain's tanker fleet.[17] The Admiralty's intervention had the desired result. It can hardly have been a coincidence that the day after Baldwin's government was overwhelmingly re-elected on a calculated pro-League platform the rules were changed. Merchant ships carrying supplies for Italian forces in East Africa were excluded from the definition of a 'warship', a move which brought Britain back into line with the French (whose restrictions applied only to Djibouti).

In February 1936 the British Resident at Aden sought advice after an Italian merchant ship, carrying 41 Italian army personnel and 203 civilian passengers, had been allowed to refuel. Again, the Admiralty manifested its anxiety to avoid provoking an incident; as a result, on 24 March, all British ports were ordered to further amend their instructions. The word of the Italian consul was now to be accepted; if doubts arose reference should be made home. Further, the description 'vessels engaged in transporting troops' was altered to read 'vessels employed as troop transports, that is vessels the main purpose of whose voyage is the conveyance of an organised body of troops'.[18]

THE REASONS WHY

Looking back, an incumbent British Foreign Secretary noted of the League's failure to rescue Abyssinia: 'the reluctant lifeguards had plenty of arguments in their locker'.[19] Some were public, others private. A highly convenient public argument, as it turned out, was the prerequisite that Britain was not prepared to go any further militarily than other League members. This was in fact the main message of Sir Samuel Hoare's Geneva speech of 11 September 1935 which, to the British Foreign Secretary's dismay, was misinterpreted as a clarion call for decisive action.[20]

Britain desired concrete reassurances of French military support if sanctions led to war. The Admiralty insisted that it must have the use of French bases at Toulon and Bizerta. It also desired an undertaking that the French air force would attack targets in northern Italy to draw off Italian air power from the eastern Mediterranean.

This view assumed a worst case scenario: that the *Regia Aeronautica* would render Malta, the main British Mediterranean base, unusable. Pierre Laval, France's deceitful Foreign Minister, prevaricated, drawing a distinction between provocation due to reasonable League action and the massed British naval forces which, in his view, were disproportionate to the sanctions in hand. France's ambivalence did not disguise the message that she was not prepared to fight in defence of the British Empire. Above all, Laval was determined to preserve the recent Franco-Italian military agreements which appeared to give France what Britain would not promise – military support against the growing German menace.[21]

Britain could still have gone it alone had she so desired in the knowledge that at the very least the League's Mediterranean powers would have provided tacit support against Italy. But ever since its inception, British governments had been apathetic towards the League, fearing that they would be called on repeatedly to play the role of policeman of the world. Rather they saw it as a forum for debating and moderating the peace treaties, whereas the French had traditionally preferred to view the League as a means of upholding the Versailles diktat.[22] In the final analysis, if the League floundered, Britain's vital interests were not perceived to be under threat.

As far as the Italo-Abyssinian dispute was concerned, the fighting services constantly pressed the view that to take military action in support of Abyssinia would be to put at risk the security of Britain and the Empire. In November 1935 the Chiefs of Staff warned that even with French support the Royal Navy would inevitably suffer losses in a conflict with Italy which might render it temporarily incapable of meeting its world-wide responsibilities, specifically the defence of the Far East. Similarly, any Royal Air Force losses would adversely affect the aim of attaining parity with the *Luftwaffe* by April 1937. Again, the War Office believed that a war against Italy would undermine its mechanisation programme aimed at readying the army for possible war with Germany.[23]

The 'men on the spot' were left in no doubt as to their superiors' views. Before he returned to Egypt the General Officer Commanding British Troops, Major-General George Weir, was informed by the Chief of the General Staff: 'It's no good Rosie, the Army can't play'.[24] Privately, Lord Chatfield, Chief of Naval Staff, denigrated his government's pro-League stance as disastrous. Before the Italian incursion into Abyssinia, Chatfield disclosed his real views to Admiral Sir William Fisher, Commander-in-Chief of the Mediterranean Fleet:

the bumptiousness of Italy is so great that it may be worth fighting her now to reassert our dominance over an inferior race. But against that a hostile Italy is a real menace to our imperial communications and defence system. We have relied on practically abandoning the Mediterranean if we send the Fleet east. For that reason I do not want to go to extreme measures.[25]

Just as the Italo-Abyssinian war erupted, a Suez Canal defence plan was finalised, a vital piece in the Admiralty's cherished contingency plans to despatch a main fleet to the Far East. If Japan became hostile, the last thing the Admiralty wanted to contend with was the prospect of its Singapore-bound fleet coming under Italian air attack in the Red Sea after passing through the vital imperial artery.[26] The profound irritation felt by the services at what they regarded as an unnecessary diversion from their preparations against Nazi Germany and Japan was epitomised by an intelligence officer's caustic reference to this 'silly African business'.[27]

An important factor for both Britain and France which has received little attention was the fear that an outright Abyssinian defeat of Italy, a fellow imperial power, could prove disastrous to western interests in the region. The famous Abyssinian rout of Italian forces at Adowa in 1896 had encouraged the victors to embark on their own expansion drive. A repeat of that triumph could stimulate a movement for outright independence within the French and British areas.

Japan and Nazi Germany were not slow to recognise in the contemporary situation the potential for weakening the western empires, and they actively encouraged the Abyssinians to stand up to the Europeans. Hoare was fully alive to the administrative difficulties liable to arise from an Abyssinian victory.[28] Britain's global over-extension required that only minimal forces were deployed in the Middle East while the French saw their forces in North Africa as a manpower reservoir to draw on in case of need against Nazi Germany. Already, there were stirrings of revolt in Egypt, Palestine and Syria. Nationalist uprisings on the back of another Adowa would jeopardise both assumptions. Even Lord Robert Cecil, President of the League of Nations Union, conceded it 'would be a great disaster if the Italians were entirely defeated by the Abyssinians', for which reason he felt it imperative that a League-sponsored solution should prevail.[29] In 1896 the Abyssinians received French arms with which to achieve their remarkable victory. Almost four decades later, western armed support was conspicuous by its absence

The Italo-Abyssinian emergency 91

(apart from limited armaments provided by the mischievous Germans).

When the Italians suffered serious setbacks at the hands of the Abyssinians in December 1935 (see pp. 95–6), the British and French colonial authorities became noticeably concerned. That month General Hutzinger, Commander-in-Chief of French forces in the Levant, dined with Sir Arthur Wauchope, British High Commissioner in Palestine. The latter predicted that if a European war were to break out over Abyssinia, then the Arabs, encouraged by Italian bribes, would revolt. On no account must sanctions be strengthened for none of the colonial powers could afford to see 'the triumph of a Black country against a European nation. The moral consequences would be terrible'. British officers serving in Egypt and the British High Commissioner in Cairo held similar views.[30]

Finally, it requires emphasis that the British galvanised their defensive resources not, primarily, as a means of enforcing sanctions, but to safeguard their interests in the Mediterranean and Middle East lest Mussolini turn 'mad dog' and snap in all directions. In August 1935 the Italian military build-up against Abyssinia, as evidenced by the increasing number of supply vessels and troop transports passing through the strategically sensitive Suez Canal, plus Italian threats against Malta, persuaded Baldwin's government to pour substantial reinforcements into the Mediterranean theatre. Apart from a residue of destroyers and submarines, Malta was evacuated by the Mediterranean Fleet in favour of Alexandria.

This followed the Chiefs of Staff's warning that sanctions could lead to war with Italy. That possibility was heightened when, much to the consternation of Britain and France, Canada proposed oil sanctions. Such a prospect, the British Naval Plans Division warned, meant 'that the possibility of an attack on this country by Italy will be greater than at any previous period since, faced by certain defeat, Italy may prefer to go down with her colours flying fighting this country than be ignominiously defeated by League action'. Accordingly, the anti-aircraft resources of the Mediterranean Fleet were augmented, with 50,000 additional rounds being despatched.[31] A few months later, having brought his command up to a high state of efficiency, Admiral Fisher wrote proudly that 'the fleet was completely ready and [I] hope that this fact was indeed a contribution to the preservation of peace'.[32] Thus had the Baldwin government achieved its main aim – the Empire's preservation – at the expense of Abyssinia's independence and the League's integrity.

THE VIEWS OF THE MEN ON THE SPOT

Rosario Quartararo's examination of the British Chiefs of Staff's papers prompted the conclusion that 'in 1935–1936 Britain could not defend Egypt or the Suez Canal, let alone fight in defence of the Covenant'.[33] It is true that the Chiefs of Staff presented a confusing picture to their government of Britain's prospects should war with Italy ensue. But Quartararo pushes her arguments too far, implying that if an Anglo-Italian war had broken out then the results of 1940–41 would have been reversed. This is palpable nonsense.[34]

There are three principal flaws in Quartararo's case. First, she fails to allow sufficiently for the fact that the Chiefs of Staff wanted to avoid a war not through any fear of defeat but because Italy was mistakenly dismissed as a transient threat whereas Nazi Germany and Japan were considered the real dangers. This is the theme of the Third Report of the Defence Policy Requirements Sub-Committee which deprecated Britain's involvement in League disputes 'in which our national interest was at most quite secondary, even if it be true that young Italy has long been jealous of our Mediterranean position and potentially hostile'.[35]

A review of the minutes of the Chiefs of Staff Sub-Committee of the Committee of Imperial Defence is instructive as to the real views of the participants which did not find their way into Cabinet papers (save in very diluted and qualified form). On 13 September 1935 the 'value of the Italian fighting man' was the main subject of discussion. All three participants took the view that any outward veneer of efficiency shown by the Italian fighting services would vanish once hostilities broke out. The Director of Military Operations and Intelligence even feared for the fate of the Italian army in Abyssinia.

> Once it was cut off from communications with the outside world it would not be in a position to stand on the resources that had already accumulated, and it would ultimately be forced to surrender. This raised a problem for us in that we should have to consider the steps required for the control of this demoralised force, and even possibly for its protection against the Abyssinians.[36]

On 13 May 1936 another meeting found Chatfield going into considerable detail about planned offensive naval operations against Italy. Once more the likely outcome of a conflict was raised. Chatfield 'had no doubts as to the ability of the Royal Navy to carry out its tasks'. The army and air force were of a similar view.[37] But by this point, with Italian forces having recently taken Addis Ababa, such discussion was purely academic. Indeed, not long before, the Deputy Chief of Naval Staff underscored the absurdity of the situation: 'Surely Italy has no intention of attacking us when she has got all she wanted without doing so'.[38]

The second weakness of Quartararo's thesis is its failure to examine the opinions and planned strategy of the Italian high command. On 14 August 1935 Mussolini was warned by his Chiefs of Staff that a war with Britain would be nothing short of disastrous.[39] This followed the complete failure of high altitude exercises involving bombers against target warships. Indeed, even if the *Regia Aeronautica* had been able to score multiple hits, the results were likely to have been derisory. Quite simply, the calibre of its standard bomb was far too small to penetrate armoured decks. A few years before, Italian experiments had correctly suggested that torpedo bombers were a better form of attack against warships, but inter-service rivalry had delayed their development. Moreover, the much vaunted SM 81 bomber, the best the Italians could boast, was in fact seriously flawed in design and almost certainly would not have greatly troubled the Royal Navy. It did not bear comparison with the American B–17 heavy bomber which played such a prominent role in the Second World War, by which time the SM 81, having been tried and found wanting, could act only in a transport role. The Italian bomber in fact possessed just half the range, one-third of the bomb-carrying capacity and a quarter of the defensive armaments of the B–17. The vulnerability of Italian aircraft generally was exposed by the Abyssinians. Despite possessing only limited anti-aircraft artillery, their effective hits compelled the *Regia Aeronautica* to fly sorties out of range at above 2,000 feet.[40]

In stark contrast to the British, Italian contingency planning for war with Britain in 1935–36 was sketchy and poorly co-ordinated.[41] The navy was caught off guard, finding difficulty in adjusting its planning away from a long expected confrontation with the French and Yugoslav navies. What strategy it developed was defensive, reflecting an inferiority complex *vis-à-vis* the Royal Navy, which was compounded by a shortage of battleships. Had war come, then the sea lanes to Libya and the Dodecanese Islands demanded protection, but only flimsy plans were laid for this eventuality. As for the army, its confidence of prevailing in an Anglo-Italian fight was unique among the services. Although Mussolini reinforced Libya whenever he wanted to threaten the British position in Egypt, no

94 *Steven Morewood*

serious or realistic invasion plans were laid. The Italians only had the pathetic thinly armoured CV 35 tank, with just two machine guns for armament; its inherent vulnerability would soon be exposed in Spain. The *Regia Aeronautica* was advanced only in the use of mustard gas but, unlike the defenceless Abyssinians, British forces were equipped with protective gas masks. Italy's desperation in the eventuality of an Anglo-Italian war was epitomised by the request for pilots to volunteer to crash their aircraft onto British warships.[42]

The third flaw in Quartararo's case is her failure to examine the views of the British 'men on the spot'. Had she done so, then Quartararo would have encountered a gung-ho mentality, a frustration at the Baldwin government's pusillanimity, and clearly defined and realistic plans. There is ample evidence to show that the 'men on the spot' were never anything but ultra-confident of dealing with the Italians. Admiral Sir Roger Backhouse, Commander-in-Chief Home Fleet, made frequent visits to Admiralty House during the emergency and discerned that 'the Mediterranean atmosphere [was] quite different from what it was at home. Their *one* thought was operations'.[43]

The Mediterranean Fleet, then the most efficient in the Royal Navy, was led by Admiral Sir William Fisher, known affectionately by his men as 'the tall Agrippa' or 'W.W.' A subsequent appraisal of Fisher, who, but for his premature death, might have become Chief of Naval Staff, would describe him 'as having got excessive wind up' at this time.[44] In August 1935 he was incensed upon reading the Chiefs of Staff's highly pessimistic report which alluded to the 'weakness' of his fleet and stipulated the need to secure certain French support before any military action could be entertained. The historian H.A.L. Fisher learned of his brother's incomprehension at the reinforcements he was receiving because he felt able to 'blow the Italians out of the water with the ordinary Mediterranean Fleet'.[45]

The irate Commander-in-Chief flashed back a dissenting signal. He favoured moving the Home Fleet from Gibraltar to Malta as a prelude to launching a major offensive against Italian shore bases on the mainland and Sicily. Soon afterwards Fisher informed his superiors that he was considering using the Fleet Air Arm for a dawn attack against Italian ships at Port Augusta and Catania. Shortly, a torpedo-bomber attack against the main Italian naval base at Taranto, foreshadowing the eventual raid of November 1940, came into Fisher's plans. The Admiralty was horrified at the prospect of situating both its prize fleets at Malta where they might come under Italian air attack and rejected this ambitious scheme. Fisher's other plans were humoured, but he was not to know that his superiors were exerting every pressure to ensure they never came into effect.[46] Significantly, the Italian naval command feared an 'English battle fleet, escorted by a powerful mass of destroyers... able to ramble about the Mediterranean inflicting whatever damage it wants to our scarcely defended coast'.[47]

Following the collapse of the Hoare-Laval Pact, the Chiefs of Staff requested a combined appreciation from the 'men on the spot'. Weir proposed to base the Mobile Force, formed during the emergency, at Sollum, on the Egyptian-Libyan frontier, where it would be well placed to push into Libya to establish advanced landing grounds for the Royal Air Force and to cut Italian communications. But the timid Chiefs of Staff took fright, seeing such a move as provocative, and ruled it out.[48]

Like Fisher before him, Weir could not understand his superiors' attitude. He was clearly contemplating an imminent offensive to coincide with the imposition of oil sanctions which were now back on the political agenda after the political storm caused by the leakage of the Hoare-Laval Pact. Weir responded with detailed and cohesive arguments in support of his proposed disposition. Since mid-December the Italians had suffered a series of setbacks in Abyssinia. In the north an Abyssinian offensive caught a squadron of CV 35s in the Dembegiuna Pass and destroyed it using iron bars. This success encouraged Emperor Haile Selassie to throw further forces in, leading a panic-stricken Marshal Badoglio, who was directing the campaign against Abyssinia, to seek the assistance of three further divisions and Mussolini's authorisation to use mustard gas. By Christmas Eve Badoglio was being pushed back on all fronts. On 28 December Mussolini gave his blessing to unlimited gas attacks to stem the tide. The *Regia Aeronautica*, at first uncertain as to the most effective means of utilising the 400 tons of gas at its disposal, soon found that saturation spraying, using groups of nine to eighteen aircraft, was the best method. By 9 January 1936 this tactic had succeeded in halting the Abyssinian advance.[49]

Weir correctly pointed out that due to their recent setbacks in East Africa, Italian dispositions were in a state of flux. The *Assietta* division was being transferred from Libya to Eritrea and would not be replaced until early in March; the *Trento* mechanised division was held back at Benghazi; the native forces in Libya were in process of reorganisation. The conclusion to be drawn was that the war potential of the Italian army would be at a low ebb for some six weeks, providing ample time to consolidate the forward position at Sollum.[50] Intelligence sources supported Weir's argument, suggesting that there was then no military activity in the Italian forward area in Cyrenaica and that Libya's weak garrison would be incapable of mounting a serious invasion of Egypt.[51]

All the evidence points to panic in the Italian camp at this critical juncture. With his ally Laval in deep political trouble, Mussolini conceded to the German ambassador that the Italo-French agreements were no longer relevant. Fearing the prospect of war with Britain, the dictator began hinting at the possibility of an agreement with Germany which might include his abandonment of the Austrian cause. His nervousness was only increased by Royal Navy exercises in the Straits of Sicily and by the publication, after Laval's fall from power, of the Anglo-French Declaration of Mutual Assistance in the Mediterranean. One authority suggests that Mussolini's rival, Air Marshal Balbo, the Governor of Libya, in alliance with Badoglio and Alessandro Lessona, the Colonial Under-Secretary, who was in East Africa, was readying a military coup. Mussolini's desperation was epitomised by his publication of the Baldwin government's secret Maffey Report, thereby seeking to expose British 'hypocrisy' with its revelations that there were deemed to be no vital British interests in Abyssinia. In so doing he risked compromising his access to the invaluable archive of the British Embassy in Rome.[52] Another indication of Mussolini's plight was his renewed attempt to stir up the Sino-Japanese dispute. Since November 1935, British intelligence had followed Italian efforts to capitalise on Italy's leading role in assisting China's air rearmament and persuade the Chinese to appeal to Geneva over Japanese encroachments. The fact that China was also applying sanctions against Rome was regarded by the Italians as an 'inconvenience [which] would not outweigh the advantages accruing to Italy from the League's becoming embroiled in a Sino-Japanese conflict'. But, to Mussolini's intense annoyance, the Chinese refused to play ball, leading, in January 1936, to strong intimations to China that Italy might reverse its pro-China policy and seek an accommodation with Japan. In delivering this message, the Italian ambassador emphasised that 'China, being equally threatened by a powerful neighbour, ought better than any other nation to understand Italy's position in the face of British pressure in the Mediterranean'.[53]

'We are sitting in a circle of fire', Balbo lamented to the German consul in Naples.[54] He was not to know that the British Chiefs of Staff were about to play the fire brigade role. The Chief of the Imperial General Staff refused to be swayed by Weir's case. Field-

Marshal Sir Archibald Montgomery-Massingberd insisted that it would not be his government but the Italians who would initiate any hostilities.[55] A report on the defence of Egypt, which correctly suggested that logistical problems and maintenance difficulties would greatly restrict any Italian advance into Egypt, found its way to the Chiefs of Staff in late February.[56] But they did not consider it until a month later, underlining once more their reluctance to risk a war with Italy and the subsequent supervention of the Rhineland crisis.

The latter was used by the Chiefs of Staff and their ministers to finally drown out any prospect of oil sanctions. On 2 March 1936 Eden, by now Foreign Secretary, indicated British support for an oil embargo, but the still ambivalent French put off consideration of the issue until the 10th. Three days earlier German forces marched into the demilitarised Rhineland. Notwithstanding the fact that the British Cabinet had been considering restoring the zone to Berlin as part of a *modus vivendi*, the Chiefs of Staff seized their opportunity. Without instructions they instigated a report from the Joint Planning Committee on Britain's immediate prospects in a war with Nazi Germany.[57] Not surprisingly, a pessimistic picture was drawn: Mediterranean commitments arising from the Italo-Abyssinian emergency rendered Britain incapable of despatching a field force to France, of defending herself in the air, or engaging German pocket battleships. The inference was clear:

> if there is the smallest danger of being drawn into commitments which might lead to war with Germany, we ought at once to disengage ourselves from our present responsibilities in the Mediterranean, which have practically exhausted the whole of our meagre forces.[58]

The Chiefs of Staff's views were strongly represented in Cabinet by service ministers. The Secretary of State for Air bemoaned that 'with so many aircraft and airmen in Egypt the air position at home was deplorable'. The Secretary of State for War criticised the proposed international police force for the Rhineland, an undertaking which would render the position 'worse than ever'.[59] Italy's judicial participation in the Locarno conversations (sanctions provided a good excuse not to participate in staff talks) threw a welcome spanner into the works for the services. On 20 March, the Chief of Air Staff informed his 'man on the spot' in Egypt of his thinking:

> I do not see how there can be, in reality, sanctions against Italy

at the same time as we are actively co-operating with them on the Franco-German frontier.... You can take it that there is no chance of a war with Italy over Abyssinia at the present time. However, if the German affair is settled in the next few months, and the Italians and Abyssinians continue to fight, the situation which has obtained during recent months might again exist in the autumn, when campaigning... becomes possible again in North East Africa.[60]

The premises of this assessment – that the Abyssinians would hold out indefinitely, making Italy conclude that victory was not worth the candle – soon looked increasingly shaky.

The Italian offensive, begun 11 February, was driving the Abyssinians back in a haze of mustard gas. Nor was their cause helped by suicidal head-on clashes. The use of gas was a flagrant breach of Italy's adherence to the Geneva Protocol of 1925. Publicly, the Baldwin government maintained that it had no firm evidence on the gas attacks. In fact, conclusive proof had been received from the Assistant Military Attaché in Abyssinia. He had sent some of the liquid from a fallen bomb; after examination, the Chemical Defence Research Department concluded it did indeed contain mustard gas.[61] On 4 April the Cabinet decided not to concede Italian violations publicly but rather seek to defuse outraged public opinion by pointing out that the subject was under investigation at Geneva.[62] There, predictably enough, Italo-French procrastination sidetracked the issue, in particular through the raising of the counter-issue of alleged Abyssinian atrocities. The subject remained a hot debating point in Parliament, but to criticism of inaction Eden responded that his government's policy 'has throughout been based upon collective action through the League, and they cannot therefore take any unilateral action in this matter'.[63]

The assumption that the onset of the rainy season would halt the Italian military campaign in April was belatedly realised to be false – heavy impeding rains did not fall until June. On 6 April Eden suggested in Cabinet that the only effective action would be to close the Suez Canal. But neither he nor his colleagues were keen to grasp this nettle.[64] One month later, with Italian forces within sight of Addis Ababa, the Foreign Secretary warned an angry House of Commons: 'If honourable Gentlemen wish to take military action I must warn them that you cannot close the Canal with paper boats'.[65] Privately, Eden had already given up, though it was to be the Chancellor and future Prime Minister, Neville Chamberlain, who

The Italo-Abyssinian emergency

publicly signalled his government's wish to lift sanctions. For once, the British were prepared to take the lead and it was at their instigation that Geneva removed sanctions against Italy.

THE IMPLICATIONS

The Chiefs of Staff's rose-tinted view of the future course of events at the end of the 'silly African business' are a matter of record:

> Our hopes lie in a peaceful Mediterranean, and this can only be obtained by returning to a state of friendly relations with Italy.... One of the objects of raising sanctions is to enable us to withdraw our extra forces at present in the Mediterranean and to a state of normal distribution which will permit us to be more ready to defend our interests at Home and in the Far East.[66]

These hopes were to be frustrated. Soon after these words were written Mussolini, buoyed by his success, sent his forces into Spain. The western powers' failure to respond in kind was a further blow to their credibility. Prior to his moment of triumph in winning the Italo-Abyssinian war, Mussolini had been restrained by the military leadership from undertaking a whole series of rash foreign adventures, including the invasion of Turkey (1924–26), Yugoslavia (on two occasions) and France (1932–33). Now, his popularity was at an all time high. His successful bluff of Britain during the Mediterranean crisis of 1935–36, combined with his conquest of Ethiopia, greatly increased his prestige and his power over the Italian armed forces.[67]

The British services' unspoken assumption that Mussolini would be so grateful for Britain's inaction over Abyssinia that Italy could once more be counted on as a friendly power proved illusory. In fact, despite claiming that Italy's imperial ambitions were now satisfied, the dictator's appetite for achieving his dream of *mare nostrum* had only been whetted. His military commanders, by and large, were happy to go along for 'The Ethiopian confrontation had taught the service [army], and the military as a whole, to see Britain as the enemy'. Planning for a future Anglo-Italian war commenced in 1937. Even the conservative Admiral Cavagnari began to hope that the German and the Japanese threats would draw off sufficient British forces from the Mediterranean and Middle East to allow Italy to become the dominant power in the theatre.[68] Moving ever closer to Adolf Hitler, the next few years would see Mussolini instigate a series of crises which threatened and further subverted the British position in the Middle East. Some response was demanded, not least because in the region Italy now evoked fear and respect as a ruthless nation which had 'defeated' a Britain which dare not oppose her. Mussolini was able to play the numbers game, pouring thousands of troops into Libya at opportune moments. The frightened Egyptians demanded that Britain respond in kind, an impossibility given the growing German and Japanese menaces and the smallness of her army. British prestige in the Arab world therefore continued to decline.

This outcome was not unforeseen by everyone in the Baldwin government. As the Italo-Abyssinian crisis deepened, the head of the Egyptian Department of the Foreign Office, Ronald Campbell, warned that British authority in the Middle East would greatly suffer if Italy was not checked.[69] The Secretary of State for the Colonies, Ormsby-Gore, went even further. Anglo-Italian coexistence was impossible. Ultimately Britain would 'have to meet the Italian challenge to our prestige, power and interests by force or go under in Africa and the Mediterranean'.[70] Such views predictably met with indifference from the services, who refused to regard the Italians as a serious threat. In fact, the Foreign Office had to make the running in building up the defences of Egypt. 'It was like extracting eye-teeth, and the War Office professed complete complacence and faith in their ability to cope with clouds of Italians on unrevealed resources', recorded a leading Foreign Office official after one particularly tense meeting of the Defence Policy Requirements Committee.[71]

One of the third Marquis of Salisbury's better foreign policy dictums suggests that it is a fatal mistake to stick to the carcasses of dead policies. In this instance the corpse was represented by the idea of a conveniently friendly and inconsequential Italy. As Wesley Wark has noted:

> the easy references to Italian military inefficiency served to deflect the British authorities from a serious reading of the lessons of the Mediterranean affair in 1935–1936. The Italian strategic situation was not surveyed as a whole, nor was any effort made to conduct an appreciation of the situation as it might be seen from Italian eyes. . . . In terms of grand strategy, the result of this inattention was to leave Italy as an ambiguous military factor in British defence planning: a threat to British control of the Mediterranean, but perhaps not a serious enemy.[72]

Italian ambivalence contributed to the pursuit of appeasement by Britain in the later 1930s. Although the policy was never officially

The Italo-Abyssinian emergency 101

abandoned, the knock-on effect of the uncertainty over Italy's position was to scupper the long-standing Admiralty policy of reinforcing Singapore with the so-called 'Main Fleet'.

Documents released in 1993 reveal that little over a month after Italy entered the Second World War the Governor of the Straits Settlements, Sir Shenton Thomas, then visiting Britain, made his acute unease over Singapore's exposed position apparent in official quarters. Criticising an Overseas Defence Committee memorandum, dated 20 March 1940, Thomas pointed out that the period that Singapore needed to hold out before a fleet arrived had been tripled from 30 to 90 days, affording the Japanese

> plenty of time to come through to Singapore from any part of the Malay Peninsula, including Thailand. The entry of Italy into the war would seem to give the Japanese even longer time, because, so long as the Italian Fleet remains in being, the Mediterranean Fleet must presumably stay in European Waters.[73]

Thomas's conclusions are an effective commentary on the barrenness of British politico-strategic thinking during the Italo-Abyssinian crisis. The impact of the League's failure to deal decisively with Italy was profound. Abyssinia was a decisive test and Geneva never recovered its authority. Had Mussolini been halted in his empire-building tracks a Second World War would probably still have come about given the forces for change which existed in Germany and Japan. At the same time, success for the League in 1935–36 would almost certainly have delayed the onset of the Second World War. This ought to have placed Britain, France and the Soviet Union in a better position to contain Nazi Germany while the United States might also have begun to come into the reckoning the longer a world war was delayed.

In practice, through its abandonment of collective security, the Baldwin government ensured that rearmament was delayed, dictating that diplomacy could be pursued only from a position of weakness. Besides, the labour movement at the time would support only a League policy and was horrified by what it saw as the craven policy of appeasement pursued by the Chamberlain government. In March 1938, for instance, when the government was anxious to intensify its rearmament efforts following the *Anschluss*, the Trades Union Congress refused to consider 'dilution'. The shortage of skilled labour, a major spanner in the rearmament works, should have been addressed more practically, but the government and trade unions were not at one on foreign policy.[74]

Britain, then, might have checked Italy to the advantage of her grand strategy in 1935–36. The overthrow of Mussolini – which would probably have been accomplished, as in 1943, by a collection of disgruntled military commanders anxious to avoid a suicidal confrontation with the British Empire – could have turned Italy into a friendly power once more, or at least one which so respected Britain that war with her was unthinkable. But instead of sitting on the sidelines, as Spain did, Italy could not resist plunging in against the 'decadent' British Empire in June 1940. In a prophetic paper written shortly afterwards, the Joint Planning Staff foresaw the collapse of Italy and the occupation by Nazi Germany of the Italian mainland to preclude Britain from obtaining air bases within range of southern Germany.

Instead, the Abyssinian crisis would mark the height of Mussolini's success. He had triumphed against all the odds. Choosing to ignore the doubts of his service chiefs, Mussolini had refused to be deflected from his empire-building venture. The opposite was true in Britain, where political resolve was in short supply. Hoare had briefly favoured imposing oil sanctions but felt compelled to engage in humiliating diplomatic manoeuvrings with the French because of the positions of service chiefs whom he privately described as 'the worst pacifists and defeatists in the country'.[75]

The efforts of the Chiefs of Staff to paint as black a picture as possible emerges from the minutes of a secret meeting between Baldwin and the Executive Committee of the League of Nations Union. Astounded at the Hoare-Laval Pact, the latter had demanded an audience with the Prime Minister, reminding him of his electoral promise to 'continue the policy of sanctions until they are effective and to support no settlement of the Abyssinian dispute which fails to make it clear that aggression does not pay'. Using background notes, Baldwin was extremely pessimistic, even warning that the *Regia Aeronautica* could inflict more casualties in Malta harbour than all the fatalities from the Abyssinian campaign.[76] These were unconvincing arguments. As the Union's chairman wrote to his deputy the next day:

> In League matters if this country wants to lead it can lead. I recognise the dangers of the situation, but if it allows its policy to be dictated simply by fears of a 'mad dog' attack on the part of Mussolini, I do not see much future hope either for the League or for the British Empire.[77]

The Empire had been founded on risk-taking and military triumphs

The Italo-Abyssinian emergency 103

against the odds. By the 1930s, however, the service chiefs had become risk-averse even when, as over Abyssinia, ultimate success was not in doubt. As A.J.P. Taylor put it, 'the successors of Nelson put their names to a craven opinion which would have earned them instant dismissal from an earlier Board of Admiralty'.[78] This could not be said of the 'men on the spot' whose view was epitomised by Viscount Cunningham, then a Rear Admiral under Fisher, who would later lead the Mediterranean Fleet against Italy. In 1935–36 that fleet was anxious to see its government take effective action against Italy, principally through the closure of the Suez Canal. Fisher showed him the Chiefs of Staff's prognosis of the situation and shared his anger at their 'very pessimistic, not to say defeatist, view of the Mediterranean Fleet's capacity to deal with the Italians'.[79] A few days after Eden faced an angry House of Commons to announce the end of sanctions, Hugh Dalton saw Admiral Fisher and found him 'very insistent that the Italians would have had short shrift in the Mediterranean'.[80] The eventual clash with Italy when, because of other commitments, the Royal Navy was not as strong as in 1935–36 (especially in Fleet Air Arm aircraft), would completely vindicate this view.

As it was, Britain's humiliation over Abyssinia was to prove a turning point, which was increasingly regretted. On 13 April 1937, Sir Eric Phipps, Britain's departing ambassador from Berlin, assessed Britain's changing fortunes in German eyes during his four-year tenure.

> The victory of Italy opened up a new chapter. It was inevitable in a country where Might is worshipped [that] English prestige should then fall. The German began to ask himself whether it was necessary to conciliate a power, without whose favours Italy seemed to be doing very well.... British influence and prestige reached its height towards the end of 1935 (when, for a brief space, it was thought that England, at the head of the League, might succeed in stopping Mussolini's Abyssinian adventure). I reported at the time that in existing circumstances the policy of Anglo-German understanding would be abandoned only with the greatest reluctance.[81]

Eden, too, came to conclude that the failure to check Mussolini had been a turning point, 'a fatal mistake'.[82]

At the end of 1937 a foreign affairs debate found Neville Chamberlain staunchly defending his proactive appeasement policy, soon after Lord Halifax's visit to Berlin to express British sympathy for German grievances. Italy's recent withdrawal from the League hardly caused a ripple – there had in fact been no Italian delegation to Geneva since May 1936, with Italy playing no part in League activities for over a year. As the international situation deteriorated – Italy having joined Nazi Germany and Japan in the Anti-Comintern Pact and fascist involvement in Spain showing no signs of diminishing – the Labour leader, Clement Attlee, accused the government of betraying the League 'because it has always considered only the narrow imperial interest and not the world interest'. Sir Archibald Sinclair, for the Liberals, echoed these sentiments, 'regretting the fact that the government, in the Hoare-Laval negotiations, threw it all away. They stabbed the League in the back. It is from that moment that the difficulties of this country have increased and the world situation has deteriorated'.[83] Within two years of these words being uttered, the helter-skelter of international events which appeasement could not stop had propelled Britain into yet another unwanted world war which would ultimately deal a fatal and premature blow to the empire.

ACKNOWLEDGEMENT

The author expresses grateful thanks to the Twenty-Seven Foundation for its generous financial assistance.

NOTES

1 Mandrake column, *Sunday Telegraph*, 9 September 1990, p. 20.
2 Quoted in Douglas Hurd, 'Why Iraq's challenge has to be crushed', *Daily Telegraph*, 14 January 1991, p. 16.
3 Mussolini speech, 2 October 1935, quoted in C.F. Delzell (ed.) *Mediterranean Fascism, 1919–1945*, New York, Harper & Row, 1970, p. 194.
4 C. Andrew, *Secret Service: The Making of the British Intelligence Community*, London, Heinemann, 1985, p. 403.
5 Baldwin's address, *The Times*, 1 November 1935.
6 Neville to Ida Chamberlain, 8 December 1935, Neville Chamberlain Papers, NC18/1941. These papers are located at the Library of the University of Birmingham.
7 There are numerous publications which deal in detail with these events. See, for example, D.C. Large, *Between Two Fires: Europe's Path in the 1930s*, New York, Norton, 1990; R. Pankhurst, 'The Italo-Ethiopian War and League of Nations sanctions', *Genève-Afrique*, vol. 13, 1974; R.A.C. Parker, 'Great Britain, France and the Ethiopian Crisis, 1935–1936', *English Historical Review*, vol. 90, 1974, pp. 293–332.
8 Commander-in-Chief East Indies to Admiralty, 27 October 1935, ADM

1/8804. The *El Amin* was part of the local coastal trade run by the Halal Shipping Co-British Company.
9 Admiralty to Foreign Office, 21 September 1935, India Office Records IOR/L/P&S/12/1529.
10 Meeting of 30 September 1935, IOR/L/P&S/12/1529.
11 Drummond to Hoare, 7 October 1935, IOR/L/P&S/12/1529.
12 Drummond to Hoare, 29 October 1935, IOR/L/P&S/12/1529.
13 Philip Noel-Baker to Henry Cummings, 12 February 1936, Noel-Baker Papers. These papers are located at the Archive Centre, Churchill College, Cambridge.
14 Naval Plans Division, 22 July 1935, ADM116/3487. For details of the reinforcements see AIR5/308.
15 F. Chiaverelli, *L'opera della Marina Italiana nella guerra Italo-Etiopica*, Milan, 1969, pp. 142–3.
16 Drummond to Hoare, 7 November 1935, IOR/L/P&S/12/1519.
17 Admiralty to Foreign and Colonial Offices, 24 March 1936, IOR/L/P&S/12/1519.
18 Ibid.
19 Hurd, op. cit.
20 Hoare to Wigram, 14 September 1935, Templewood Papers VIII/4. These papers are located at the University of Cambridge Library.
21 W.I. Shorrock, *From Ally to Enemy: The Enigma of Fascist Italy in French Diplomacy, 1920–1940*, Kent, Ohio, Kent State University Press, 1988, pp. 145–57.
22 See F.S. Northedge, *The League of Nations: Its Life and Times 1920–1946*, Leicester, Leicester University Press, 1986.
23 Defence Requirements Committee meeting, 5 November 1935, CAB16/112.
24 Sir David Kelly, *The Ruling Few*, London, Hollis & Carter, 1952, p. 228.
25 Chatfield to Fisher, 25 August 1935, Chatfield Papers, CHT4/4/1. These papers are located in the National Maritime Museum, Greenwich.
26 For details see S. Morewood, 'Protecting the jugular vein of empire: the Suez Canal in British defence strategy, 1919–1941', *War and Society*, vol. 10, 1992, pp. 82–7.
27 Squadron-Leader Ivelaw-Chapman, Royal Air Force Intelligence, to Group-Captain Dacre, Air Attaché, Rome, 31 December 1935, AIR2/1681.
28 Hoare to Clerk, 29 July 1935, *Documents on British Foreign Policy 1919-1939*, 2nd series, vol. XIV, no. 403. Hereafter *DBFP*.
29 Lord Cranborne's record of conversation with Lord Cecil, 14 January 1936, *DBFP*, 2nd series, vol. XV.
30 This section derives from an unpublished chapter from Esmonde Robertson, *Mussolini as Empire-Builder: Europe and Africa 1932–36*, London, Macmillan, 1977, kindly supplied in part by the author.
31 Naval Plans Division, 'Summary of present situation in regard to Italo-Abyssinian Crisis', 11 December 1935, ADM116/3049.
32 Fisher to Admiralty, 19 March 1936, ADM116/3468.
33 R. Quartararo, 'Imperial defence in the Mediterranean on the eve of the Ethiopian crisis (July-October 1935)', *Historical Journal*, vol. 20, 1977, pp. 185–220.

34 Esmonde Robertson held a similar view of Quartararo's premise.
35 Third Report of the Defence Policy Requirements Committee, 21 November 1935, CAB16/139.
36 Chiefs of Staff Sub-Committee, 150th meeting, 13 September 1935, CAB53/5.
37 Chiefs of Staff Sub-Committee, 174th meeting, 13 May 1936, CAB53/5.
38 Admiral Little to Chatfield, 27 April 1936, ADM 116/3468.
39 G. Baer, *The Coming of the Italo-Ethiopian War*, Cambridge, Mass., Harvard University Press, 1967, pp. 253–4.
40 B.R. Sullivan, 'A thirst for glory: Mussolini, the Italian military and the fascist regime, 1922–1936', unpublished DPhil thesis, Columbia University, New York, 1984, pp. 371–2, 378, 568.
41 B.R. Sullivan, 'The Italian armed forces, 1918–40', in A.R. Millett and W. Murray (eds) *Military Effectiveness, vol. II: The Interwar Period*, London, Allen & Unwin, 1988, p. 176.
42 Sullivan, 'A thirst for glory', p. 456.
43 Backhouse to Chatfield, 3 February 1936, Chatfield Papers, CHT4/4/1.
44 Summary of the Senior Admirals, c.1936, Viscount Norwich Papers, DUFC2/12. These papers are located at Churchill College, Cambridge.
45 Quoted in Noel-Baker to Hugh [Dalton], 16 December 1935, Noel-Baker Papers.
46 See A. Marder, 'The Royal Navy and the Ethiopian crisis of 1935–36', *The American Historical Review*, vol. 75, 1970, pp. 1327–56.
47 Baer, op. cit., p. 360.
48 Chiefs of Staff Sub-Committee, 161st meeting, 13 January 1936, CAB53/5.
49 Sullivan, 'A thirst for glory', pp. 477–80.
50 Weir, 'Appreciation of the possibility of offensive action', 8 February 1936, WO106/284.
51 War Office Intelligence Summaries, January 1936, WO106/284.
52 Sullivan, 'A thirst for glory', pp. 482–4, 507–8, 512.
53 Notes by M12, 17 January 1936, WO106/5140.
54 C.G. Segre, *Italo Balbo: A Fascist Life*, Berkeley, University of California Press, 1987, p. 340.
55 Chiefs of Staff Sub-Committee, 162nd meeting, 24 January 1936, CAB53/26.
56 Dill, 'Defence of Egypt: the situation in the Western Desert', 26 February 1936, CAB53/26.
57 Chiefs of Staff Sub-Committee, 166th meeting, 12 March 1936, CAB53/5.
58 Joint Policy Committee Report, *DBFP*, 2nd series, vol. XVI, no. 3.
59 CM17(36), 11 March 1936, CAB23/86.
60 Ellington to Brooke-Popham, 20 March 1936, Brooke-Popham Papers, BPII/5/32. These papers are located at King's College London.
61 Chiefs of Staff Sub-Committee paper, 'The use of gas by Italy in the war against Abyssinia', 1 April 1936, CAB4/24.
62 CM27(36), 6 April 1936, CAB23/83.
63 29 April 1936, *Hansard Parliamentary Debates*, HC, 5th series, vol. 311, cc. 914–15.
64 CM27(36), 6 April 1936, CAB23/83.

The Italo-Abyssinian emergency 107

65 6 May 1936, *Hansard Parliamentary Debates*, HC, 5th Series, vol. 311, c. 1736.
66 Chiefs of Staff Sub-Committee, 178th meeting, 16 June 1936, CAB53/5.
67 Sullivan, 'The Italian armed forces', p. 181.
68 M. Knox, 'Fascist Italy assesses its enemies, 1935–1940', in E.R. May (ed.) *Knowing One's Enemies: Intelligence Assessment before the Two World Wars*, Princeton NJ, Princeton University Press, 1984, pp. 366–7. See also B.R. Sullivan, 'The impatient cat: assessments of military power in fascist Italy, 1936–1940', in W. Murray and A.R. Millett (eds) *Calculations: Net Assessments and the Coming of World War II*, New York, The Free Press, 1992.
69 Campbell memorandum, 19 August 1935, *DBFP*, 2nd series, vol. XIV, no. 420.
70 Ormsby-Gore to Baldwin, 8 September 1935, Baldwin Papers, vol. 123. These papers are located at the University of Cambridge Library.
71 Vansittart minute, 27 September 1935, FO371/19052.
72 W.K. Wark, 'British intelligence and small wars in the 1930s', *Intelligence and National Security*, vol. 2, 1987, p. 70.
73 L.C. Hollis to Colonel Cornwall-Jones, 29 July 1940, CAB21/2625.
74 For the labour movement's commitment to collective security, through the League of Nations, see Peter J. Beck, Chapter 7 in this volume.
75 Hoare to Eden, 17 September 1935, FO800/295.
76 Minutes of meeting, 13 December 1935, PREM1/177. Sir Maurice Hankey, Secretary to the Cabinet and Committee of Imperial Defence and very much an ally of the Chiefs of Staff, had prepared Baldwin's briefing notes.
77 Professor Gilbert Murray to Cardinal Bourne, 14 December 1935, Murray Papers. These papers are located at the Bodleian Library, Oxford.
78 A.J.P. Taylor, *The Origins of the Second World War*, Harmondsworth, Penguin, 1961, pp. 173–4.
79 Viscount Cunningham of Hyndhope, *A Sailor's Odyssey*, London, Hutchinson, 1951, pp. 173–4.
80 Hugh Dalton diary entry, 25 June 1936. Dalton's diaries are located at the British Library of Economics and Political Science, London.
81 Sir Eric Phipps report, 13 April 1937, *DBFP*, 2nd series, vol. XVIII, no. 399.
82 Oliver Harvey diary entry, 22 April 1938, J. Harvey (ed.) *The Diplomatic Diaries of Oliver Harvey 1937–1940*, London, Collins, 1970, p. 131.
83 Foreign affairs debate, House of Commons, *Hansard Parliamentary Debates*, HC, 5th series, vol. 330, cc. 1810–11, 1814.

5 The 'proffered gift'
The Vatican and the abortive Yugoslav concordat of 1935–37

Peter C. Kent

On 25 July 1935, the agreed text of a concordat between Yugoslavia and the Holy See was signed in Rome between Lujevit Auer, the Yugoslav Minister of Justice, and Cardinal Eugenio Pacelli, the Vatican Secretary of State.[1] The concordat was designed to replace all earlier concordatory agreements which had governed the role and position of the Roman Catholic Church in the component parts of what became Yugoslavia in 1918. Once signed, the concordat had to be ratified by the Yugoslav parliament. Two years were to pass, however, before it was ratified by the lower house, the Skupstina, and it was not even considered by the upper house, the Senate, with the result that it was never ratified and ultimately proved to be an abortive exercise.

In December 1937, when it became apparent that the concordat was not likely to be ratified, Pope Pius XI rewarded Monsignor Pellegrinetti for long service as apostolic nuncio in Belgrade by making him a cardinal. When presenting him with his red hat, the Pope expressed the conviction that the time would come when Yugoslavia's rejection of his 'proffered gift' would be regretted by many 'and not only from religious reasons, but from political and social considerations too'.[2]

From the perspective of 1993, with Yugoslavia currently in the process of violent disintegration, fired by the memory of the brutalities associated with the creation of an independent Croatia between 1941 and 1945, the Pope's remarks of 1937 appear to be particularly prophetic. This raises the question of whether the 1935 concordat might, in fact, have prevented much subsequent bloodshed had it been ratified and implemented by the Yugoslav government.

While such speculation is not the terrain of historians, it might be argued that if the concordat contained sufficient bases of agreement between the various interest groups in Yugoslavia – Serbs, Croats,

Slovenes, Roman Catholics, Serb Orthodox and Muslims – then the failure of the concordat could have been a missed opportunity for national integration. Examination of the evidence in this case, however, demonstrates exactly the opposite. The concordat had been negotiated between King Alexander of Yugoslavia and the Holy See with little reference to religious or ethnic sensibilities inside Yugoslavia. Consequently, when the time came for ratification, not only was the concordat strongly opposed by Serb politicians and by the hierarchy of the Serb Orthodox Church, but also it elicited little enthusiasm from the Croat and Slovene communities or from many Roman Catholics including significant members of the Yugoslav Catholic hierarchy. If there was any basis of agreement between domestic factions, it lay in opposition to the concordat and, particularly, in opposition to the royal dictatorship of Alexander which had produced it.

The Corfu Declaration of 1918, which established the new Kingdom of the Serbs, Croats and Slovenes, declared that the three major religions, Serb Orthodox, Roman Catholic and Muslim, would enjoy equality of status in the new state. The Holy See recognised the new state in 1919 and established diplomatic relations with it. Negotiations for a new concordat between the kingdom and the Holy See opened in 1922 but achieved little under the parliamentary regimes of the 1920s.[3] The Serbs in government were little interested and Stephen Radic and the leaders of the Croat Peasant Party were anti-clerical, 'conscious of the influence of the church on the Croats and [fearing] that clerical elements in the church might try to take over political leadership in Croatia'.[4] Consequently, when King Alexander instituted his royal dictatorship in January 1929 in an effort to force the integration of the component parts of his state into a new Kingdom of Yugoslavia, negotiations for a concordat were still in progress.

Rather than relying on political institutions to build and integrate the nation, Alexander sought to use other institutional structures for his programme. In order to carry out the commitment that all religions should be equal in the eyes of the state, the king set out to regulate the position of each of the three major religions. Relations with the Serb Orthodox were regulated by a law of 1929 and with the Muslims by a law of 1936.[5] A concordat would regulate the position of the Roman Catholic Church and, for this reason, the king himself took up the development of a concordat. He started by engaging Professor Charles Loiseau of France, 'the leading expert on concordats', to advise him.[6]

In Alexander's calculations, if the Croat political leaders were unwilling to work for an integrated Yugoslavia, he might be able to enlist the religious leaders of the Croats to achieve the same ends. A generous settlement with the Vatican to protect the status of the Catholic Church in Yugoslavia might, the king calculated, secure the allegiance of the Catholic bishops and clergy for the Yugoslav state and might, thereby, convince the Croat people to set aside their autonomist and separatist predilections in favour of national unity. Moreover, the king recognized that Catholic priests were better educated and organised than the Orthodox. If the Catholic Church could be harnessed as an *instrumentum regni*, Alexander believed it could also be helpful in using its organisational strength to prevent the spread of communism in Yugoslavia.[7]

Alexander made a considerable show of support for the Catholic Church. In February 1931 he decorated Monsignor Ante Bauer, the Catholic Archbishop of Zagreb and, in return, Bauer demonstrated his loyalty to Yugoslavia by issuing a pastoral letter calling for prayers for those Catholic Slavs being persecuted in fascist Italy. In December 1933, Alexander celebrated his 45th birthday by attending high mass in Zagreb cathedral. Yet, it became apparent that it would be difficult for the king to develop satisfactory negotiations for a concordat through the Catholic bishops, many of whom were active supporters of Croatian political autonomy. The king concluded that the most effective approach to the concordat would be through direct negotiations in Rome with representatives of the Vatican Secretariat of State. In this way, the Yugoslav Catholic bishops could be bypassed and, with the conclusion of a concordat, the king expected that the Holy See would insist that Catholic bishops and clergy demonstrate their loyalty to the Yugoslav state. Through his integration of Catholic culture with the Yugoslav political entity, Alexander hoped to contend with continuous Croat demands for autonomy and independence.

By the beginning of 1934, it was becoming apparent that Alexander's experiment with royal dictatorship was less than a strategic success. The Croat political opposition had not been weakened, but had been consolidated behind the Croat Peasant Party under the leadership of Vladko Macek, while the traditional Serb governing parties had been fragmented and alienated from the royal regime.[8] The conclusion of a concordat seemed a necessity for shoring up Alexander's weakening position.

Negotiations with the Holy See proceeded with the utmost secrecy during 1934, carried out in Rome by Monsignor Moscatello, counsellor to the Yugoslav Embassy there, as Alexander's representative.[9] At the same time, the king acted to set aside the objections of the Serb Orthodox patriarch. Late in the year, when the negotiations were almost concluded, the king sent for the patriarch and told him of his determination to come to terms with the Holy See. 'The Catholic Church', he said, 'is more powerful than our Church and Yugoslavia needs her support'. When the patriarch protested, the king hurried through the negotiations in the face of potential Serb Orthodox opposition.[10] The negotiations were virtually completed and the concordat was in its final draft when Alexander was assassinated in Marseilles by an agent of the Croatian separatist Ustasa in October 1934.[11]

A major achievement of the pontificate of Pius XI had been the conclusion of the 1929 Lateran Agreements with Mussolini's Italy which re-established the temporal power of the papacy through the creation of the Vatican City State and also regulated the position of the church in Italy. Such close working relationships with the Italian fascist regime had their price, however, and one was that the Vatican had to be circumspect in its dealings with the enemies of Mussolini. Relations between Italy and Yugoslavia had been difficult since the creation of the latter denied to Italy territory that she considered her due after her contributions in the First World War. As Italy sought to weaken Yugoslav influence in the Balkans, Belgrade had turned, in 1927, to France for support and Italo-Yugoslav relations had become entwined with Franco-Italian relations, which were frequently hostile. The Vatican had learned at first hand of the problem that the Catholic Church in Yugoslavia could create for the Holy See when Archbishop Bauer's anti-Italian pastoral of 1931 became one of the factors inspiring a fascist attack on Italian Catholic Action in that year.[12] If there were to be negotiations for a concordat with Yugoslavia, they should be secret and they should be worth the risk of negotiating.

The evidence indicates that because Alexander desperately wanted a settlement with the Holy See, the latter extracted a very high price for its agreement. The Yugoslav concordat was later described by one of its critics, the Bishop of Gloucester, in the following way:

> If the Concordat as a whole is examined it will be seen that it not only grants to a minority Church in Yugoslavia all the privileges accorded to the Roman Catholic Church in countries like Austria and Italy, where the population is overwhelmingly Roman

Catholic, but also contains privileges which are not contained in any other Concordat, and have, in fact, been firmly refused even in a country like Austria.[13]

The Holy See was asked to name its terms for an agreement, which it did, asking for extensive guarantees for church property, education and marriage rights, including a legal guarantee that the children of mixed marriages would be raised as Catholics. Not only did King Alexander accept all that was asked, to the apparent surprise of the Holy See, but also his counter-proposals were minimal.[14]

Specifically, Yugoslavia sought permission to use the Old Church Slavonic language in the Catholic liturgy. This had been an approved practice in certain parts of Dalmatia and was now desired as a symbol that the Catholic Church was prepared to recognise Slavic traditions which could serve as a bridge to the Serb Orthodox. Yugoslavia also sought to regularise the situation of the Institute of St Jerome of the Slavs in Rome, which had been the subject of debate between the Vatican and the Belgrade government since the First World War.[15]

In previous years, the Vatican relationship with Belgrade had been complicated by disagreements between Italy and France over the Balkans and Yugoslavia in particular. Thus, the Franco-Italian Agreement of January 1935 helped to clear the way for a treaty between the Vatican and Yugoslavia. In fact, King Alexander's fatal visit to France had been part of the French strategy to improve relations with Italy. The Franco-Italian rapprochement was welcomed by Pius XI as a high point of interwar diplomacy since, for the first time, it brought together the two major powers of Catholic Europe in defence of the European status quo and against the antireligious statolatry of Adolf Hitler.

Alexander was succeeded on the throne by his son Peter, then a child of 11. A regency was necessary during the king's minority and Alexander's brother, Prince Paul, became the chief regent. Paul realised that Alexander's dictatorial policies had weakened support for the monarchy among both Serbs and Croats and, accordingly, he sought to improve relations with both. For the Serbs, he began to restore parliamentary government while, at the same time, he sought to reach out to the Croats in order to bring their political leaders into the government.

Immediately, however, the incomplete Yugoslav concordat was before Prince Paul and his Prime Minister, Jeftic. The Vatican's terms were considered again by the Jeftic government in the spring of 1935, and, after considerable debate,[16] Jeftic announced, only a week before national elections on 5 May, that negotiations for the concordat had been concluded and that it would be signed after the election.[17] The government gambled that they might glean some votes in Catholic areas by agreeing to the conclusion of the concordat. However, after winning the elections, Jeftic was replaced as Prime Minister on 25 June 1935 by Milan Stoyadinovich. Prince Paul believed that Stoyadinovich, also a Serb, would be more able than Jeftic to resolve the problem of Croat dissidence. Jeftic duly passed on the concordat to the Stoyadinovich government which, in turn, despatched Auer, the Minister of Justice, to Rome for the signing of the concordat on 27 July 1935.

The concordat replaced all earlier concordatory agreements which preceded the foundation of Yugoslavia and defined new diocesan boundaries, making them co-terminous with the frontiers of the state. The Holy See agreed to consult the Yugoslav government on the appointment of bishops and to have these bishops take an oath of allegiance to the state. Yugoslav religious orders would not report to foreign provincials except in exceptional circumstances. The concordat guaranteed church property and the government agreed to indemnify the church for property lost through earlier land reforms. An annual governmental subsidy of 35.5 million dinars was to be provided to the Roman Catholic Church.[18] Religious instruction was to be provided in schools and had to be approved by religious authorities. In predominantly Catholic schools, the teachers were to be Catholic, while, in other schools, Catholic teachers were to be in the same ratio as Catholic students. The government recognised degrees earned from the pontifical universities in Rome as the equal of Yugoslav degrees and agreed that episcopal approval was needed for anyone teaching theology in Yugoslavia. The Holy See agreed to appoint a Catholic military bishop to head a Catholic chaplains' corps and it recognized the use of Old Slavonic in the liturgy.

The most controversial articles in the concordat were those dealing with marriage and with Catholic Action. Article XXXII on marriage recognised church marriages as the equivalent of civil marriage even when the spouses were of different religions. Nullification of marriage was to be carried out by an ecclesiastical and not a civil tribunal and, in mixed marriages, the concordat stipulated that all children would be raised as Catholics. Article XXXIII provided for Catholic Action to have the freedom to carry out a full range of religious, cultural and athletic programmes, subject only to the direction of the Catholic hierarchy.[19] Critics saw this as a potential agency for Catholic proselytising and political indoctrination.

The conclusion of this concordat did not impress the Catholic Croats and Slovenes who saw the Vatican making a deal with the Yugoslav government in order to preserve the institution and property of the church rather than acting to protect and promote the interests of Yugoslav Catholics. The Croats and Slovenes pointed to the Italian concordat of 1929 as an example of Vatican interest in the fate of Croats and Slovenes. In 1929, the Holy See had worked out a complex arrangement with the Italian state such that the Vatican was forced to look the other way when the fascist regime carried out its active programme of Italianising Catholic Slavs in Venezia Giulia and the Catholic German-speaking population of the South Tyrol. If the Holy See was not prepared to agitate on behalf of Catholics in Italy lest it lose its favoured position there, it was reasoned that little could be expected from the Holy See by Catholics in Yugoslavia.

Neither the Slovenes nor the Croats had any time for Italy and they saw no particular advantage to be gained from the concordat. The leaders of the Croatian Peasant Party, including Vladko Macek, were anti-clerical and even the Croatian clergy were not 'by any means disposed blindly to follow the precept of the Vatican whose Italian affiliations are viewed with misgiving in ecclesiastical circles'.[20] In fact the Croat Catholics were 'disappointed with the Vatican for signing the Concordat which they regard as in the nature of a surrender to Belgrade'.[21]

The concordat might have been received more positively by the Yugoslavs had it been set against the background of a serious effort to improve relations between Italy and Yugoslavia, but, in spite of the Franco-Italian rapprochement, there was no real improvement in Italo-Yugoslav relations in 1935. Two issues were of particular concern to Yugoslavia. One was the Italianisation programme in Venezia Giulia – which Italy gave no sign of wishing to abate – and the other was the Italian protectorate over Albania.[22] In both these areas, the Vatican was seen to be clearly on the side of the Italians.

The Italianisation programme in Venezia Giulia was especially active in 1935 and the Italians expected and received Vatican assistance in its implementation. On the conclusion of the Yugoslav concordat, the Vatican assured the Italians that the use of Old Slavonic would be restricted to very limited areas of Yugoslavia and would not set a precedent which might encourage priests in Venezia Giulia to use the Slavic language in their services.[23] When the Lazarist monastery at Montegrado in Venezia Giulia was promoting anti-Italian Slovene irredentist propaganda, the Vatican Secretariat of State indicated its willingness to replace Slovene monks in Montegrado with monks from the Piedmontese province of the Lazarist Order 'who can be trusted to be good Italians'.[24]

In June 1935, the Pope sent Cardinal Hlond, the Primate of Poland, to Ljubljana, the capital of Slovenia, to preside over a National Eucharistic Congress, choosing him because, as a Slav, it was felt that he would be welcome in Yugoslavia. In his sermon, Hlond spoke of 'the mission of Catholic Slavdom', saying that 'the riches of the Slav soul, still largely asleep and inactive, constituted a magnificent reserve of moral strength for Europe which the Catholic Slavs must endeavour to save from Western materialism, "raciste" paganism and Soviet atheism'.[25]

Following the Congress, some Slovene youth leaders took Hlond at his word and asked him to convey to the Pope their concerns for the Slavs of Venezia Giulia.[26] Some days later, the Vatican lodged a half-hearted protest with the Italian foreign ministry about police action against Slovene priests in Pola, only to back off when told that the pulpit was often the source of anti-Italian propaganda in these Slovene churches.[27] The Italian authorities recognised that the Holy See was too concerned about maintaining its friendship with Italy to mount a strong protest on behalf of the Slovenes of Venezia Giulia.[28]

As the Holy See was unwilling to challenge the treatment of Slav Catholics in Venezia Giulia, it also worked closely with the Italian government in extending its own and that government's influence in Albania, where the small Catholic population, mostly congregated around the northern city of Scutari, was recognised as an element of Italian support and influence.[29]

On 22 April 1933, the government of King Zog had secularised the schools of Albania, ordering the immediate closure of all minority private schools, including thirty-five Catholic schools, many with Italian teachers.[30] The schools question was the subject of ongoing negotiations between Italy and Albania and between Albania and the Holy See.[31] Meeting an Albanian emissary in February 1935, Mussolini told him that, in the school question, Italy would accept whatever solution should be reached between Albania and the Holy See on this issue.[32] When a stalemate developed in these latter negotiations, Cardinal Pacelli advised Mussolini that it would be better for Italy not to try to mediate between Albania and the Vatican, but just to keep Vatican goals in mind as the Italians conducted their own negotiations.³³ On 9 May 1936, the Albanian government issued a decree-law on private schools which provided rather less than the Roman Catholic had hoped for but did go some distance towards addressing their concerns.³⁴ In June 1936, the apostolic delegate to Albania told the Italian ambassador to the Holy See that he would be counting on Italian assistance and pressure to resolve the schools question in favour of the Vatican and also that he intended to give the Albanian priesthood an Italian orientation by seeing that all new priests received part of their education in Italy.³⁵

The apparent collaboration of the Vatican with Italian interests in Venezia Giulia and in Albania was enhanced and confirmed by the active and enthusiastic support given to the Italian invasion of Abyssinia in October 1935 by Italian bishops and clergy. While the papacy sought to preserve the appearance of neutrality and to act as a mediator in the crisis, the Catholic Church in Italy outdid itself in demonstrating support of Mussolini.³⁶ From the perspective of the Yugoslavs, who supported the League of Nations at great personal expense by imposing sanctions on Italy,³⁷ the Vatican appeared to be little more than a mouthpiece for the disliked Italian regime.

When Austrian Nazis staged a coup in Vienna in July 1934 which resulted in the murder of Chancellor Engelbert Dollfuss, Mussolini had moved Italian troops to the Brenner frontier as a warning to Hitler to respect Austrian independence. Kurt von Schuschnigg, Dollfuss's successor as Chancellor and a devout Catholic, continued to look to Italy for support against a possible *Anschluss*. The Italian invasion of Abyssinia meant, however, that Italian troops would not be able to spring so readily to Austrian defence.

With the threatened extension of German power towards the south-east after 1934, the Holy See sought to secure the position of the Catholic Church in central Europe and the Balkans. Austria, under the chancellorship of the devout von Schuschnigg and with a constitution based on Catholic principles, could be expected to resist Nazi incursion as long as it was able. With the Abyssinian war, the Vatican recognised that the Austrians would need support from friendly governments and looked to the states of the Little Entente, especially Yugoslavia and Czechoslovakia, to support the independence of Austria. Previously, the Vatican had supported Hungarian revisionism and had been reluctant to recognise the frontiers of the successor states after 1918. The concordat with Yugoslavia represented a changed strategy, serving as it did to bring diocesan boundaries into line with the 1918 boundaries of Yugoslavia.

In January 1936, von Schuschnigg paid an official visit to Czechoslovakia where he spoke of the need for economic co-operation between Austria and Czechoslovakia 'as a preliminary to an Economic Danube Confederation, consisting of Austria, Hungary, Czechoslovakia, Yugoslavia and Roumania'. Since Schuschnigg visited Cardinal Kaspar in Prague and since President Beneš of Czechoslovakia was known to be trying to fashion a Roman Catholic bloc of supporters, the rumour spread 'that the Roman Catholic Church is endeavouring, through its devoted son, Dr. Schuschnigg, and its new ally, Dr. Beneš, to build up the nucleus of a common Catholic front in Central Europe against Germany'.[38]

Once again, Yugoslav suspicions were aroused. Prince Paul received this rumour with great alarm, believing that Austria was determined to restore the Habsburgs, that France was supporting the plan and that the Pope had sent instructions to all papal nuncios to work 'for a fusion of Austria, Hungary and Czechoslovakia under a Habsburg ruler'.[39] Paul's distress came from his belief that a Habsburg restoration would attract the Croats and possibly the Slovenes out of the Yugoslav union at a time when that union was none too secure. Prince Paul saw the *Anschluss* as a lesser evil than a Habsburg restoration.[40]

In July 1937, at the same time as the Yugoslav concordat was ratified by the Skupstina, Father Korosec, the Yugoslav Minister of the Interior and the leader of the Catholic Slovenes, travelled to Vienna for a meeting with von Schuschnigg in what appears to have been an attempt to improve relations between Austria and Yugoslavia.[41] The Vatican may well have been behind the initiative since, when Cardinal Pacelli was asked about an anti-German Catholic front he replied enigmatically that Vatican relations with Germany were as bad as ever, that the secretary of state had heard that Germany was encouraging the Serb Orthodox in their opposition to the Yugoslav concordat, that the Nazis worked against Catholicism in countries other than Germany, that he had confidence in the Austrians and that he doubted that Mussolini would again move his troops if there were another threat of *Anschluss*.[42]

In 1927, Czechoslovakia and the Vatican concluded a *modus vivendi*, designed to bring diocesan boundaries into line with the national boundaries of Czechoslovakia as soon as church lands sequestrated by the Czech government had been restored to the church. The *modus vivendi* was to be implemented by a papal bull but negotiations between the Vatican and Czechoslovakia regarding implementation of this agreement went on for several years. The

Vatican was a reluctant negotiator because neither the Hungarians, with irredentist claims on Czechoslovakia, nor the Slovaks, who were looking for autonomy from Prague, wanted the Holy See to confirm the existing structure of Czechoslovakia. Negotiations resumed with some promise in 1936, however, and on 2 September 1937 the papal bull was finally promulgated.[43] By this action, the Pope officially recognized the Czech borders and gave a blow to Hungarian aspirations for boundary revision.[44] In fact, by the Yugoslav and Czech agreements, the Holy See attempted to stem the spread of Nazism by placing itself firmly in the European anti-revisionist camp.

Since the First World War, the Church of England had taken a paternal interest in the Serb and Romanian Orthodox Churches. Many of the Serb Orthodox clergy had received their training in England during the war and, after 1917, when the Russian Orthodox Church was unable to provide its traditional support to other Slav Orthodox churches, the Church of England deliberately took up this role. Spear-headed by the Anglican Bishop of Gibraltar, the Church of England was especially concerned about the vitality of the ministry of the Serb Orthodox Church and about its ability to 'withstand the missionary appeal of Rome'.[45]

One of the goals of the Church of England was to bring the Slav Orthodox churches together to provide mutual support for each other and also to explore with them ecumenical possibilities between the Orthodox and Anglican communions. In May 1935, an important conference of the Orthodox churches of Yugoslavia, Bulgaria and Romania was held at Karlovci, the seat of the Serbian Patriarchate.[46] The Orthodox patriarchs were joined at this meeting by a delegation from the Anglican Communion, headed by the Bishop of Lincoln who had formerly been the Bishop of Gibraltar. Included in the delegation were a representative of the Episcopal Church of New York and the current Bishop of Gibraltar, who had been instrumental in engineering the rapprochement between the Bulgarian and Yugoslav churches as well as the rapprochement between the Orthodox and Anglican churches. This delegation was en route to Bucharest to discuss the possible recognition of Anglican orders by the Romanian Orthodox Church.[47]

The leaders of the Church of England suspected that the Roman Catholic Church was acting in many places in league with the Italians and, for this reason, the Anglicans sought to strengthen the Orthodox in the Balkans just as, following Mussolini's October

The abortive Yugoslav concordat of 1935–37 119

invasion of Abyssinia, the Archbishop of Canterbury sought to force the Pope to declare himself publicly in favour of peace.[48]

The Stoyadinovich government viewed the concordat as a domestic political liability and was in no hurry to move towards ratification while the Holy See, who stood to gain much, patiently waited for the government to choose the right moment for ratification.[49] While the concordat was in limbo in 1936, the international environment was changing radically. With the conclusion of the Abyssinian campaign in 1936, Italy sought to improve relations with Yugoslavia, starting with the conclusion of an economic and financial agreement in September 1936. When Mussolini announced the creation of the Rome-Berlin Axis in a speech in Milan on 1 November of that year, he pointedly invited Yugoslavia to join Germany and Italy in their anti-Bolshevik campaign. In December, formal negotiations began with the Stoyadinovich government for a wide-ranging settlement of issues between Italy and Yugoslavia.[50] Prodded by the rapprochement with Italy, Stoyadinovich announced at the end of November 1936, that the concordat would be placed before the Skupstina for ratification on 10 December.

In a pre-emptive move, on 26 November, the Assembly of Bishops of the Serb Orthodox Church issued a statement that they found the Yugoslav concordat to be completely unacceptable.[51] They prepared and submitted to the government a lengthy memorandum setting out their objections to the concordat. The memorandum asserted that

> the Concordat places the Church of a minority ... in a privileged and, indeed, in a dominant position.... Some of its provisions are ... of a kind unknown in a modern State, others give the Roman Catholic minority advantages denied to the other Christian communities.

In citing specific sections of the concordat, the memorandum referred to Article XIII, 'an astonishing proposal' which was not available to other denominations

> that where an ecclesiastic is convicted of an offence against public order, and his religious superiors are not in agreement on this point with the civil authorities, the matter shall be referred to a mixed commission of representatives of the Ministry of Justice and of the Episcopate.

Article XXXII, providing civil enforcement of the requirement that children of mixed marriages be raised as Catholics, had 'no parallel in any valid Concordat' and represented 'a one-sided intervention by the State in a matter hotly contested between the Roman Catholic and other Churches'.

The economic provisions of the concordat were also criticised as having the effect of 'putting the Roman Catholic Church into a dominant position'. Article XVI provided 'that the possessions and institutions of the Roman Catholic Church remain the property of that Church, even if the population which these possessions and institutions serve joins another religious denomination'. It was pointed out that no similar guarantee existed for the property of the Serb Orthodox Church. While a government subvention to the Roman Catholic Church was considered reasonable, the compensation for church property confiscated in the past and the guarantee against future expropriation of church property were again rights which were not enjoyed by any other church as were the privileges in education, in the army and in public institutions.[52]

As a result of this memorandum, Stoyadinovich deferred the presentation of the concordat to the Skupstina. Given the promise of his negotiations with Italy, he did not now feel that there was any point in joining battle with the Serb Orthodox Church over the concordat until the Italo-Yugoslav negotiations had been completed. Ratification of the concordat had not been a condition imposed by the Italians and these negotiations culminated in the Italo-Yugoslav Agreement of 25 March 1937, which ushered in a new age of Italo-Yugoslav amity.

When Stoyadinovich finally presented the concordat for ratification in the summer of 1937, he did so as part of his strategy for coping with the Croatian question. In January 1937, urged on by Prince Paul, the Prime Minister had had an unsuccessful meeting with Macek who refused to negotiate with the government unless they were prepared to change Yugoslavia into a federal state.[53] Since neither Stoyadinovich nor Prince Paul were prepared to consider this course, Stoyadinovich tried instead to isolate Macek and to reduce his influence within Yugoslavia. Macek and the intellectuals of the Croatian Peasant Party were wary of the additional power which the concordat would provide to the church. In particular, Catholic Action would be given full scope for its activities and could thereby develop, so it was believed, into a political arm of the Croatian Clericals under the 'energetic leadership of Monsignor Stepinac, the Acting Archbishop of Zagreb'.[54] The Yugoslav treaty with Italy, a new treaty with Bulgaria and negotiations with Hungary were attempts to isolate the Croats from their erstwhile foreign supporters, while the ratification of the concordat was designed to split the Croats from within by trying to secure the support of Bishop Stepinac and the Croat clergy against the anti-clerical Macek and his followers. Stoyadinovich calculated that, if Macek could be isolated in this way, he could eventually be pushed into a settlement with Belgrade.[55]

The Serb Orthodox Church sought assistance in its campaign against the concordat from the Church of England.[56] On 18 March 1937, Bishop Ireney of Dalmatia wrote to his good friend Arthur Cayley Headlam, the Bishop of Gloucester, to urge him to place the concerns of the Serb Orthodox before the Council on Foreign Relations of the Church of England, to write to the press, and to send copies of his articles for distribution in Yugoslavia. Headlam did as requested, presented the matter to the Council on Foreign Relations and, on 4 May 1937, published an article in *The Times*, entitled 'Yugoslavia and Rome: An Astonishing Concordat', designed to enlist British opinion against the ratification of the concordat. In this article, Headlam summarised the arguments which had been made by the synod of the Serb Orthodox Church in their formal submission to the Stoyadinovich government.[57]

Serb Orthodox Patriarch Varnava himself led the campaign against the concordat within Yugoslavia. After the November 1936 meeting of the Assembly of Bishops, church leaders 'issued circulars urging their flock to protest against [the concordat] by every means in their power'. On 26 May 1937, Varnava reconvened the Assembly of Bishops which reiterated the view that the concordat was 'injurious to the vital interests of the Serbian Church'.[58] All Serb Orthodox legislators were threatened with excommunication should they vote to ratify the concordat.[59] When it was announced that the concordat would be placed before the Skupstina for ratification on 19 July 1937, the Orthodox Church planned a major demonstration in Belgrade for that day, including a religious procession which turned into a riot and was eventually broken up by the police with considerable brutality.[60]

Before placing the concordat before the Skupstina, Stoyadinovich publicly asserted how important the ratification would be to the Croats and also stressed the need for equality of treatment of the three main religious groups of Yugoslavia. On 7 July, the government added a supplementary clause to the concordat to provide that, by simple ministerial order, the government could extend the privileges given to the Catholics to all the other religious communities.[61] The concordat was ratified in the Skupstina by a comfortable majority of thirty-eight votes on 23 July 1937, two days short of two years from the original signing. Before the introduction of the motion to parliament on 19 July, Patriarch Varnava had fallen ill, and he died on the very day that the vote was taken, which provided a dramatic emphasis to the parliamentary decision. Stoyadinovich and the Serb Orthodox legislators who had voted for ratification were duly excommunicated by church authorities.

Full ratification of the concordat required approval by the Yugoslav Senate as well as the Skupstina. Because of the strong opposition of the Serb Orthodox Church, Stoyadinovich decided to delay presenting the concordat to the Senate until the autumn, in hopes that some prior agreement could be reached with that church.[62] Yet, Stoyadinovich's hopes did not materialise. The Serb Orthodox Church continued its public campaign of protest and demonstration against the concordat into the autumn, being assisted by members of the former governing party, who saw a continuing opportunity to embarrass the government.[63] Nor, for that matter, did Macek and his Croatian followers remain isolated since, on 8 October, they finally reached an agreement for united political action with the Serb Opposition group, thereby breaking out of the isolation that Stoyadinovich had tried to impose on them.[64] Consequently, Stoyadinovich, recognising that the religious situation and his own political situation had not improved since July, announced in October that he would not be placing the concordat before the Senate for ratification.[65]

Stoyadinovich had also found that he could not even elicit statements of support for the concordat from the Catholic bishops. On 21 August, he sent a personal representative to Bishop Stepinac to ask him to make a public declaration in favour of the concordat, but Stepinac temporised, knowing, as president of the bishops' conference, that the Catholic bishops were not united in their views. Archbishop Saric of Sarajevo, in fact, was a strong Croatian nationalist and had openly spoken against the concordat, for which he received a reprimand from the papal nuncio.[66]

The Catholic bishops met in Zagreb on 22 October 1937 for their annual conference. The important issue at this meeting was the extent to which the bishops and clergy should become involved in political issues. Some bishops were active Croatian nationalists and were sympathetic to the right-wing Frankist movement which had links with the Ustasa. These bishops wanted considerable freedom for Catholic Action to be able to indoctrinate urban youth with Croatian nationalism. They were also opposed to the concordat, which they saw as a sell-out to Belgrade. Other bishops did not believe that the church should be involved in politics and favoured a rural as opposed to an urban emphasis in the church. With opinions divided, the bishops decided that it was best not to react to the public attacks by the opponents of the concordat and to see that blame for opposition fell on the political centralisers, the Marxists and the freemasons, and not on any lack of enthusiasm on the part of the Croat movement.[67]

The Vatican believed that the concordat provided real advantages to both Yugoslavia and the Holy See and were initially optimistic that Prince Paul and Stoyadinovich could secure full ratification.[68] In December 1937, Stoyadinovich paid a formal visit to Italy and to the Vatican and, while there, assured the Pope that he still intended to take the concordat to the Senate for ratification at the appropriate time.[69] Yet, in spite of Stoyadinovich's assurances, the Pope was not pleased. When Monsignor Pelligrinetti ended his service as Nuncio to Belgrade in December, the Pope, in order to show his displeasure and disappointment, deferred the naming of his replacement for four months.[70] On a subsequent review of the failure of the Yugoslav concordat, the Vatican placed the blame squarely on the Croat politicians who had been so determined to achieve political autonomy that they did not support the concordat lest its ratification should weaken their claim for autonomy.[71]

By the beginning of 1938, Stoyadinovich placed a higher premium on resolving the dispute with the Serb Orthodox Church than on ratifying the concordat. The hierarchy of the Serb Orthodox Church was bitterly divided about whether and on what terms they should settle with the government. Some, including the bishops, who had maintained the closest relations with the Church of England, were opposed to any reconciliation except on terms which amounted to a virtual capitulation by the government. The majority, however, were willing to settle on condition that they receive 'a definite assurance ... that the Concordat would not be resuscitated in its present form, together with a promise that ... amends would be made to persons who had suffered fines or imprisonment on account of their support of the Church'. The government were interested in having the excommunication against those who had voted for the ratification lifted and also wanted the cessation of anti-government propaganda which continued to be disseminated by the Orthodox clergy.

Although the Skupstina had previously been told that the

concordat could not now be ratified,[72] on 1 February 1938, Stoyadinovich assured the Episcopal Council

> firstly, that the concordat in its present form would not again be brought before Parliament, and, secondly, that the Government would always in future, when regulating their relations with the Vatican and the position of the Roman Catholic Church in Yugoslavia, fully respect and apply the principle of equality for all recognized confessions guaranteed by the Constitution.

On 9 February, a royal decree amnestied all who had been punished or fined since January 1937 for offences connected with the concordat. The Episcopal Council accordingly announced on 10 February that the excommunication of those who had voted for ratification of the concordat was being lifted.[73] With this lifting of the ban, the dispute between the Serb Orthodox Church and the Yugoslav government was brought to a final conclusion.

The Vatican expressed its dissatisfaction with the treatment it had received, especially when an agreement which had been duly and properly signed had not been submitted to parliament for full ratification, and it lodged a formal protest with the Yugoslav government on 15 February.[74] Yet Vatican disappointment with the failure of the Yugoslav concordat was tempered within the month by the much greater threat to central European Catholics posed by the *Anschluss* which brought Nazi Germany into the centre of central and southern European affairs.

The Yugoslav concordat represented an attempt by King Alexander to use the religious institutions of his country to force its political integration. In so doing, he was prepared to deal with a foreign power, the Holy See, in the expectation that it could force Yugoslav Catholics to do the bidding of the king. The Holy See, aware that improved relations with Yugoslavia would arouse the suspicions of the Italian fascists, was willing to deal with Alexander on condition that the Catholic Church was adequately compensated for its trouble. The assassination of Alexander in October 1934 removed the one person who sincerely believed in the advantages of the concordat. While his successors went through the motions of concluding the negotiations and signing the document, they soon realised that the concordat was a domestic political liability. The non-ratification of the concordat in 1937 signified the rejection by Yugoslavs of the centralised direction given by Alexander's royal dictatorship and, at the same time, indicated the rejection by Yugoslav Catholics of political tutelage by the Vatican.

NOTES

1 N. Alex Dragnich, *The First Yugoslavia: Search for a Viable Political System*, Stanford, Calif., Hoover Institution Press, 1983, p. 107.
2 Annual Report on the Holy See for 1937, 10 February 1938, FO371 series, R1681/1681/22.
3 S. Alexander, *Church and State in Yugoslavia since 1945*, Cambridge, Cambridge University Press, 1979, pp. 4–5.
4 S. Alexander, *The Triple Myth: A Life of Archbishop Alojzije Stepinac*, New York, Columbia University Press, 1987, p. 30.
5 ibid., p. 30.
6 Dragnich, op. cit., pp. 106–7.
7 Montgomery (Holy See) to Hoare, 8 August 1935, FO371 R4997/81/22; Annual Report on the Holy See for 1935, 9 January 1936, FO371 R217/217/22.
8 Dragnich, op. cit., ch. 5.
9 Pignatti (Holy See) to Ciano, 1 December 1936. Archives of the Ministero degli Affari Esteri, Rome, busta 30, Santa Sede 5 – Jugoslavia. Hereafter ASMAE.
10 Montgomery (Holy See) to Hoare, 8 August 1935, FO371 R4997/81/22; Annual Report on the Holy See for 1935, 9 January 1936, FO371 R217/217/22.
11 P.C. Kent, *The Pope and the Duce: The International Impact of the Lateran Agreements*, London, Macmillan, 1981, pp. 117, 166.
12 ibid., pp. 116–121.
13 *The Times*, 4 May 1937.
14 Wingfield (Holy See) to Simon, 16 March 1935, FO371 R1985/1365/92.
15 A. Rhodes, *The Vatican in the Age of the Dictators, 1922–45*, London, Hodder & Stoughton, 1973, pp. 158–9; Alexander, *Triple Myth*, p. 20.
16 Henderson (Belgrade) to Simon, 1 April 1935, FO371 R2293/1365/92.
17 Telegram from Balfour (Belgrade), 30 April 1935, FO371 R2958/1365/92.
18 This sum should be compared with 46 million dinars given to the Serb Orthodox and 13 million dinars to the Muslims.
19 Henderson (Belgrade) to Hoare, 22 July 1935, FO371 R4620/1365/92; Pignatti (Holy See) to Ciano, 1 December 1936. ASMAE, busta 30, Santa Sede 5 – Jugoslavia.
20 Campbell (Belgrade) to Hoare, 7 December 1935, FO371 J9210/8550/1.
21 ibid.
22 Henderson (Belgrade) to Simon, 31 January 1935, FO371 R850/241/92; Drummond (Rome) to Simon, 12 May 1935, FO371 R3197/241/92.
23 Taramo (Holy See) to Mussolini, 24 July 1935. ASMAE, busta 24, Santa Sede 5 – Jugoslavia.
24 Taramo (Holy See) to Mussolini, 27 February and 4 June, 1935. ASMAE, busta 25, S6 – 3/4.
25 Annual Report on the Holy See for 1935, 9 January 1936, FO371 R217/217/22.
26 Natali (Ljubljana) to Mussolini, 11 July 1935. ASMAE, busta 25, S6 – 3 (PG).
27 Suvich to the Minister of the Interior, 16 July 1935. ASMAE, busta 25, S6 – 3/3.

28 Taramo (Holy See) to Mussolini, 3 August 1935. ASMAE, busta 25, S6 – 3 (PG).
29 Muslims made up 70 per cent of the population of Albania while the Christians were divided between the Orthodox, who represented 20 per cent of the population, and the Roman Catholics, representing 10 per cent. Most of the Orthodox belonged to the Greek Orthodox Church, which came directly under the Patriarchate of Constantinople, although a small group had been encouraged by the government to separate from Constantinople in 1922 and to create the Albanian Autocephalous Church. The Roman Catholics were mostly of the Latin rite with the exception of a Uniate Church which had been opened at Elbassan in 1929. The religious distribution of the Albanian population in 1936 of 1,001,500 was:

Bektash Muslims	250,000
Other Muslims	450,000
Greek Orthodox	200,000
Albanian Orthodox	1,000
Roman Catholics – Latin rite	100,000
Roman Catholics – Uniate	500

Report by LaTerza, 6 June 1936, ASMAE, busta 29, Santa Sede 5 – Albania.
30 Petition to the League of Nations, 31 January 1936, FO371 R682/12/90.
31 Kent, *Pope and Duce*, pp. 157–8, 169–70.
32 Suvich to the Minister to Albania, 5 February 1935. ASMAE, busta 24, Santa Sede 5 – Albania.
33 Talamo (Holy See) to Mussolini, 15 February 1935. ASMAE busta 24, Santa Sede 5 – Albania.
34 Foreign Ministry to Embassy to the Holy See, 13 June 1936. ASMAE, busta 29, Santa Sede 5 – Albania.
35 Pignatti (Holy See) to Ciano, 13 June 1936. ASMAE, busta 31, Santa Sede 12 – Albania.
36 P.C. Kent, 'Between Rome and London: Pius XI, the Catholic Church and the Abyssinian Crisis of 1935–36', *International History Review*, vol. 9, 1989, pp. 252–71.
37 Italy was the main trading partner of Yugoslavia before 1935.
38 Hadow (Prague) to Eden, 21 January 1936, FO371 R468/424/67.
39 Eden to Campbell (Belgrade), 6 February 1936, FO371 R681/125/67.
40 Campbell (Belgrade) to Eden, 2 March 1936, FO371 R1288/42/92. See also N. Balfour and S. Mackay, *Paul of Yugoslavia: Britain's Maligned Friend*, London, Hamish Hamilton, 1980.
41 Shone (Belgrade) to Nichols, 1 and 12 August 1937, FO371 R5334/R5707/5160/92; Torr (Holy See) to Nichols, 13 August 1937, FO371 R5597/5160/92; Mack (Vienna) to Nichols, 24 August 1937, FO371 R5931/5160/92.
42 Torr (Holy See) to Nichols, 16 August 1937, FO371 R5628/5160/92.
43 De Facendis (Prague) to Ciano, 3 August 1936; Bratislava to Prague Legation, 9 December 1936; De Facendis to Ciano, 15 December 1936. ASMAE, busta 29, Santa Sede 5 – Cecoslovacchia.
44 Foreign Ministry to the Embassy to the Holy See, etc., 17 March 1937;

The abortive Yugoslav concordat of 1935–37 127

ASMAE, busta 38, Santa Sede 5 – Cecoslovacchia (1938); Newton (Prague) to Eden, 8 September 1937, FO371 R6188/2032/12.
45 Kent, *Pope and the Duce*, p. 65. See also R. Jasper, *Arthur Cayley Headlam; Life and Letters of a Bishop*, London, Faith Press, 1960.
46 Cora (Sofia) to Mussolini, 19 January 1935. ASMAE, busta 24, Santa Sede 5 – Jugoslavia.
47 Jasper, op. cit, p. 231.
48 Kent, 'Between Rome and London'.
49 Foreign Ministry to Embassy to the Holy See, 23 May 1936; ASMAE, busta 31, Santa Sede 12 – Austria.
50 See J.B. Hoptner, *Yugoslavia in Crisis, 1934 – 1941*, New York, Columbia University Press, 1962, pp. 52–63.
51 Dragnich, op. cit., p. 108; Pignatti (Holy See) to Ciano, 1 December 1936. ASMAE, busta 30, Santa Sede 5 – Jugoslavia.
52 The Bishop of Gloucester, 'Yugoslavia and Rome: an astonishing concordat', *The Times*, 4 May 1937. The British Minister to Belgrade, Sir Ronald Campbell, attested that this article gives an excellent précis of the Serb Orthodox position. Campbell (Belgrade) to Eden, 10 May 1937, FO371 R3283/3283/92.
53 Dragnich, op. cit., ch. 6.
54 Campbell (Belgrade) to Eden, 10 May 1937, FO371 R3283/3283/92.
55 Campbell (Belgrade) to Eden, 4 June 1937, FO371 R4041/175/92.
56 Telegram from Shone (Belgrade), 28 July 1937, FO371 R5218/175/92.
57 *The Times*, 4 May 1937; Jasper, op. cit., pp. 227–30.
58 Dragnich, op. cit., p. 108.
59 Shone (Belgrade) to Eden, 18 July 1937, FO371 R5002/175/92.
60 Balfour and Mackay, op. cit., p. 145; Rhodes, op. cit., p. 159–60.
61 *The Times*, 8 July 1937.
62 *The Times*, 23 and 24 July 1937, Shone (Belgrade) to Eden, 27 July 1937, FO371 R5235/175/92. Foreign Ministry to Prague, Bucarest, etc., 8 August 1937, ASMAE, busta 35, Santa Sede 5 – Jugoslavia.
63 Zuccolin (Serajevo) to Foreign Ministry and the Embassy in Belgrade, 14 September 1937. ASMAE, busta 35, Santa Sede 5 – Jugoslavia.
64 Telegram from Campbell (Belgrade), 8 October 1937, FO371 R6699/175/92.
65 Telegram from Campbell (Belgrade), 9 October 1937, FO371 R6836/175/92.
66 Alexander, *Triple Myth*, pp. 35–6; J.J. Sadkovich, *Italian Support for Croatian Separatism, 1927–1937*, New York, Garland, 1987, pp. 203–4.
67 Gobbi (Zagreb) to Foreign Ministry and the Embassy in Belgrade, 27 and 29 October 1937. ASMAE, busta 35, Santa Sede 5 – Jugoslavia.
68 Foreign Ministry to the Embassy in Belgrade, 29 October 1937. ASMAE, busta 39, Santa Sede 5 – Jugoslavia (1938).
69 Foreign Ministry to the Embassy in Belgrade, 13 December 1937. ASMAE, busta 35, Santa Sede 5 – Jugoslavia.
70 Osborne (Holy See) to Eden, 5 January 1938, FO371 R260/260/92; Osborne to Halifax, 21 April 1938, FO371 R4225/260/92.
71 Osborne (Holy See) to Eden, 10 February 1938, FO371 R1277/260/92.
72 D.N. Ristic, *Yugoslavia's Revolution of 1941*, University Park, Pennsylvania State University Press, 1966, p. 24.

73 Campbell (Belgrade) to Eden, 14 February 1938, FO371 R1457/260/92.
74 Osborne (Holy See) to Halifax, 24 February 1938, FO371 R1890/260/92.

6 Britain, France and the Spanish problem, 1936–39

Glyn Stone

For many years after the Second World War there was a tendency to characterise French foreign policy in the late 1930s as being subservient to that of Britain; that France obeyed her 'English governess'.[1] The Franco-British appeasement of Nazi Germany in 1938, initiated by Neville Chamberlain, the British Prime Minister, and culminating in the Munich Agreement of September, appeared the classic confirmation of this view. Anthony Adamthwaite, however, has demonstrated convincingly that as far as the appeasement of Germany was concerned France was not dragged along unwillingly on the coat tails of Britain, rather that 'in practice French policy was much more assertive and independent than supposed'. Certainly this was true of France's relations concerning fascist Italy, as William Shorrock has demonstrated.[2] For example, Edouard Daladier, the French Prime Minister, was resisting British pleas to get on better terms with the Italian dictator, Benito Mussolini, as late as July 1939. In view of this re-evaluation of French foreign policy, it is surprising that some historians still persist in seeing Britain as the only real villain responsible for the demise of the second Spanish Republic in 1939, with France cast as an unwilling, almost innocent accomplice unable to resist British demands to maintain non-intervention in the Spanish Civil War even if occasionally she took action or adopted a stance which would benefit the Republican cause.[3]

The fact that France was capable of taking action which was contrary to non-intervention would indicate a certain independence of mind and at least question the assertion of French subservience to British policy in the Spanish case. Clearly, France was less neutral in the Spanish conflict than Britain. During the civil war she sold between 100 and 150 obsolete aeroplanes to the Republicans, provided facilities for the export of gold from the Bank of Madrid between July 1936 and March 1937, permitted the Soviet Banque

Commerciale pour l'Europe de Nord to operate under French laws in order to facilitate international payments for war *matériel* on behalf of the Spanish Republic, and at various times opened the French Pyrenean frontier for the transportation of arms to Spain. Moreover, the largest contingent of foreign combatants in the International Brigades which supported the Spanish Republic was composed of Frenchmen, some 10,000 in all.[4] If the French were capable of taking independent action over Spain when it suited them, it is reasonable to suppose that when they conformed to non-intervention and co-operated closely with the British they did so because it was perceived to be in their interests to do so; in which case they should share responsibility with the British for the outcome of the Spanish conflagration to a greater extent than acknowledged hitherto. Accordingly, it is the purpose of this essay to re-examine Franco-British relations in the context of the Spanish problem, both during the civil war and its immediate aftermath, so as to ascertain the degree of convergence and divergence of policy and the extent of France's complicity in the failed non-intervention policy.

The creation of the non-intervention policy in Spain in August 1936 has long been a source of controversy among historians, the majority of whom, until the archives were opened in the 1960s, remained convinced that Britain was its originator rather than France.[5] While it is no longer disputed that it was the French who invented the policy, the prevailing view continues to be that Léon Blum's Popular Front government proposed non-intervention under intense British pressure.[6] To quote Dante Puzzo: 'It was the Quai d'Orsay which proposed but No. 10 Downing Street which disposed'.[7] It is sometimes forgotten that the French had several reasons for wishing to avoid involvement in the Spanish struggle. The fear of a right-wing backlash in France which could threaten further civil disorder and ideological divisions and possibly civil war, and which might also jeopardise the social reform programme of the *Front Populaire* as enshrined in the Matignon Agreements of June 1936, was a major consideration.[8] So, too, was the Quai d'Orsay's view that French intervention in Spain would alienate her East European allies, notably Yugoslavia and Romania.[9] At the same time, the French military, while recognising the strategic dilemmas and risks of intervention and non-intervention alike, supported the latter, partly because the sympathies of the high command lay with the insurgents in Spain.[10] In this connection, Nicole Jordan has revealed recently the effect of the Spanish Civil War in heightening the military's concern over France's volatile internal situation in the summer of 1936; a concern which the Germans sought to exploit including the preaching of anti-Bolshevism to General Gamelin's staff by the German Military Attaché in Paris.[11]

Blum, no less than the British government, feared that any intervention in Spain by either Britain or France might jeopardise irretrievably their efforts to reach a general European settlement based on a new Locarno, which had been proceeding since Hitler's reoccupation of the Rhineland in March 1936.[12] French ministers, including Blum himself, Yvon Delbos (the Foreign Minister), Edouard Daladier (the Minister of Defence), and others, such as the Secretary-General of the Quai d'Orsay, Alexis Léger, genuinely feared, like their British counterparts, a general European war if intervention in Spain proceeded unchecked. This danger could not be discounted. When Blum referred to the possibility in a major speech at Luna Park in Paris on 6 September 1936, and urged that non-intervention was the best means of preventing such a calamity, there was little dissent, and he was able to maintain Socialist party support for the non-intervention policy.[13] It was as a compromise that the French government, led by the personally troubled Blum,[14] proposed a non-intervention agreement in the vain hope that, starved of outside assistance, the rebellion of the Spanish generals would be short-lived.

There can be no doubt about the commitment of the British government to maintain non-intervention in the Spanish Civil War even though they did not invent the policy itself. They were committed in thought and deed to non-intervention before the French made their proposal for a non-intervention agreement on 1 August 1936, and they adhered strictly to it throughout the thirty-two months of the civil war. Moreover, during the early weeks of August, faced with the prospects of a collapse of French resolve to pursue non-intervention in the face of escalating German and Italian intervention on the side of the rebel forces, a possibility carefully cultivated by the Quai d'Orsay, the Foreign Office – notably the Secretary of State for Foreign Affairs, Anthony Eden, his stand-in during part of August, Lord Halifax, the Permanent Under-Secretary of State, Sir Robert Vansittart, his deputy, Sir Alexander Cadogan, and two Assistant Under-Secretaries of State, Sir George Mounsey and Sir Orme Sargent – offered full support to the urgent French requests for diplomatic assistance; in particular it sought to persuade other powers (Italy, Germany and Portugal) to adhere to the Non-Intervention Agreement.[15] However, when the British authorities appeared to be applying pressure on the French to maintain their resolve in favour of their own policy of non-intervention in August and September 1936, they were acting not only in accordance with their own predilictions but also in response to requests for support from Delbos and his officials who feared that without it the more extreme elements in the *Front Populaire* would succeed in forcing France to intervene in Spain with all of its attendant risks.[16]

In short, the origins of non-intervention in Spain can be summed up as an exercise in collaboration and collusion by the respective foreign ministries of France and Britain in pursuit of their respective great power interests. In this regard many of the reservations held by the French concerning intervention in Spain were shared by the British, notably the fear of a general European war arising from the Spanish conflagration; the disruption to the appeasement process as it related to Germany, and subsequently Italy; the pro-Franco sympathies of the British Foreign Office and military authorities, in particular the Admiralty, who backed the non-intervention policy as the best means of protecting British strategic interests; and the need to avoid polarising British society any further than was necessary.[17]

Just as the initiative for a non-intervention agreement had come from the French, so too did the idea of an international committee to supervise non-intervention. Charles Corbin, the French ambassador in London, told the British Foreign Secretary, Anthony Eden, that his government was convinced that if non-intervention was to work it was essential that some committee be established to deal with the many technical details which would arise, and that the best place for such a committee was London. The French government attached great importance to the committee's location in London because in Eden's words: 'to be frank, they felt that our capital was more neutral than the capitals of any of the other great Powers in this difficult business'.[18] The British government raised no objection, but in accepting the committee's location in London ministers were to saddle themselves before history with the burden of its failures. The French escaped this fate.[19]

From September 1936 until July 1937 the British and French governments co-operated closely in the work of the Non-Intervention Committee, which was the locus of Spanish Civil War diplomacy. Both sought to make non-intervention more effective even if the French were less sanguine about its success. Paris continued to make pro-republican gestures. For example, in the autumn of 1936 and the winter of 1936–37, the French refused to consider giving *de facto* recognition to General Franco's forces even if Madrid fell, which seemed likely for a few weeks in October and November 1936. They also withheld the granting of belligerent rights to both Spanish belligerents; a move which would have benefited the insurgents more than the Republicans. The British on the other hand both considered giving *de facto* recognition to the insurgents if Madrid fell and the granting of belligerent rights to both combatants. In the event they did neither.[20] But in practice there was no substantive difference with the French government. The latter did nothing positive or substantial to aid the Republicans in this period, relying instead on the Soviet Union to act as their saviour. When the German Condor Legion was sent to Spain in December 1936, Delbos apparently warned Berlin that if Germany sent further troop transports in addition to the Legion such action 'would necessarily lead to war'.[21] According to American sources, however, Delbos denied issuing such a warning and the Quai d'Orsay was at great pains to stress that there was 'a good deal of exaggeration' in *The Times* reports which emphasised that the French government had advised the German government that if the latter's assistance to Franco increased perceptibly France would abandon the non-intervention policy.[22] In the event, no further German troops were sent and France remained with the British on the sidelines of the Spanish conflict.

Within the Non-Intervention Committee, which was chaired by Lord Plymouth, Parliamentary Under-Secretary of State at the Foreign Office, and administered by a largely British Secretariat headed by Francis Hemming, it was the British government which, in the winter of 1936–37, took the initiative in attempting to make non-intervention more effective. The aim was to lessen the impact of foreign intervention on the outcome of the Spanish conflict including that of Germany, Italy and Portugal on the side of the anti-Republican forces as well as Soviet support for the Republic. The French government fully supported this initiative, which envisaged a control scheme for the supervision of the land and sea frontiers of Spain and her dependencies, and even joined in a proposal with the British for mediation in the civil war. Although the latter lapsed, because of German, Italian, Portuguese and Soviet reservations and their continued intervention in Spain,[23] the scheme for controlling the entry of arms into the Spanish arena was developed within the Non-Intervention Committee.

Eden also recognised that, following the despatch of the Condor Legion and of further Italian 'volunteers' to Spain, something would have to be done about the alarming increase in the number of foreign combatants engaged on both sides in the Spanish conflict. The Foreign Secretary argued forcibly that Britain should take action in the form of Royal Navy supervision of 'all approaches to Spanish ports both in Spain and in the Spanish overseas possessions with a view to preventing the access to these territories either of volunteers from foreign countries or of war material which is subject to prohibition under the agreement of the Non-Intervention Committee in London'.[24] The Foreign Secretary's proposal was rejected by the British Cabinet, on the grounds that it amounted to nothing less than a unilateral blockade of the whole Spanish coast by the Royal Navy.[25] Consequently, the Non-Intervention Committee was charged with the task of producing a control scheme prohibiting the entry of arms and munitions into the Spanish theatre while the question of extending the scheme to include volunteers was conveniently put to one side. The French government did not cavil at this priority. On the contrary, in March 1937 they readily agreed to the supervision of the Franco-Spanish frontier by a team of international observers which would result in the frontier being closed permanently to the transit of arms (essentially from Soviet Russia and Czechoslovakia) to the Spanish Republic. The French also consented to the establishment of a four-power naval patrol of Britain, France, Germany and Italy which excluded the Soviet navy.[26]

This Franco-British success was to be short-lived. The control scheme remained operational for a mere three months until June 1937 and the withdrawal of Germany and Italy from the naval patrol and Portugal's suspension of land observation on the Hispano-Portuguese frontier. The withdrawal of Germany and Italy from the naval patrol followed the bombing, by unidentified aircraft on 29 May, of the German battleship *Deutschland* while on patrol off the coast of Spain. The Germans accompanied their withdrawal by bombarding the undefended port of Almeira, killing many civilians in the process. The Italians immediately followed the Germans and withdrew from the patrol. Both announced that they would no longer participate in the business of the committee.[27] After a period of intense diplomatic activity, and with French support, Eden succeeded, on 12 June, in persuading the Italian and German governments to resume their places on the Non-Intervention Committee and to participate in the naval patrol. On 19 June, however, the Germans claimed that their cruiser *Leipzig* had been attacked by Spanish Republican submarines north of Oran on the African coast.[28] Supported by the Italians, they demanded a firm response, including a strong naval demonstration by the four naval powers before Valencia, the seat of the Republican government. Although considerable sympathy was expressed for the German view by senior members of the Cabinet, including the Prime Minister, Neville Chamberlain, and Lord Swinton, Secretary of State for Air, the British government rejected the call for a demonstration because they recognised that the French would not countenance such action.[29] Consequently, Germany and Italy withdrew again from the naval patrol – this time retaining their places on the Non-Intervention Committee – while Portugal suspended observation on the Hispano-Portuguese frontier.[30]

Throughout this crisis the French and British governments maintained their co-operation and kept their respective responses in step with each other. They continued to do so for a short while after the withdrawal of Italy and Germany from the naval patrol. However, recognising that the withdrawal of the Axis powers left the Republican-held coastline of Spain without supervision, the French and British governments proposed to extend their own patrol. The German and Italian governments rejected this proposal, also an alternative one which envisaged German and Italian observers on board French and British ships.[31]

Faced with this apparent deadlock, the British and French governments appeared to diverge in their respective policies for the first time. The French wanted a firm response to the effect that they and the British should proceed with their proposals, taking neutral observers on board regardless of German, Italian and Portuguese abstention. If Germany, Italy and Portugal absolutely opposed the plan, they should resume their complete freedom of action and make it public, leaving the responsibility for the breakdown of non-intervention with those powers; and in that case observation on the Franco-Spanish frontier would cease.[32] The British government refused to accept that breakdown of non-intervention was inevitable and they were prepared to sacrifice to some degree their previous co-operation with France in order to achieve a measure of compromise with Germany, Italy and Portugal. The compromise took the form of what became known as the 'British Plan' which explicitly linked naval observation with the withdrawal of foreign volunteers and the recognition of belligerent rights to the contending parties in Spain.[33]

The decision of the British authorities to distance themselves from the French was only partly based on a desire to achieve a workable compromise amongst the international powers in the Non-Intervention Committee. They did not believe this shift in policy would involve a real breach with France because the essential interests of both countries were too closely bound up.[34] Thus from Britain's point of view, the deadlock in the Non-Intervention Committee provided the opportunity to deal effectively with the long-standing and important questions of foreign volunteers and belligerent rights. The question of the withdrawal of foreign volunteers had been one of common agreement between the British and French governments, who had sought on a number of occasions since November 1936 to effect their withdrawal. On the last occasion, in May 1937, the Foreign Office had suggested a temporary cessation of hostilities in Spain for a period 'sufficient to enable the withdrawal of volunteers to be arranged'.[35] However, apart from the French government, the suggestion had been received with little enthusiasm by Germany, Italy, Portugal and Soviet Russia, even before the *Deutschland* incident rendered it out of court.[36]

There was less common ground between Britain and France with regard to the granting of belligerent rights, with the latter vehemently opposed to such a step. The British government had failed to recognise Franco's belligerency in November 1936 only because Madrid did not fall to his forces. They further considered granting belligerent rights during the Nationalist siege of Bilbao in April 1937, which included a naval blockade by Franco's navy, and were dissuaded only by the advice of the Foreign Office.[37] By July 1937, however, both the Admiralty and the Foreign Office had become more inclined towards conceding Franco's wish for belligerent rights.[38] This change of heart, which put them at odds with the French government, was largely based on their recognition of the realities of the war – the recent Nationalist conquest of Basque territory – and a growing conviction that Franco was by no means wedded irrevocably to the Axis powers.[39]

Despite their disappointment at the shift in Britain's position, the French government confined their response to the suspension of international observation on the Franco-Spanish frontier, which meant that it was once more open as an entry point into and escape route from the Spanish arena.[40] France maintained her role within the naval patrol and was able, in co-operation once more with Britain, to make it more effective as a result of the successful Nyon Conference of September 1937. The conference was held between 10 and 14 September to deal with the growing menace of submarine attacks, mainly by Italy, in the Mediterranean.[41] After refusing initially to attend the Nyon Conference, the Italians relented and agreed to participate in the revised patrol scheme. They were allotted the Tyrrenhian Sea while the British and French navies together patrolled the main Mediterranean trade routes from Suez to Gibraltar, from the Dardanelles to Gibraltar and from the North African ports to Marseilles. The Soviet navy was excluded from the revised patrol duties in the Aegean Sea in deference to the wishes of Greece and Turkey. The Germans, who refused to attend at Nyon, ceased to be involved in the patrol. Subsequently, the French government agreed to close their frontier once more with Spain.[42]

Having come into line once more with British policy as a consequence of Nyon, the French were greatly disappointed to learn of Chamberlain's intention to open separate conversations with Italy.[43] Towards the end of September they insisted on a joint Anglo-French approach to the Italians with a view to tripartite negotiations on the non-intervention policy in Spain and in particular the withdrawal of volunteers. The British complied, albeit reluctantly, and on 2 October a joint Anglo-French note was sent to Mussolini. A reply was received on 9 October which rejected tripartite negotiations and which advised that the question of withdrawal of volunteers should be dealt with at the Non-Intervention Committee.[44]

British reluctance to comply with the French request stemmed partly from the growing weight of opinion in government circles in favour of giving Mussolini the benefit of the doubt in Spain, demonstrating the importance they attached to the Italian end of their general appeasement policy. The corollary was a more critical view of French policy.[45] When the French government threatened to reopen the Pyrenees frontier on 22 September, senior officials in the Foreign Office – Cadogan, Mounsey and Rex Leeper – and Lord Plymouth, Chairman of the Non-Intervention Committee, expressed consternation and opposition to falling in with the French suggestion.[46] Similar sentiments were expressed later by Howard Smith, an Assistant Under-Secretary attached temporarily to the League of Nations and Western Department, and by Orme Sargent. The former favoured sending a categorical warning to the French that if they opened their frontier and war (presumably with Italy and possibly Germany) were to follow, His Majesty's government would have 'no part or lot with them and they must face the consequences alone'.[47] The permanent head of the Foreign Office, Vansittart, refused to endorse the growing anti-French attitude of his colleagues, as did Eden himself, but they were in a minority. Vansittart did not favour the French opening their frontier officially because the only effect would be to precipitate the victory of Franco – which was the very thing both Britain and France should wish to avoid.

However, he thought they would be wise to open their frontier to the extent that they were able to say nothing about it, for he doubted the ability of the French to send across the Pyrenees frontier anything like the quantity of men and material that would be sent in by Mussolini.[48]

Eden definitely sympathised with the French, having little faith in Mussolini's promises concerning Italy's lack of ambition in the Spanish conflagration. He was particularly incensed on receiving reports, on 5 October, that Italian troops and arms had landed at Cadiz and Seville, two weeks after the Italian Foreign Minister, Galeazzo Ciano, had given assurances that no further volunteers would be sent. In these circumstances, he felt that the French should not be restrained from opening the frontier and he hoped to find some means of helping the Valencian government since he had become convinced that its survival was in Britain's interest and that it would put a bar to Mussolini's progress.[49] By the time he saw Corbin on 12 October, Eden's militancy had been modified. The French ambassador announced that his government, while accepting that the Italian rejection of tripartite conversations placed the onus once more on the Non-Intervention Committee, wished for joint Anglo-French pressure to expedite the work of the committee on the volunteers issue; such pressure to be accompanied by a statement which would emphasise Italian duplicity and open support for Franco in contravention of non-intervention. In the interim it was proposed that both the French and British governments should temporarily authorise the transit of arms across the frontier to Spain. Eden offered no hope that his government would take similar action.[50] The following day the majority of Cabinet expressed strong disapproval of the tenor of the French proposals, in particular their anti-Italian bias and all that that entailed for appeasement in Spain and the Mediterranean. Chamberlain hoped Eden would do his best to ensure that the French 'should not persist in their intention to harp on past events which could only produce discord when the real object was to secure an improvement in the future'.[51] In taking this line the Prime Minister was influenced, in part, by the results of an inquiry by Francis Hemming, Secretary to the Non-Intervention Committee, which seemed to dispose of the allegations concerning the disembarkation of Italian troops at Cadiz and Seville.[52]

It must be emphasised, however, that what appeared to be a growing rift at this time between the British and French governments over non-intervention and the means of dealing with Italian involvement in Spain was more apparent than real. The French government kept the Pyrenees frontier closed only partly in deference to British wishes. Apart from Socialist politicians, whose influence in the French government had diminished following Blum's resignation as Prime Minister in June 1937, there was not a great deal of enthusiasm for opening the frontier. Indeed, the French Chargé d'Affaires, Roger Cambon, told Orme Sargent on 12 October that the Quai d'Orsay, in particular its Secretary-General, Alexis Léger, and its Political Director, René Massigli, disliked the proposal to reopen the Franco-Spanish frontier because 'it would be completely ineffective in so far as it was intended to help the Valencian government to free Spain from the Italian stranglehold'. In addition, the Quai d'Orsay shared Vansittart's view that it might make the position of the Republican government worse if, as was possible, Mussolini retaliated by sending further troops to Spain. Cambon also hinted that in place of opening the frontier the Quai d'Orsay favoured the occupation of Minorca as a *gage*. The French government insisted, however, that the withdrawal of volunteers from Spain should not be done on a man-for-man basis but should be proportionate taking into account the higher proportion of effectives serving on Franco's side.[53] The British government agreed and on 14 October Eden informed the Italian representative on the Non-Intervention Committee, the ambassador in London, Dino Grandi, of the British intention to press within the committee for an immediate start to be made on the withdrawal of volunteers taking account of proportions. The following day Vansittart brushed aside the complaint of the Portuguese representative on the Non-Intervention Committee, the ambassador in London, Armindo Monteiro, concerning proportionate withdrawals and his protestations that there were at least as many volunteers on the Valencian side as on the Nationalist side. Vansittart told Monteiro that he did not accept any such view; all their information went to prove that there was a very considerable majority on the Nationalist side.[54]

The realignment of French and British policy in October 1937 continued until the commencement of the short-lived second ministry of Léon Blum in March 1938, which heralded a temporary modification of the non-intervention policy by the French authorities. The one exception was Britain's decision to exchange Special Agents with Franco's regime in November 1937, a decision which was taken essentially to protect British commercial and strategic interests in Spain. The French studiously avoided following the British example.[55] With this not unimportant exception both governments continued until March 1938 to insist, in the face of objections from Germany, Italy, Portugal and Franco himself, on proportionate withdrawals and the granting of belligerent rights only after a considerable proportion had been withdrawn from each side; in the order of 75 per cent. In March this figure was modified considerably to less than 30 per cent, which represented a major concession by Britain and France. The Soviet Union, however, rejected this revised figure and prevented a consensus from emerging in the Non-Intervention Committee.[56]

Meanwhile, for the first time during the Spanish Civil War, there was a fundamental divergence of policy between Britain and France. The former opened conversations with Mussolini's Italy in March in search of an Anglo-Italian Agreement, which was achieved in April but not ratified until November owing to the lack of progress made in withdrawing Italian volunteers from Spain. Moreover, despite the lack of progress made with the 'British Plan', Chamberlain's government maintained their commitment to non-intervention through the spring and summer of 1938. The French remained unimpressed by the signing of the Anglo-Italian Agreement. Duff Cooper, the British First Lord of the Admiralty, who visited Paris during Easter, found great scepticism among French ministers as to the value of the agreement in view of Italy's past betrayal of agreements and allies. Daladier, who had just become Prime Minister, went so far as to argue that the British government had saved Mussolini from disaster following his passive response to the *Anschluss* in March 1938.[57]

Chamberlain's government could afford to ignore French scepticism over the Italian accord, but they could not ignore the very real prospect that, faced with the possible collapse of Republican forces on the Aragon Front in northern Spain in March 1938, the French might be compelled to intervene and abandon non-intervention. On 16 March the Cabinet confirmed their support for non-intervention and acting on the advice of Lord Halifax, who had succeeded Eden as Foreign Secretary, refused to encourage the French to take the offensive.[58] In the event, Blum's short-lived government did not intervene but opened the Pyrenees frontier and covertly supplied the Republican forces.[59] The Socialist Prime Minister went no further because General Maurice Gamelin, Chief of the French General Staff and National Defence, advised against intervention on the grounds that France had insufficient forces to risk war and Léger had expressed his conviction that both Italy and Germany would regard French intervention in Spain as a *casus belli*.[60]

The failure of Blum's second ministry and its successor, led by

Daladier, to go further and intervene directly in Spain, because they wished to avoid taking a high risk which might provoke a European war, was entirely consistent with previous French policy in the Spanish affair. Throughout the entire period of the civil war, successive French governments stopped well short of taking action that might provoke such an outcome and failed to sustain what limited action they did take. This was again the case in the summer of 1938. Having opened the Pyrenees frontier in March, they closed it again in mid-June despite the Hispano-Portuguese frontier remaining open. Contrary to the views of certain historians, the decision was not taken in response to strong British pressure.[61] It is true that in June 1938 the British ambassador, Sir Eric Phipps, strongly advised the French government to close their frontier with Spain, but the French needed little persuasion. As Georges Bonnet, the Foreign Minister, later admitted to Phipps, his government were convinced that if they did not close the frontier the risk of war would have been increased by 100 per cent because they had heard that a large shipment of war *matériel* had left or was about to leave the Soviet Union for Le Havre and Bordeaux for trans-shipment to Spain. Bonnet deplored 'Russia's renewed and unhealthy wish to fish in troubled Spanish waters far removed from her own territory, which would therefore be immune from the disturbances and damage she wished to cause others'.[62]

Although the 'British Plan' finally received the endorsement of the Non-Intervention Committee in July 1938, it was recognised that the contending parties in Spain, and in particular Franco, remained unconvinced. The Secretary of the Non-Intervention Committee, Francis Hemming, was eventually sent to Spain in October, to try to persuade both parties to give serious consideration to the plan. Meanwhile, Chamberlain, buoyed by the apparent success of the Munich Conference, sought to secure Mussolini's help in bringing about an armistice in Spain.[63] The French complied with this objective and supported the British insistence that belligerent rights could not be granted to Franco unless progress was made on the withdrawal issue. The Spanish *Caudillo* had insisted to Hemming that, despite the unilateral withdrawal of all foreign volunteers from the Republican side, which had been completed by November, he would not accept any further withdrawal of volunteers – other than the 10,000 Italians recently withdrawn by Mussolini as the price to be paid for the ratification of the Anglo-Italian Agreement – unless belligerent rights were conceded in advance. It was also clear that

Germany, Italy and Portugal supported Franco's position in this matter.[64]

The British and French governments continued, however, to insist that the withdrawal of the 10,000 Italians in October constituted insufficient grounds for conceding belligerent rights. The Foreign Office was convinced that, confronted with Franco's intransigence, British opinion could not countenance any such concession. Moreover, as Corbin told Halifax on 5 January 1939, opinion in France had hardened considerably in favour of the Spanish Republicans and his government had information that the Italians had been sending considerable reinforcements of men and material for Franco's offensive on Catalonia.[65] Halifax agreed that a similar shift in opinion had taken place in the United Kingdom, which put the issue of the immediate grant of belligerent rights out of the question as practical politics.[66] Both governments agreed, however, that the 'British Plan' and the prospects of an armistice were doomed unless Mussolini was prepared to make a positive response in their favour. In the event, during the visit of Chamberlain and Halifax to Rome in mid-January, the Italian dictator made no positive response to the British Prime Minister. Even if he did not say so directly, it was apparent that he had no intention of withdrawing any further troops and remained committed to a Franco victory in Spain.[67]

The prospects for an armistice had evaporated and to all intents and purposes the 'British Plan' was doomed. This Anglo-French failure was compounded by the receipt in London of disturbing intelligence reports, to the effect that German policy had as its ultimate objective the breaking of the Anglo-French entente and the creation of a European bloc to include Spain and which was to be directed primarily at the British Empire. The reports also pointed out that Italy and Germany were in full agreement that the Spanish problem should be resolved at the earliest possible moment and that with this end in view considerable supplies of material were being sent by both powers to the aid of Franco.[68] In addition, on 16 January, Ciano warned the British ambassador in Rome, Lord Perth, that if France intervened in Spain Italy would land thirty battalions at Valencia even if a European war resulted.[69]

This intensification of German and Italian support for Franco threatened to create a divergence in the French and British commitment to maintaining non-intervention. The British realised that the French might be tempted, even at this late hour, to intervene to save the Spanish Republic. Even Halifax had wished to protest against Ciano's warning and to demand the withdrawal of 5,000

Italian volunteers, but Chamberlain had prevented him from doing so.[70] However, the Prime Minister and the Foreign Secretary were in complete agreement in wishing to dissuade the French government from open intervention in Spain. In this respect Halifax chose to accept the advice of his Permanent Under-Secretary, Cadogan, rather than that of the Chief Diplomatic Adviser, Vansittart, who wished to encourage the French to supply arms and munitions to the Republican forces. The Cabinet Foreign Policy Committee on 23 January endorsed the advice of Chamberlain and Halifax and refused to consider the abandonment of non-intervention or to encourage the French to do so.[71]

There was, however, no question of the French abandoning non-intervention. The response of the French government to the growing crisis of the Spanish Republic in January 1939 was both predictable and unremarkable; they opened the Pyrenees frontier once more to allow Russian war *matériel* into Catalonia.[72] But this action was taken too late to save the Republic. At the same time, the French opened conversations with the Nationalist authorities in Spain and these culminated with the Bérard-Jordana Agreement of 25 February 1939. The Agreement was accompanied by France's *de jure* recognition of the Franco regime, demonstrating a willingness to abandon the Republic in the interests of improving relations with the future government of Spain; this despite a substantial minority in the French Chamber of Deputies refusing to recognise Franco's regime.[73] Unsurprisingly, the British authorities were just as quick to grant *de jure* recognition to Franco as the French. Indeed, both countries had concerted their actions in February and agreed that recognition as soon as it was feasible was in the best interests of both countries.[74] In recognising Franco's regime the French went further than the British since included in the Bérard-Jordana Agreement was an affirmation on the part of both governments of their determination to maintain friendly relations, to be good neighbours and to apply in Morocco a policy of frank and honest collaboration.[75]

Following the end of the civil war in Spain in March 1939, the British and French governments both sought to improve their relations with Franco in order to prevent him from becoming irrevocably wedded to the Axis powers. Spain's adhesion to the Anti-Comintern Pact in April 1939 was interpreted as an ideological gesture and not as confirmation of Spanish intentions to ally with Germany and Italy. Genuine improved relations, however, proved elusive and the British government blamed the French for failing to follow through on the Bérard-Jordana Agreement owing to their refusal to return Spanish gold lodged previously in France by the Republican authorities. The return of the gold was clearly incorporated as a French commitment in the agreement, but the French government was split over the issue of improving relations with Franco's Spain by fulfilling their obligations under the agreement. The Foreign Minister, Bonnet, and the French ambassador in Spain, Marshal Philippe Pétain, urged the return of the gold without conditions, whereas Daladier, Léger and the Finance Minister, Paul Reynaud, insisted on Spain accelerating the return of the half million refugees who had fled into France during the dying throes of the Spanish Republic.[76] The British government, and Chamberlain in particular, were much irritated by Daladier's attitude and, encouraged by the Portuguese government, urged him to return the gold to Spain while negotiating a solution to the refugee problem.[77]

In the event, the French government returned the gold to Spain in July without insisting on an immediate solution to the refugee problem. In case it may be assumed that this was yet again another example of a beleaguered France wilting under British pressure to conform over Spanish policy, it should be noted that the French authorities themselves were divided. Moreover, Daladier's resistance to fulfilling the Bérard-Jordana Agreement had less to do with hostility towards Franco, or his lack of faith in the General's declarations of Spanish intentions to remain neutral in the event of a European conflict, and more to do with the fact that the refugee crisis was an immense problem for France which was causing domestic repercussions and the French Treasury to dig deep into its purse.[78] The French Prime Minister sought to use the return of the gold to Spain as a means of pressurising Franco to accelerate the process of repatriating the refugees, and conceded this position in July only because by then it had become essential to use Spanish labour in the rapidly expanding rearmament economy in France.[79] The remaining refugees had ceased to be a liability and had become an asset and there was therefore less urgency to accelerate the process of repatriation.

Naturally, the British were highly satisfied at the turn of events, but neither they nor the French succeeded in making Franco's Spain a friendly neutral in the summer of 1939. Spain did declare her neutrality when the Second World War broke out in September 1939, but it was a neutrality which was benevolent towards the Axis powers and the primary reason why Franco did not go further in his support was because Spain was in no condition to do so, exhausted and broken as she was by almost three years of bloody civil

Britain, France and the Spanish problem 145

war. The demise of the Spanish Republic had ensured this outcome. A hostile but not belligerent Spain was the price to be paid for the failure of both Britain and France to uphold Spanish democracy between 1936 and 1939.

In conclusion, it is not difficult to criticise the British government for their persistence in maintaining non-intervention while Germany and Italy intervened to destroy Spanish democracy. The case against is overwhelming and there are few if any defenders amongst the historical community. Certainly, I am not one of them. However, France was barely less culpable. In mitigation of France it can be claimed that she at least was prepared to modify her commitment to non-intervention to take action which would serve the Spanish Republican cause even if it did fall short of actual involvement compared with Germany, Italy, Soviet Russia and even Portugal. However, it is precisely this comparison with the far more substantial intervention of these other powers which puts the French commitment and contribution into proper perspective. It is only when compared to Britain's unrelenting commitment to non-intervention, which incidentally did not prevent the British from protecting their own economic interests, that the French emerge with any credit from a debate which since the Second World War has consistently excoriated the non-intervention policy of one of the two European democratic powers.

When scrutinised closely, it is clear that there was far more convergence than divergence in the relations of Britain and France with regard to the Spanish problem. The French willingly aligned themselves with the British because it was politic to do so since of their two potential allies – Britain and Soviet Russia – they preferred the former.[80] It might be argued that it is this factor which accounts for the ability of the British government to apply pressure on France and explains why France ultimately complied with it, for example in the establishment of the non-intervention policy itself and in cancelling action which might be seen as contravening non-intervention, such as opening the Pyrenees frontier. However, it has been demonstrated that whenever the argument of British pressure is raised it by no means tells the whole story. France invariably had other more compelling reasons for maintaining non-intervention, not least the constant fear of provoking a European war or of encouraging civil war at home should she become too heavily involved on the side of the Spanish Republic. In view of the foregoing it would not be unreasonable to conclude by asking that in future, when examining the causes of the failure of Spanish democracy to endure and emerge triumphant from the Spanish Civil War, the French should appear together with the British in the dock as co-defendants and should not be permitted to plea bargain or to turn Queen's evidence.

NOTES

1 See A. Adamthwaite, 'France and the coming of the Second World War', in W.J. Mommsen and L. Kettenacker (eds) *The Fascist Challenge and the Policy of Appeasement*, London, Allen & Unwin, 1983, p. 246.
2 ibid., p. 250. See also A. Adamthwaite, *France and the Coming of the Second World War, 1936–1939*, London, Frank Cass, 1977; W.I. Shorrock, *From Ally to Enemy: The Enigma of Fascist Italy in French Diplomacy 1922–1940*, Kent, Ohio, Kent State University Press, 1988.
3 Historians who see the British government as the real villain of the piece include: J. Edwards, *The British Government and the Spanish Civil War, 1936–1939*, London, Macmillan, 1979; D. Little, *Malevolent Neutrality: The United States, Great Britain, and the Origins of the Spanish Civil War*, Ithaca, NY, and London, Cornell University Press, 1985 (in Little's case the United States is also regarded as culpable in the demise of the Spanish Republic); H. Thomas, *The Spanish Civil War*, London, Hamish Hamilton, 3rd edn, 1977; E. Moradiellos, *Neutralidad Benévola: El Gobierno Británico y la Insurrección Militar Española de 1936*, Oviedo, Pentalfa, 1990; M.D. Gallagher, 'Léon Blum and the Spanish Civil War', *Journal of Contemporary History*, vol. 6, 1971, pp. 56–64; D. Little, 'Red Scare, 1936: anti-Bolshevism and the origins of British non-intervention in the Spanish Civil War', *Journal of Contemporary History*, vol. 23, 1988, pp. 291–311; E. Moradiellos, 'British political strategy in the face of the military rising of 1936 in Spain', *Contemporary European History*, vol. 1, 1992, pp. 123–37.
4 H. Thomas, op. cit., pp. 943, 981–3; A. Viñas, 'The financing of the Spanish Civil War', in P. Preston (ed.) *Revolution and War in Spain 1931–1939*, London, Methuen, 1984, pp. 268–70.
5 One source for this view was Ivan Maisky, the Soviet ambassador in London during the 1930s, who continued to insist that the British government invented non-intervention in Spain. He wrote later: 'the idea of non-intervention in Spanish affairs... was born in the depths of the British Foreign Office immediately after the start of Franco's rebellion', I. Maisky, *Spanish Notebooks*, London, Hutchinson, 1966, p. 27.
6 Naturally, there are exceptions to this view which often fails to distinguish between positive and negative pressure. One exception is Robert J. Young, who asserts that British pressure was negative and minimal and that if this was the key consideration in the French decision to propose non-intervention then France was 'decked by a feather': *In Command of France: French Foreign Policy and Military Planning, 1933–1940*, Cambridge, Mass., Harvard University Press, 1978, pp. 140–1.
7 D. Puzzo, *Spain and the Great Powers, 1936–1941*, New York, Arnos Press, 1972 reprint, p. 120.
8 For a discussion of the domestic considerations see Young, op. cit.,

pp. 139–41; J.E. Dreifort, *Yvon Delbos at the Quai d'Orsay: French Foreign Policy during the Popular Front 1936–1938*, Wichita, University Press of Kansas, 1973, pp. 38–43; D. Carlton, 'Eden, Blum, and the origins of non-intervention', *Journal of Contemporary History*, vol. 6, 1971, pp. 46–7; N. Haywood Hunt, 'The French Radicals, Spain and the emergence of appeasement', in M.S. Alexander and H. Graham (eds), *The French and Spanish Popular Fronts*, Cambridge, Cambridge University Press, 1989, pp. 38–49.
9 J. Néré, *The Foreign Policy of France from 1914 to 1945*, London, Routledge & Kegan Paul, 1975, p. 215; N. Jordan, *The Popular Front and Central Europe: The Dilemmas of French Impotence, 1918–1940*, Cambridge, Cambridge University Press, 1992, pp. 203–4. According to Jordan, within two weeks of the outbreak of the civil war in Spain, Yugoslavia's regent, Prince Paul, was 'almost unhinged' by the fear of the spread of the communist menace to France. He also had nightmares of being dragged by the recently concluded Franco-Soviet pact into a war provoked by the Soviets in which Yugoslavia would be compelled to fight Germany without effective French aid.
10 Young, op. cit., pp. 136–9 and nn. 22 and 25, p. 286; M.S. Alexander, *The Republic in Danger: General Maurice Gamelin and the Politics of French Defence, 1933–1940*, Cambridge, Cambridge University Press, 1992, p. 101.
11 Jordan, op. cit., pp. 208–9.
12 Franco-British efforts to reach a general settlement between March and August 1936 are well documented in W.N. Medlicott, *Britain and Germany: The Search for Agreement 1930–1937*, London, Athlone Press, 1969, pp. 25–30.
13 Dreifort, op. cit., pp. 52–3; D.A.L. Levy, 'The French Popular Front 1936–37', in H. Graham and P. Preston (eds) *The Popular Front in Europe*, London, Macmillan, 1987, p. 73. For the impact of Blum's speech see *The Times*, 4, 5 and 7 September 1936. A month earlier, at Sarlat, Blum had declared to his constituents: 'At no cost must a new ideological crusade materialise in Europe, a crusade which would inevitably lead to war', G. Warner, 'France and non-intervention in Spain, July-August 1936', *International Affairs*, vol. 38, 1962, p. 207.
14 Blum's personal crisis of conscience is well documented. For example, on 11 August 1936 the British ambassador at Paris, Sir George Clerk, reported that the French Prime Minister was 'in torture' at having been obliged 'for reasons of high international policy' to place an embargo on the despatch of arms and ammunition to Republican Spain. G.A. Stone, 'Britain, non-intervention and the Spanish Civil War', *European Studies Review*, vol. 9, 1979, p. 144.
15 ibid., pp. 139–42.
16 See, for example, Foreign Office Minute, 4 August 1936, FO371/20527, W7748/62/41; Lloyd Thomas, British Minister at Paris, to Sir Alexander Cadogan, Deputy Under-Secretary of State at the Foreign Office, 5 August 1936, FO800/294; Lloyd Thomas to Cadogan, 11 August 1936, FO371/20531, W8676/62/41.
17 G.A. Stone, 'The European Great Powers and the Spanish Civil War, 1936–1939', in R. Boyce and E.M. Robertson (eds) *Paths to War: New*

Essays on the Origins of the Second World War, London, Macmillan, 1989, pp. 213–16. Tom Buchanan has shown how the British labour movement itself was divided over the issue of intervention in Spain and he argues convincingly that trade union leaders supported non-intervention to maintain the unity of their members: *The British Labour Movement and the Spanish Civil War*, Cambridge, Cambridge University Press, 1991.
18 Eden to Clerk, 24 August 1936, *Documents on British Foreign Policy 1919–1939*, 2nd series, vol. XVII, no. 128, p. 161. Hereafter *DBFP*.
19 The French, as Delbos told Clerk, were most grateful to the British government for allowing the meetings of the Non-Intervention Committee in London, FO371/20573 W9986/9549/41, At the time, French gratitude probably stemmed from relief at having avoided the committee's location in Paris where it would have been a considerable embarrassment to the government given the strongly interventionist views of *Front Populaire* militants.
20 Edwards, op. cit., pp. 184–6.
21 D. Smyth, 'Reflex reaction: Germany and the onset of the Spanish Civil War', in Preston (ed.), op. cit., pp. 258–60.
22 William Bullitt, Ambassador at Paris, to the Acting Secretary of State, Washington, 24 December 1936, *Foreign Relations of the United States, 1936*, vol. II, pp. 614–15. Hereafter *FRUS*.
23 For details of the mediation proposals see *DBFP*, 2nd series, vol. XVII, nos 417, 434 and 443, pp. 600–1, 636, 647–8. See also *Documents diplomatiques français 1932–1939*, 2nd series, vol. IV, no. 39, pp. 53–4. Hereafter *DDF*.
24 Memorandum by Eden on Spain, 8 January 1937, CAB24/267 CP(37).
25 *DBFP*, 2nd series, vol. XVIII, no. 33, pp. 42–51. See also S. Roskill, *Naval Policy between the Wars vol. II, The Period of Reluctant Rearmament*, London, Collins, 1976, pp. 376–7; Edwards, op. cit., pp. 110–12.
26 For full details of the Non-Intervention land and sea control scheme see *Parliamentary Papers 1936–1937*, vol. XXVIII, Cmd 5399.
27 H. Thomas, op. cit., pp. 685–6. Thomas claims that the aircraft were piloted by Russian airmen. A few days previously, the Italian auxiliary vessel *Barletta* had been hit during Spanish Republican bombing raids on Parma; six Italian officers were killed.
28 A German note communicated to the Foreign Office on 19 June admitted that 'while no submarine was actually seen by those on the *Leipzig* tracks of torpedoes were observed', CAB23/88 CM25(37). Later, on 24 June, Vansittart told the Labour MP, Hugh Dalton, that he was extremely doubtful whether any torpedo had been fired at the *Leipzig* and the Admiralty shared his opinion: unpublished *Dalton Diaries*, 1.18, entry 24 June 1937. These diaries are located at the British Library of Economics and Political Science, London.
29 CAB23/88 CM25(37) and CM26(37). In a speech to the House of Commons on 25 June 1937 Chamberlain went out of his way to express sympathy for German losses on the *Deutschland*, and, seemingly oblivious of the bombardment of Almeira, not to speak of German complicity in the bombing of Guernica, Bilbao and other Republican held towns, to praise the German government for 'showing a degree of restraint

which we all ought to recognise', *Hansard Parliamentary Debates*, HC, 5th series, vol. 325, cc. 1548–9.
30 *DBFP*, 2nd series, vol. XVIII, nos 655 and 656, pp. 938–9; *DDF*, 2nd series, vol. VI, no. 136, p. 213; *Dez Anos de Política Externa 1936–1947: A Nação Portuguesa e a Segunda Guerra Mundial*, vol. IV, no. 1124, pp. 353–4. Hereafter *DAPE*.
31 Memorandum by Bismarck, Deputy Director of the Political Department of the German Foreign Ministry, 29 June 1937, *Documents on German Foreign Policy 1918–1945*, series D, vol. III, no. 367, p. 380. Hereafter *DGFP*.
32 Telegrams 125, 127, 376, 379 Sir Eric Phipps, Ambassador at Paris, to the Foreign Office, 1–3 July 1937, FO371/21339, W12645/W12652/W12735/7/41 and FO371/21340, W12787/7/41.
33 Foreign Office to Sir Charles Wingfield, Ambassador at Lisbon, 14 July 1937, FO371/21342, W13561/7/41.
34 Minute by Lord Cranborne, Parliamentary Under-Secretary of State for Foreign Affairs, 17 July 1937, FO371/21341, W13250/7/41.
35 *DBFP*, 2nd series, vol. XVIII, no. 499, p. 753. See also *DAPE*, vol. IV, nos 976 and 980, pp. 294, 298.
36 See e.g. the German and Portuguese replies, *DBFP*, 2nd series, vol. XVIII, nos 522 and 525, pp. 785–6, 791–2.
37 Minutes by Beckett, Mounsey, Vansittart and Eden, 7–10 April 1937, FO371/21352, W6481/23/41, CAB23/88 CM15(37). Foreign Office to Sir Henry Chilton, Ambassador to the Republican government at Hendaye, 11 April 1937, FO371/21352, W6936/23/41.
38 Minutes by Cranborne, Plymouth, Vansittart and Eden, 30 June–1 July 1937, FO371/21294; W11685/1/41; Roskill, op. cit., pp. 380–1.
39 This conviction was based on a number of sources. Franco's brother, Nicholás, the Anglophile Duke of Alba, and the Portuguese government provided assurances that the *Generalissimo* desired improved relations with Britain, that it was his desire that the Iberian nations should work together within the orbit of British policy and that nationalist indebtedness to the Axis powers would be paid only in the commercial sphere. Chilton to Mounsey, 14 June 1937, FO371/21295, W11819/1/41; *DBFP*, 2nd series, vol. XVIII, no. 664, pp. 948–9; CAB27/622 FP(36) 15th meeting, 28 June 1937; *DAPE*, vol. IV, no. 1145, pp. 475–8; *FRUS*, 1937, vol. I, p. 354.
40 By keeping the frontier open the French government could assist the Republican cause by enabling its forces to retreat to safety within France, to regroup and then return replenished to Spain. Such action was clearly at odds with non-intervention, and when the British discovered in early September 1936 that the French authorities had permitted several hundred militiamen fleeing from Irun to enter France and then to return refreshed in special trains to the Pyrenees frontier, where they were able to join the Catalan Anarchists, they issued a strong reprimand, which had the desired effect of preventing a repetition in the future. Stone, 'Britain, non-intervention', p. 135 and n. 27, p. 147.
41 For details of the Italian submarine attacks see J.F. Coverdale, *Italian Intervention in the Spanish Civil War*, Princeton, NJ, Princeton University Press, 1975, pp. 306–8, 311–13. See also M. Muggeridge (ed.) *Ciano's*

Diary, 1937–1938, London, Methuen, 1952, entries 23 August, 31 August, 2 September, 4 September, pp. 3, 6–9.

42 For details of the Nyon Conference and its aftermath see Roskill, op. cit., pp. 383–7; P. Gretton, 'The Nyon Conference – the naval aspect', *English Historical Review*, vol. 90, 1975, pp. 103–12; W.C. Mills, 'The Nyon Conference: Neville Chamberlain, Anthony Eden and the appeasement of Italy in 1937', *International History Review*, vol. 15, 1993, pp. 1–22.

43 For a discussion of Chamberlain's initiative to improve Anglo-Italian relations in the summer of 1937, which did so much to alienate Eden from him, see K. Feiling, *The Life of Neville Chamberlain*, London, Macmillan, 1946, pp. 330–1; Lord Avon, *The Eden Memoirs: Facing the Dictators*, London, Cassell, 1962, pp. 452–5; D. Carlton, *Anthony Eden: A Biography*, London, Allen Lane, 1981, pp. 107–8; R. Rhodes James, *Anthony Eden*, London, Weidenfeld & Nicolson, 1986, pp. 176–9; V. Rothwell, *Anthony Eden: A Political Biography*, Manchester, Manchester University Press, 1992, pp. 38–9; N. Rose, 'The resignation of Anthony Eden', *Historical Journal*, vol. 25, 1982, pp. 913–15; R. Douglas, 'Chamberlain and Eden, 1937–1938', *Journal of Contemporary History*, vol. 13, 1978, pp. 99–104; see also *DBFP*, 2nd series, vol. XIX, nos 64, 65, 80, 81, 82, 90, 91 and 115, pp. 118–20, 142–7, 155–73, 219–27.

44 CAB23/89 CM35(37), CAB24/271 CP234(37). See also *Parliamentary Papers 1936–1937*, vol. XXIX, Cmd 5570.

45 Edwards, op. cit., pp. 156–9; Stone, 'Britain, non-intervention', p. 135.

46 Unpublished Cadogan Diaries, entries 22 and 28 September 1937. These diaries are located at the Archives Centre, Churchill College, Cambridge.

47 Minute by Howard Smith, 4 October 1937, FO371/21346, W19006/7/41. For Orme Sargent's views see his letter to Phipps of 8 October 1937; Phipps Papers, PHPP2/16. These papers are located at the Archives Centre, Churchill College, Cambridge. See also FO800/274.

48 Vansittart's marginal comments on Howard Smith's minute of 4 October and a separate minute of 5 October 1937, FO371/21346, W19006/7/41.

49 J. Harvey (ed.) *The Diplomatic Diaries of Oliver Harvey 1937-1940*, London, Collins, 1970, entry 5 October 1937, pp. 49–50.

50 CAB23/89 CM37(37).

51 ibid.

52 Maurice Hankey, Secretary to the Cabinet, to Chamberlain, 6 October 1937, PREM1/360. See also *Ciano's Diary 1937–1938*, p. 20.

53 Minute by Orme Sargent, 12 October 1937, Phipps Papers, PHPP1/19.

54 NIS(C)(36) 64th meeting of the Chairman's Sub-Committee [of the Non-Intervention Committee], 16 October 1937, Hemming Papers and FO849/28. Hemming's papers are located at the Bodleian Library, Oxford. Eden to Lord Perth, Ambassador at Rome, 15 October 1937. Minute by Vansittart, 15 October 1937, FO371/21346 W19109/W19235/7/41.

55 Stone, 'The European Great Powers', p. 212. Britain's special agent to the Nationalist administration was Sir Robert Hodgson while the Duke of Alba represented Nationalist interests in London.

56 NIS(C)(36) 83rd meeting of the Chairman's Sub-Committee, 31 March 1938, FO849/29 and Hemming Papers.

Britain, France and the Spanish problem 151

57 A. Duff Cooper, *Old Men Forget*, London, Hart-Davis, 1953, p. 219.
58 CAB23/93 CM14(38).
59 The fall of Blum's short-lived government did not halt the supply of arms via the French frontier. On the contrary, during April and May the Pyrenees frontier remained open allowing the transit of 25,000 tons of war material and 300 Russian aircraft into Spain. Thomas, op. cit., pp. 804–5, 832.
60 Eleventh session of the Comité Permanent de la Défense Nationale, 15 March 1938, in A. Adamthwaite (ed.) *The Making of the Second World War*, London, Allen & Unwin, 1977, p. 182. See also Jordan, op. cit., pp. 316–17. According to Jordan, Blum concluded from the meeting that little could be done to save the Spanish Republic and that the Spanish situation had reached a point at which Franco no longer needed foreign military aid.
61 See in this context Edwards, op. cit., p. 174, and Thomas, op. cit., p. 825.
62 Phipps to Halifax, 16 July 1938, Phipps Papers PHPP1/20. Note of an interview with Lord Halifax at the Foreign Office, 29 July 1938. Cecil of Chelwood Papers MSS 51084. These papers are located at the British Library, London.
63 The British Prime Minister had taken the opportunity during the Munich Conference to solicit Mussolini's support for an armistice in Spain. The *Ducé* had promised to think about it. P. Stafford, 'The Chamberlain-Halifax visit to Rome: a reappraisal', *English Historical Review*, vol. 98, 1983, p. 63.
64 'Hemming Report', 17 November 1938, Hemming Papers. See also the unpublished Hemming Diaries, entries 21 and 22 November 1938.
65 During January 2,035 army officers and troops were despatched and in February another 1,857. At the same time, 920 members of the fascist militia also left for Spain and during March close to 5,500 men were sent, the army accounting for 3,776 and the militia for 1,090. Coverdale, op. cit., pp. 374, 381.
66 Foreign Office memorandum (unsigned), 2 January 1939; Halifax to Phipps, 5 January 1939, FO371/24114, W312/W475/5/41.
67 'The Visit to Rome of the Prime Minister and the Secretary of State for Foreign Affairs from January 11 to January 14, 1939', CAB24/282 CP8(39). See also Stafford, op. cit., p. 93.
68 CAB27/624 FP (36) 35th meeting.
69 Stafford, op. cit., p. 93.
70 ibid., p. 93.
71 Minute by Cadogan to Halifax, 18 January 1939, FO371/24115, W1464/5/41; CAB27/624(36) 35th meeting.
72 Thomas, op. cit., pp. 869, 871, and Edwards, op. cit., pp. 207–9.
73 The vote in the Chamber was 323 for recognition, 261 against, with 17 abstentions.
74 For details of the recognition decision see Edwards, op. cit., pp. 206-9. See also CAB 24/283 CP46(39) 'Situation in Spain: Memorandum by the Secretary of State for Foreign Affairs 13 February 1939' and *DDF*, 2nd series, vol. XIV, nos 92, 97, 174 and 175, pp. 166, 177-8, 298–300.
75 For the full text of the Bérard-Jordana Agreement see *DDF*, 2nd series, vol. XIV, no. 211, pp. 372–4. Léon Bérard was a member of the French

Senate and a friend of Pierre Laval; later he became Vichy Ambassador to the Vatican. General Francisco Gómez Jordana y Sousa was Franco's Foreign Minister.

76 Details of the dispute concerning the Spanish gold and refugees as they affected French policy and Anglo-French relations can be found in the author's unpublished paper, 'Britain, France and Franco's Spain in the aftermath of the Spanish Civil War', presented to the inaugural conference of the British International History Group at Bristol Polytechnic in September 1988.

77 The extent of Chamberlain's irritation with the French at this time is clearly revealed in a letter to his sister Hilda on 17 June: 'The French for their part continue to keep up a quarrel with everyone whom they ought to make friends, Italy, Spain, Turkey. And we inevitably get tarred with the same brush', Neville Chamberlain Papers, NC18/1/1103. These papers are located in the Library of the University of Birmingham.

78 The impact of the Spanish refugee crisis within France is thoroughly documented in Louis Stein's admirable book, *Beyond Death and Exile: Spanish Republicans in France, 1939–1955*, Cambridge, Mass., Harvard University Press, 1979. According to Léger, during May 1939 the French authorities were spending between 5 million and 6 million francs a day on the refugee problem. Phipps to the Foreign Office, 19 May 1939, FO371/24159, W8031/3719/41.

79 Sir Maurice Peterson, Ambassador at Madrid, to Halifax, 8 July 1939, FO371/24159 W10599/379/41. Bullitt to Secretary of State Cordell Hull, 18 July 1939. Roosevelt Papers, President's Secretary's File 25. These papers are located in the Franklin D. Roosevelt Library in New York.

80 Alexander, op. cit., pp. 297–302. In March 1937 the French Minister of Defence, Edouard Daladier, told his generals that 'in a conflict, France could do without Soviet aid but not that of the British, who were profoundly averse to Franco-Soviet military ties', Jordan, op. cit., p. 264.

7 Britain and appeasement in the late 1930s
Was there a League of Nations' alternative?

Peter J. Beck

On 21 October 1939 Sean Lester, Deputy Secretary-General of the League of Nations, used a radio broadcast to the New York World Fair to discuss the organisation's adjustment to a world at war.[1] The outbreak of the Second World War, the very war the League had been created to prevent, had resulted already in the postponement of the Assembly and Council sessions scheduled for September 1939.

The apparent failure of the League-based 'new diplomacy' in the face of the enduring strength of the 'old diplomacy' was illustrated most graphically in September 1938 when the German threat to Czechoslovakia came to a head. The League Assembly and Council were in scheduled session between 12–30 and 26–30 September respectively, but neither was seized of the Czech problem, which was dealt with instead by bilateral Anglo-German exchanges at Berchtesgaden (15–16 September) and Godesberg (22–23 September) followed by the four-power Munich conference (29–30 September). British and French priorities were indicated by the presence at Munich of Neville Chamberlain and Edouard Daladier, their respective Prime Ministers, whereas the simultaneous League session received a British delegation led by only a junior minister (Richard, later Lord, Butler, parliamentary Under-Secretary of State at the Foreign Office). Georges Bonnet, the French Foreign Minister, spent merely a few days in Geneva at the start of the Assembly, where the French delegation was led by Joseph Paul-Boncour, a former Foreign Minister. Germany and Italy, the other two players at Munich, were no longer members of the League, whose jurisdiction they refused to respect.

The League was steering, or rather being steered by its key members, clear of major international problems. According to the Czech President, Dr Eduard Beneš, 'Geneva as an instrument of European democracy was already dead'; thus, the Czech government, albeit a

League member, looked to Munich rather than Geneva 'to see what the Great Powers... were going to do' about the German threat to its territorial integrity.[2] Even delegates present at Geneva realised that the key developments were occurring elsewhere, as implied by Butler's resentment about being 'off-stage discussing minor issues like European road signs' or the complaints of Sir Henry Channon, his parliamentary private secretary, about 'unsitthroughable' meetings of 'that absurd Assembly'.[3] On 29 September 1938, when the Munich conference was generally perceived to have world peace in its hands, the League merely adopted a resolution expressing anxiety about the international situation in spite of prompting to do more from the Soviet and other delegations.[4] Butler, writing from Geneva to his mother, felt 'sure we haven't appreciated the intense drama that has been going on in England'.[5] British opinion, though uneasy about the sacrifice of Czech territory, seemed more relieved at the peaceful outcome of the crisis than annoyed by the marginalisation of the League.[6]

Within a year the outbreak of the Second World War pushed the League further outside the international mainstream, at least until a brief period between 9 and 14 December 1939, when Finland's appeal against Soviet aggression made Geneva the focus of world attention.[7] This League session occupied centre stage for governments, the media and opinion, especially as the 'phoney war' in the west allowed attention to move eastward, as indicated by reports that in King George VI's office a map of the Russo-Finnish border replaced one covering the western front.[8] Even non-members, like the USA, were drawn into the question.

Nevertheless, the British government was opposed in principle to League involvement in the 'Winter War'.[9] The League was perceived – to quote a typical view expressed earlier in the year by Sir Alexander Cadogan, Permanent Under-Secretary of State at the Foreign Office – as 'a forum where the utmost provocation is given with the least possible practical effect'.[10] Britain, having shown a reluctance throughout the past decade to antagonise Japan, Italy and Germany for the sake of the League, had no desire to add the USSR to the list; indeed, Lord Halifax, the British Foreign Secretary, was 'very frightened' about a conflict adjudged likely to extend beyond the Baltic.[11] There were also fears that the special session would prompt unwelcome debates about recent League victims of aggression, like Albania, Austria, China, Czechoslovakia or Poland[12] In the event, the Finnish action, forcing the issue, faced Britain with an unwelcome *fait accompli*.

On 14 December 1939 the Assembly, adopting a resolution expelling the USSR from the League for placing itself 'outside of the Covenant', concluded the special session. The apparent speed, efficiency and decisiveness with which the dispute was handled brought back the League into the international limelight in a manner suggesting its ability to perform an active and meaningful peacekeeping role, even in disputes involving a major power. On the surface, the episode contrasted markedly with the organisation's recent history; indeed, some contemporaries, like Gilbert Murray, and commentators after 1945 argued that greater reliance upon the League option in preference to appeasement might have prevented the outbreak of the Second World War. In reality, nothing had changed. Expulsion served no military value, for the Soviet Union, ignoring Assembly resolutions, continued the invasion launched on 30 November. The Finnish government, though desperate for material rather than moral support, received plenty of sympathy but relatively little meaningful assistance from League members.[13] In turn, the USSR's understandable refusal to return to any League-based international organisation meant that the December session effectively killed the League as an institution.

LOOKING AT THE LEAGUE

Inevitably, historiographical controversies concerning appeasement have merged into the even more extensive debate about the origins of the Second World War. Chamberlain, fearing that historians would follow his political successors by judging him harshly, is interpreted now with a deeper understanding of his motives given the need for an over-stretched world power in decline to respond to the simultaneous threat posed by three potential aggressors, Germany, Italy and Japan. But even so, the 'Guilty Men' syndrome has never been completely pushed aside.[14] Anti-appeasers, albeit disagreeing among themselves, implied the availability of a feasible and better policy for dealing with Germany through say the use of force in 1936 or 1938, the imposition of economic sanctions, or the conclusion of alliances with the USSR or USA. The League option was also frequently commended as 'an impressive and obvious alternative to appeasement'; indeed, during 1939 Gilbert Murray, formerly President of the League of Nations Union (LNU), asserted that, if only Britain had consistently supported the League system, 'the whole course of history would have been different'.[15]

Hitherto, historical investigation has concentrated upon key disputes involving Corfu, Manchuria and Ethiopia, which also happen to represent the League's major 'failures'. Other periods have been neglected, as highlighted by the League's virtual non-role in studies of British foreign policy during the late 1930s, even if this might be rationalised as a function of its low priority.[16] The usual historical focus on the failure of the League, whose dissolution in 1946 appeared to follow on naturally from pre-1939 setbacks, means that there is nothing novel about a study reconsidering and dismissing the feasibility of the League alternative to appeasement. Nevertheless, this essay attempts also to illuminate aspects often ignored, like wide-ranging British support for collective security and the Chamberlain government's encouragement of the League's non-political work.

PRO-LEAGUE ANTI-APPEASERS

In many respects, the League, though widely supported for other reasons, offered one focus for the critics of appeasement. During the late 1930s a British policy centred upon collective security was still pressed strongly by the LNU, whose actual membership reached about 406,000 in the early 1930s (its reputed total of over 1 million included anyone who had ever been a member), as well as by a diverse group of anti-appeasers, including the Labour, Liberal and Communist parties and sections of the Conservative Party. Thus, Winston Churchill's 'Arms and the Covenant' campaign, advocating the League's use 'to address Germany collectively' with 'overwhelming force in support of international law', paralleled the Labour Party's efforts to urge the government – to quote Clement Attlee, the party's leader – 'to make support of the League the whole basis of its policy'.[17]

After 1935 Hugh Dalton, among others, pushed the Labour Party towards a more coherent and realistic policy linking collective security with the rearmament rather than the disarmament of Britain. By October 1937 the Bournemouth party conference's acceptance of rearmament provided the foundation for a determined attack upon the 'weak and vacillating policy' of appeasement.[18] Throughout 1938 the Labour Party, like the LNU, urged Britain to breathe new life into the League by using rearmament to strengthen collective security, but the campaign's efficacy was qualified by factional strife and the National government's massive parliamentary majority.

Although the Conservative Party as a whole was not known for championing the League cause, Anthony Eden enjoyed a sound

League image. Inevitably, his resignation as Foreign Secretary (February 1938) was viewed both within and outside the government as symptomatic of British antipathy towards Geneva; for instance, the unease articulated by certain junior ministers echoed that emanating from the Australian government.[19] The actual reasons for his resignation – involving disagreements about the nature and conduct of policy – were more complex than this. In the event, Eden, whose apparent 'lack of urge' was attributed by Lord Butler to an 'addiction to office', seemed more anxious to safeguard his political future than to mount an effective anti-appeasement campaign.[20] Disappointment about his 'vague and weak' speeches was voiced by MPs like Harold Macmillan who were looking for a lead.[21]

Another Conservative MP, Winston Churchill, proved a more eloquent and visible anti-appeaser, whose most telling indictment came during the parliamentary debate on the Munich agreement in which he accused the government, among other things, of discrediting the League, sustaining 'a total and unmitigated defeat', and leaving Britain inadequately armed at a time of crisis.[22] Subsequently, his wartime and postwar emphasis upon 'an unnecessary war' proved important in turning opinion against the 'Guilty Men'. During the late 1930s Churchill pressed for a 'grand alliance' under the League in response to German aggression: 'Here Geneva seems to be the centre through which Great Britain and France should apply their influence'.[23] Churchill's 'Arms and the Covenant' campaign could not be discounted by the government, but his prospects of constructing an effective critical lobby were hindered by a reputation for warmongering and party disloyalty alongside accusations of political opportunism.[24] Newly acquired League credentials failed to hide his basic character as a balance of power man pursuing purely British interests.

> He was aware of the sentimental attachment which many Britons had for the League, and correctly took the view that his own ideas for a grand alliance would be much more attractive if it flew under League colours.[25]

His espousal of collective security as 'our rock' seemed intended more to remedy Britain's disarmed state and to contain Germany than to revive the League itself.[26]

Lord Cecil of Chelwood, albeit more of a political lightweight, was also prominent in lamenting the government's 'usual attitude' of ignoring the League during major crises for 'the much less defensible policy of appeasement'.[27] Nevertheless, idealism reinforced through LNU links was not allowed to cloud his assessment of the situation after the Ethiopian dispute (1935–36):

> I put aside, personally, all hope of maintaining peace by objurgation or appeals or even the unassisted influence of world opinion.... These influences ... have never yet succeeded in preventing a war which has been determined upon by any powerful country.[28]

Only the threat of 'overwhelming' force was likely to halt German expansionism:

> If Germany were assured that any particular hostile action would be met by a combination of all forces of the members of the League she would probably refrain from it. That seems to me the only solid hope for world peace.

CHAMBERLAIN AND LEAGUE REALITIES

Despite its strong attractions to the centre and left in British politics as well as to certain members of the Conservative Party, a League-based policy was ruled out as a feasible alternative to 'appeasement' by a British government increasingly preoccupied with the German problem. The Chamberlain government (1937–40), whilst acknowledging the Covenant's 'grand and magnificent' ideals, adopted a pragmatic approach seeking to keep the League's political functions 'on ice', or rather in a state of 'suspended animation', until international conditions were adjudged more appropriate.[29] The Covenant remained in force, but what was its protection worth? Privately, the Prime Minister – he defined the concept as 'collective action of a number of States ... to prevent aggression, or if aggression is undertaken, to put a stop to it and punish the aggressor' – expressed a growing desire to bring 'the fresh air of reality into the idea of collective security'.[30]

At first, domestic political considerations persuaded the Chamberlain government to pay-lip service to an institution attracting considerable support from a range of public opinion, which after the Ethiopian dispute still believed that the League could work next time, even against Germany. Collective security's failure in the Ethiopian question was blamed on Britain and France, not the League. At the same time, while the 1935 Peace Ballot's massive majorities for League-based sanctions appeared to vindicate LNU claims that the British people strongly favoured collective security, the allegedly 'loaded' nature of the questions prompted some to regard it as a public relations exercise designed to boost an ailing League and LNU.[31] How far would British opinion, despite its 'uncritical loyalty' and 'messianic zeal' for the League, be prepared to accept collective security's practical implications?[32] Chamberlain, like Butler, branded LNU supporters as 'fanatics' and 'idealists'.[33] He confessed his astonishment 'at the lighthearted way in which people who think that they are pacifists are yet prepared to advocate measures which would almost certainly bring us into war'.[34] Were people really willing, one minister asked, to see 'our young men' fight and die for the League in a far away country, like Manchuria, Ethiopia or Czechoslovakia?[35] Perhaps Sir John Simon, speaking just before Chamberlain became Prime Minister, identified the central issue when he complained that collective security was frequently treated 'as though it were an arrangement by which you are going to receive a contribution without making one'.[36] Simon, pointing to the Labour Party's simultaneous support at this time for collective security and British disarmament, drew upon an analogy from Lewis Carroll's *Hunting of the Snark* when comparing League supporters to the man who 'at charity-meetings stands at the door. And collects – though he does not subscribe'.

Government policy, though presented in terms acceptable to the LNU and like-minded interests, was not based on the League. Despite the sizeable gap existing between public opinion and government views about the League's political role, it was not until the early months of 1938 that Chamberlain, recalling that his 1936 'midsummer of madness' speech urging the end of League sanctions against Italy provoked far more letters of abuse than of approval, was prepared openly to accuse League supporters of ignoring international realities.[37]

> At the last Election it was still possible to hope that the League might afford collective security. I believed it myself. I do not believe it now.... The League as constituted today is unable to provide collective security for anybody... we must not try to delude ourselves, and still more, we must not try to delude small weak nations, into thinking that they will be protected by the League against aggression and acting accordingly, when we know that nothing of the kind can be expected.[38]

Two weeks later, he repeated the fundamental problem:

The League today is mutilated.... it is halt and maimed.... I ask what small country in Europe today, if it be threatened by a larger one, can safely rely on the League alone to protect it against invasion?... There can only be one honest answer to it, and that it is none.[39]

Within a few days, one 'small country', Austria, seemed to prove the point. One year later, Chamberlain returned to this theme: 'It was of no use in present circumstances to appeal to the League of Nations to obtain collective security for us... *we had to trust to other means* of maintaining peace and keeping the country safe'.[40] Once again, German actions, this time conducted against Prague, soon gave substance to an assessment which underwent no revision even during the 'Winter War', when Halifax reaffirmed the government's belief that the League 'could *not* deal with political matters'.[41]

THE LEAGUE AS AN INTER-GOVERNMENTAL ORGANISATION

In May 1938 Halifax reminded the League Council that 'Great as is the League of Nations, the ends that it exists to serve are greater than itself'.[42] Despite occasional attempts (for example the Geneva Protocol for the Pacific Settlement of International Disputes in 1924) to transform it into a supernational body, the League remained an inter-governmental organisation which mirrored international conditions and the views of its leading members. For peacekeeping purposes, the League tended to be 'they', its most powerful members, rather than 'it', the League as an autonomous international actor. This inter-governmental character explained a growing dependence upon the policies pursued by Britain and France, whose influence as the leading 'producers' of security was accentuated during the 1930s by the departure of other major powers and the USA's continued absence. Anglo-French predominance was symbolized by the regular visits undertaken by Joseph Avenol, the League's Secretary-General (1933–40), and Frank Walters, a member of the secretariat and subsequently the organisation's historian, to Paris and London respectively to discuss forthcoming League business. Inevitably, divisions among the great powers were soon reflected in the League, whose successes and failures proved essentially a function of great power co-operation. For any effective League action, as happened during the 1925 Graeco-Bulgarian dispute, great power interests had either to coincide or at least not to conflict with each other.[43] Even non-members influenced its role. Just as the USA's absence from Geneva severely curtailed League activity in both functional and geographical senses, so the withdrawal of Germany (1933), Italy (1937) and Japan (1933) rendered it futile to involve the League in matters appertaining to these countries. Significantly, in October 1937 Baron Constantin von Neurath, the German Foreign Minister, delivered a lecture to the Academy of German Law at Munich about the bankruptcy of collective security and his government's preference for alternative strategies:

> In politics, even in peace politics, success is what counts, not the mere announcement of beautiful aims, which may be enticing, but which are in practice unattainable and therefore worthless.[44]

Such sentiments could easily have been expressed by Chamberlain.

The League's adaptation to a changing world – the so-called 'reform' process – was under discussion throughout the late 1930s, when the breakdown of international order, withdrawals by major powers, and growing emphasis on rearmament exacerbated existing doubts about the organisation's peacekeeping and disarmament functions. Declining confidence in the League was accompanied by budgetary difficulties consequent upon falling membership and subscription arrears. However, the chief stimulus for 'reform' arose from an appraisal of recent history, most notably the League's failure in what was often described by contemporaries like Sir Austen Chamberlain as the 'test case' provided by the Ethiopian Crisis.[45] The League's predicament was compounded by Hitler's remilitarisation of the Rhineland (March 1936), for the resulting preoccupation with the German problem reinforced the Anglo-French desire to prioritise good relations with Italy as compared to the interests of either Ethiopia or the League.[46] Naturally, during June–July 1936 the mood of the League Assembly was one of pessimism, and delegates did not need Emperor Haile Selassie to remind them that the issues at stake extended beyond the fate of his small country. Members looked elsewhere for security, as evidenced by Belgium's retreat into neutrality. By contrast, Mussolini, speaking in Rome, rejoiced about a 'great victory... a white flag has been hoisted in the ranks of world "sanctionism"... and so it will come tomorrow and always'.[47]

French domestic and military weaknesses, in conjunction with the assertive attitude assumed by Chamberlain in dealing with the dictators, contributed to British predominance in Anglo-French exchanges as far as the appeasement of Germany was concerned.

Even before becoming Prime Minister, Chamberlain expressed doubts to the 1900 Club about the merits of a League strategy. Chamberlain, believing that the Ethiopian crisis confronted the League with 'a task which was beyond its power to fulfil', thought that the continuation of sanctions would be the 'very midsummer of madness': 'All the same it [the League] is beaten, and I am anxious that we should survey the history of this affair and make up our minds what is the best way of keeping the peace'.[48] For him, 'the best way' did not involve the League, whose recent experiences 'had therefore demonstrated the failure of collective security': 'This was because collective security depended on the individual actions of members of the League, whose interests and capacities differed widely'.[49] British co-operation with France, Germany and Italy outside the League became the preferred instrument of policy, an attitude reflecting not only Chamberlain's assessment of recent international realities but also his basic antipathy towards the League as an institution, in so far as he had ever given serious thought to the subject. Within the Conservative Party there had always existed a range of feeling towards the League, and Chamberlain, refusing to subordinate British interests to it, shared the pragmatic and limited, even hostile, attitude adopted towards the League by most fellow Conservatives.[50]

The central problem derived from an awareness of defensive shortcomings alongside fears that collective security would require military action in defence of something other than a specifically British interest, as already acknowledged in November 1935 by the Committee of Imperial Defence's Defence Requirements Sub-Committee:

> We feel bound to bring to notice the very serious effect of the [collective security] system, in its present stage, on our own defence requirements, as illustrated by the Manchurian and Abyssinian episodes.... In 1932–33, and again in 1935, owing to our obligations under the Covenant and the position we occupy as the one great sea power remaining in the League, we had no alternative but to play our part – inevitably a leading part – in disputes in which our national interest was at most quite secondary.... On each occasion, we have come within sight of war and aroused the bitterness of old friends and allies, including in the recent past, not only Italy, but even France.[51]

Who would support British sanctions imposed against Germany? The sub-committee's comment that, 'If the Covenant breaker were

Germany, that support would be even less reliable than in the present case [Ethiopia]', rendered it more dangerous for Britain to use the League than not to do so, as argued by Chamberlain when addressing the 1900 Club in 1936:

> Is it not apparent that a policy of sanctions involves, I do not say war, but a risk of war? ... Is it not also apparent that, from what has happened, in the presence of such a risk, nations cannot be relied upon to proceed to the last extremity unless their vital interests are threatened?[52]

Subsequent events merely reaffirmed his view that 'the League will never be any good unless it has definitely abandoned all idea of compulsion'.[53]

Meanwhile, League members created a Committee of Twenty-Eight to advise on 'reform', and in 1938 its report, recognising the existing reality of the so-called 'intermediate League' favoured by Britain, recommended a focus upon obligatory consultations and optional sanctions.[54] Most members soon placed on record their formal contracting-out of sanctions under Article 16. The report resulted also in the formal separation of the 1919 Peace Treaties and the Covenant, although this move came too late either to moderate German and Italian hostility towards the linkage or to facilitate their return to Geneva. 'Reform' recognised rather than resolved the League's deficiencies. Indeed, in one sense, the process allowed Britain and other members to 'reform' the League out of existence as a peacekeeping body. Certainly, by this time it figured increasingly less in the thoughts and calculations of policy-makers, a point illustrated not only by the declining status of League delegations but also by the diminution of meaningful references to the League in press and archival sources for this period. In 1939 Chamberlain was denounced in Parliament for 'never saying a word about the League'; in fact, it would have been more correct to have accused him of 'never saying a good word about the League'.[55]

BRITISH LEAGUE POLICY FROM *ANSCHLUSS* TO WORLD WAR

During the late 1930s Britain and France possessed clear reasons for dealing with key events – these included the Spanish Civil War, the 1936 Rhineland Crisis, the post–1937 Sino-Japanese clash, and the Austrian, Czech, Albanian and Polish problems – away from Geneva. Even in the case of threats to or the actual invasion of

League members, Britain sought to confine the League to debate or a minor functional role (for example, protecting Spanish art treasures in the Civil War), not action. In cases involving Germany even this limited role was severely circumscribed.

In March 1938 the *Anschluss* was followed by an announcement that Austria, having become an integral part of the German Reich, was no longer a member of the League. This episode reaffirmed Anglo-French views about the League's inappropriateness for dealing with the German problem, especially as Hitler repeatedly refused their invitations either to re-join the League or to recognise its jurisdiction in any matter affecting his country's interests.[56] Cadogan, referred to League involvement in a way – he minuted 'do we want to raise the point?' – which both anticipated and prompted Halifax's negative response.[57] Given their reluctance to act directly against a breach of the 1919 Peace Treaties, Britain and France were even more opposed to Soviet and other proposals for 'collective action' through the League. Chamberlain, whilst agreeing with Cecil's assessment that Germany could be deterred only by force, saw no role for the League in this process, much to the annoyance of the LNU:

> Force is the only argument Germany understands and collective security cannot offer any prospect of preventing such events until it can show a visible force of overwhelming strength backed by determination to use it.[58]

The *Anschluss* opened the door towards Czechoslovakia, and within one year yet another League member disappeared from the map without any meaningful collective action on its behalf. Chamberlain, denying any direct British interest, refused prior commitments; instead, he merely exploited the Covenant and other obligations in ambiguous parliamentary statements designed to bluff the Germans and restrain rash action by the French.[59] Godesberg, Berchtesgaden and Munich, not Geneva, occupied centre stage during a period when the British press and newsreels presented Chamberlain, not the League, as the peacemaker.[60] Britain also had no intention of involving the Soviet Union in the Czech dispute, despite Maxim Litvinov's staunch support of collective security and multilateral co-operation against Germany.[61] Chamberlain's 'better Hitler than Stalin' attitude and under-estimation of Soviet power, combined with Halifax's 'high church' ideological reservations, cast doubt upon not only the USSR's ability to aid Czechoslovakia but also the attractions of Anglo-Soviet collaboration. In particular:

The Alliance [with Russia] would definitely be a lining up of opposing blocs and an association which would make any negotiation or discussions with the totalitarians difficult, if not impossible.[62]

In March 1939 the demise of 'rump' Czechoslovakia concentrated minds on the German threat to another League member, Poland. Resulting Anglo-French guarantee treaties, though frequently depicted as a change of direction as far as appeasement was concerned, merely continued existing trends for the League.[63] In May, Halifax's statement to the League Council epitomised the actual position:

The changes which have taken place in Europe since last September.... have imposed upon His Majesty's government a certain course of action.... The particular action which His Majesty's government have taken has not been carried through the League. This was, in the circumstances, impossible. But everything that His Majesty's government have done is in strict conformity with the spirit of the League Covenant.[64]

In any case, Poland was never a staunch believer in the Covenant, as evidenced by its chequered relationship with the League and perennial disputes with Czechoslovakia and Lithuania.[65] More recently, in 1938, it decided against seeking re-election to the League Council. Neither escalating German pressure nor the actual invasion of its territory in September 1939 elicited a Polish appeal to Geneva, and the League merely received an explanatory statement despatched from Warsaw on 29 October 1939.[66]

Soon after the outbreak of the Second World War the British and French governments, acting more out of a sense of duty than of conviction, placed on record at Geneva their case against Germany. Significantly, their declarations of war were rationalised in terms of German violations of the 1928 Kellogg-Briand Pact and the 1939 Polish guarantee treaties rather than of successive infringements of the League Covenant. In fact, the British government, avoiding any mention of League action against German aggression, seemed to put one more nail into the League's coffin: 'the Covenant has ... completely broken down in practice, thus the machinery for the preservation of peace has collapsed'.[67] The government, following pre-war trends, sought to keep the League out of the Second World War. League resolutions were rated of dubious propaganda value for the Allied cause, while Butler advised that intervention would be 'a sure way to kill the League'.[68] Significantly, Butler headed the British delegation at Geneva in December 1939, when events seemed to prove him right.

CONCLUSION

During the late 1930s the opening of the Palais des Nations, the League's grandiose lake-side headquarters, gave the impression of business as usual at Geneva. But, in reality, the organisation, though holding regular Council and Assembly sessions, was leading a shadowy existence; indeed, Avenol, lamenting the League's political paralysis at a time of '*demi-guerre*', was reportedly planting trees in the grounds of the Palais des Nations on the day of the *Anschluss*![69]

According to Neville Chamberlain, the key problems were 'how best to restore shaken confidence, how to maintain the rule of law in international affairs, how to seek peaceful solutions to questions that continue to cause anxiety?'[70] His answer assigned low priority to the League, which was deemed particularly unsuitable for discussing the activities of non-members, like Germany, Italy and Japan. Chamberlain, though sharing Churchill's instrumental view of the League in terms of the pursuit of British interests, saw it as an instrument to be either used for only a minor conciliatory role or marginalised to a virtual political non-role.[71] His basic lack of enthusiasm for the League itself was reinforced by a desire to retain direct control over decision-making in preference to slow, obstructive tiresome 'meetings at Geneva and resolutions by dozens of small nations who have no responsibilities'.[72] He never really altered his view, as expressed during the Ethiopian crisis, that the League, most notably, through its pious yet ineffective resolutions, was liable to do more harm than good:

> The League once more will have conspicuously failed to do more than exacerbate feelings all round and will be charged, not without justification, with having encouraged the Abyssinians [Ethiopians] to commit suicide.[73]

Inevitably, a leading member like Britain received a large share of the blame for the League's failure, and especially for never treating collective security as anything other than – to quote A.J.P. Taylor – 'a fifth wheel' of policy.[74] Even the Soviet Foreign Minister, Litvinov, an outspoken advocate of collective security, accepted that the League's peacekeeping role was in abeyance 'barring a decided change in policy by Great Britain'.[75] Nevertheless, the relatively wide spectrum of support for the League, though failing to determine the direction of policy, influenced the rhetoric of a government, which was forced to be defensive about its position, as demonstrated by ministerial assertions that the League failed because of intrinsic weaknesses rather than because of the action/inaction of any specific member. Even Chamberlain felt compelled publicly to acknowledge its ideals, including the hope that 'some day' the League might 'be the salvation of the world'.[76]

In particular, positive encouragement was given to both the continuation and expansion of non-political work, as pressed by the August 1939 Bruce report. According to Halifax:

> With the restriction of the political aspects of the League, it is precisely [the] education, social and humanitarian activities of the League that must be maintained and developed.[77]

Non-political work allowed the League to perform a meaningful role, which appealed to British opinion, the Dominions and even non-members, like the USA, while also providing wartime continuity for at least one form of international collaboration. Thus, the League would remain available for the reconstruction of the international system whenever 'a new start becomes possible'.[78] In the event, this 'new start' involved the United Nations, not the League, which was dissolved in 1946.

In February 1939 Chamberlain, both prompting and responding to Labour taunts that 'you destroyed it [the League]', predicted that:

> The historian will come to the conclusion that if the League failed... it was not due to the action or inaction of this country... but the real explanation was that it had been sought to impose upon the League a task which was completely beyond its powers.[79]

Chamberlain, seeking 'support for my policy' rather than either arguments about its merits or speculation about alternatives, was unmoved by anti-appeasers: 'I am completely convinced that the course I am taking is right and therefore cannot be influenced by the attacks of my critics'.[80] Despite policy misunderstandings and mistakes as well as contemporary support for collective security, most historians – these include Birn, Dilks, Henig, Hinsley and Northedge – have broadly agreed with Chamberlain's dismissal of the feasibility of the League option, even if Parker's recent book treated the League option in a more sympathetic manner.[81] According to David Dilks:

> Chamberlain would have been wiser to say much less about the League and merely to leave events to make it and collective security what they were in reality, ambitious plans which in the circumstances of the later 1930s could not be effective against challenges so determined [as those of the aggressors].[82]

In the mean time, the growing trend to view British foreign policy of the 1930s in terms of the changing balance of world power suggests that this study should be interpreted as illuminating Britain's readiness, or rather unreadiness, to abandon a world role and respond to pressures for interdependence within larger groupings. From this perspective, the late 1930s merely established the difficulties of this transformation for a country whose international power and influence was no longer decisive; thus, in February 1939 *Headway*, the LNU's mouthpiece, perceptively acknowledged that since Munich 'it is by others that the word will be given for peace – or war'.[83]

NOTES

1 *Monthly Summary of the League of Nations*, 1939, vol. 19, pp. 361–4.
2 G. Lias (transl.), *Memoirs of Dr. Eduard Benes, From Munich to New Year and New Victory*, London, Allen & Unwin, 1954, p. 37.
3 Author's interview with Lord Butler, April 1980; R.A. Butler, *The Art of the Possible*, London, Hamish Hamilton, 1971, p. 66; R. Rhodes James (ed.) *Chips: The Diaries of Sir Henry Channon*, London, Weidenfeld & Nicolson, 1967, pp. 164–8; P. Beck (ed.) *British Documents on Foreign Affairs: Reports and Papers from the Foreign Office Confidential Print, Part II, Series J: The League of Nations*, vol. 1, Maryland, University Publications of America, 1992, pp. 276–84.
4 *League of Nations Official Journal, Special Suppl. 183: Records of the 19th Assembly*, 1938, pp. 94–5.
5 A. Howard, *R.A. Butler*, London, Cape, 1987, pp. 76–7.
6 D.S. Birn, *The League of Nations Union 1918–1945*, Oxford, Oxford University Press, 1981, pp. 194–6.
7 Neville Chamberlain to Ida Chamberlain, 3 December 1939, NC18/1/1133. The Sir Austen Chamberlain (AC) and Neville Chamberlain (NC) Papers are located at the Library of the University of Birmingham, and are quoted by kind permission of the Librarian; P. Beck, 'The Winter War in the international context: Britain and the League of Nations' role in the Russo-Finnish dispute, 1939–1940', *Journal of Baltic Studies*, 1981, vol. 12, pp. 58–73.
8 *Daily Sketch*, 15 December 1939.
9 R.A. Butler to Campbell, 19 December 1939, FO371/23696, N7904/991/

38. British Foreign Office (FO), Cabinet (CAB) and Prime Minister's (PREM) papers are located at the Public Record Office, London.
10 Minute by Cadogan, 19 May 1939, FO371/24024, W8836/189/98.
11 Halifax, 1 November 1939, CAB65/1 WM67(39).
12 CAB65/2 WM103(39), 4 December 1939.
13 Beck, op. cit., pp. 68–9.
14 For Chamberlain's attitude, see Neville to Ida Chamberlain, 25 May 1940, NC18/1/1158; D. Dilks, ' "We must hope for the best and prepare for the worst": the prime minister, the Cabinet and Hitler's Germany, 1937-1939', *Proceedings of the British Academy*, vol. 73, 1987, pp. 350–2; K. Robbins, *Appeasement*, London, Historical Association, 1988, pp. 1–9. See also S. Aster, 'Guilty men: the case of Neville Chamberlain'; in R. Boyce and E. M. Robertson (eds) *Paths to War: New Essays on the Origins of the Second World War*, London, Macmillan, 1989, pp. 233–68; R.A.C. Parker, *Chamberlain and Appeasement: British Policy and the Coming of the Second World War*, London, Macmillan 1993, pp. 343–7.
15 N. Thompson, *The Anti-Appeasers: Conservative Opposition to Appeasement in the 1930s*, Oxford, Oxford University Press, 1971, pp. 49–50; G. Murray, *From the League to U.N.*, London, Oxford University Press, 1948, pp. 71–6.
16 On the League aspect, see Butler, op. cit., pp. 66–79; Maurice Cowling, *The Impact of Hitler: British Politics and British Policy 1933–1940*, Cambridge, Cambridge University Press, 1975; L.W. Fuchser, *Neville Chamberlain and Appeasement: A Study in the Politics of History*, New York, Norton, 1982, pp. 41–2, 52; R.A.C. Parker, 'The failure of collective security in British appeasement', in W.J. Mommsen and L. Kettenacker (eds) *The Fascist Challenge and the Policy of Appeasement*, London, Allen & Unwin, 1983, pp. 22–9; F.S. Northedge, *The League of Nations: Its Life and Times*, Leicester, Leicester University Press, 1986, pp. 255–77; Parker, *Chamberlain and Appeasement*, pp. 307–12.
17 M. Gilbert, *Winston S. Churchill, vol. V: 1922–1939*, London, Heinemann, 1976, pp. 663, 699, 721–3, 740, 808, 846; R.S. Churchill (ed.) *Arms and the Covenant*, London, Harrap, 1938, pp. 361–3; C.R. Attlee, *As it Happened*, London, Heinemann, 1954, p. 99.
18 H. Dalton, *Memoirs: The Fateful Years 1931–1945*, London, Muller, 1957, pp. 142–3; B. Pimlott, *Hugh Dalton*, London, Cape, 1985, pp. 225-67; M.D. Roberts, 'Hugh Dalton and the Labour Party in the 1930s', unpublished PhD thesis, Kingston Polytechnic, 1978, pp. 47-51, 61–2, 113–15, 129–35; Attlee, op. cit., p. 99; Cowling, op. cit.
19 Chamberlain to Hilda Chamberlain, 27 February 1938, NC18/1/1040; Australian Prime Minister to Dominions Office, 6 March 1938, in R.G. Neale (ed.) *Documents of Australian Foreign Policy 1937–1949*, vol. 1, Canberra, AGPS, p. 268; R. Douglas, 'Chamberlain and Eden 1937–38', *Journal of Contemporary History*, vol. 13, 1978, pp. 97–114.
20 Author's interview with Lord Butler, April 1980; Thompson, op. cit., pp. 148–9, 192-200; Earl of Avon, *The Eden Memoirs: Facing the Dictators*, London, Cassell, 1962, pp. 142–3; R. Rhodes James, *Anthony Eden*, London, Weidenfeld & Nicolson, 1986, pp. 196ff.
21 Macmillan, quoted in Hugh Dalton's Diary, 12 October 1938, Dalton

Papers. These papers are located at the British Library of Political and Economic Science, London.
22 Churchill, 5 October 1938, *Hansard Parliamentary Debates*, HC, 5th series, vol. 339, cc. 359–73; Gilbert, op. cit., pp. 916–17, 997–8; J. Charmley, *Churchill: The End of Glory*, London, Hodder & Stoughton, 1993, p. 353; R. Rhodes James, *Churchill: A Study in Failure 1900–1939*, London, Weidenfeld & Nicolson, 1970, pp. 294–8, 321–2, 342–3; Cowling, op. cit., pp. 241–53.
23 'The Austrian Eye-Opener', 18 March 1938, in W.S. Churchill, *Step by Step*, London, Odhams, 1939, pp. 211–14.
24 Charmley, op. cit., pp. 334, 342; W.N. Medlicott, *Appeasers and Warmongers*, Oulu, Finland, Oulu University Press, 1972, p. 8; Thompson, op. cit., p. 59; Birn, op. cit., pp. 145–7; Attlee, 26 March 1936, *Hansard Parliamentary Debates*, HC, 5th series, vol. 310, cc. 1531–9; Cowling, op. cit.
25 Charmley, op. cit., p. 310.
26 Churchill to Austen Chamberlain, 1 October 1935, Austen Chamberlain Papers AC41/2/46; Gilbert, op. cit., pp. 1050–2; D.C. Watt, 'Churchill and appeasement' in R. Blake and W. R. Louis (eds) *Churchill: A Major New Assessment of his Life in Peace and War*, Oxford, Oxford University Press, 1993, p. 211; Charmley, op. cit., p. 307.
27 Viscount Cecil, *A Great Experiment*, London, Cape, 1941, pp. 296–310.
28 Memorandum by Cecil, May 1936, Add MSS 51083 folios 108–9. The Cecil manuscripts (Add MSS) are located at the British Library, London.
29 Chamberlain, 7 March 1938, *Hansard Parliamentary Debates*, HC, 5th series, vol. 332, cc. 1565; author's interview with Lord Butler, April 1980; minute, A.W. Randell, adviser on League affairs, 3 May 1939, FO371/24017, W7970/164/98.
30 Chamberlain to Lord Lothian, 10 June 1936, Lothian Papers, GD40 17/445. These papers are located at the Scottish Record Office, Edinburgh; Chamberlain, 22 February 1938, *Hansard Parliamentary Debates*, HC, 5th series, vol. 332, c. 227.
31 Birn, op. cit., pp. 142–54; Robbins, op. cit., pp. 24–5.
32 G. Goodwin, 'The political role of the United Nations: some British views', *International Organization*, vol. 15, 1961, p. 581; D. Waley, *British Public Opinion and the Abyssinian War 1935–36*, London, Temple Smith, 1975, pp. 11–13, 19–22, 135–40.
33 Chamberlain to Hilda Chamberlain, 14 June 1936, NC18/1/965; author's interview with Butler, April 1980.
34 Chamberlain to Hilda Chamberlain, 29 August 1937, NC18/1/1018.
35 W.S. Morrison, Chancellor of the Duchy of Lancaster, 21 February 1939, *Hansard Parliamentary Debates*, HC, 5th series, vol. 344, cc. 333–4.
36 Sir John Simon, Home Secretary, 25 February 1937, *Hansard Parliamentary Debates*, HC, 5th series, vol. 320, c. 2334.
37 Chamberlain to Hilda Chamberlain, 14 June 1936, NC18/1/965; Chamberlain to Ida Chamberlain, 20 June 1936, NC18/1/966; Chamberlain to Hilda Chamberlain, 8 May 1938, NC18/1/1050.
38 Chamberlain, 22 February 1938, *Hansard Parliamentary Debates*, HC, 5th series, vol. 332, c. 227.
39 Chamberlain, 7 March 1938, *Hansard Parliamentary Debates*, HC, 5th

series, vol. 332, c. 1565. See also minutes by F. Roberts and H. Malkin, 11, 13 June 1938, FO371/22547, W7921/383/98.
40 Chamberlain, 21 February 1939, *Hansard Parliamentary Debates*, HC, 5th series, vol. 334, cc. 227–9.
41 Minute, Cadogan, 4 December 1939 (agreed by Halifax), FO371/23695, N7200/991/38.
42 Halifax, 12 May 1938, *League of Nations Official Journal*, vol. 19, 1938, p. 335.
43 P. Beck, 'From the Geneva Protocol to the Greco-Bulgarian Dispute: the development of the Baldwin government's policy towards the peace-keeping role of the League of Nations, 1924–1925', *British Journal of International Studies*, vol. 6, 1980, pp. 67–8.
44 Enclosed in Sir Nevile Henderson to Eden, 2 November 1937, Beck (ed.) *British Documents on Foreign Affairs*, vol. 2, p. 332.
45 Austen Chamberlain, 5 December 1935, *Hansard Parliamentary Debates*, HC, 5th series, vol. 307, c. 351; G.W. Baer, *Test Case: Italy, Ethiopia and the League of Nations*, Stanford, Calif., Hoover Institution Press, 1976.
46 Gilbert Murray to Austen Chamberlain, 4 April 1936, AC41/3/25; Drummond to Eden, 5 March 1937, FO954/13A, fo.59.
47 Mussolini, 15 July 1936, quoted in A.J. Toynbee, *Survey of International Affairs 1935, vol. II*, London, Oxford University Press, 1936, pp. 512–13.
48 Chamberlain to Hilda Chamberlain, 2 May 1936, NC18/1/959; *The Times*, 11 June 1936.
49 Chamberlain Diary, 27 April 1936, NC2/23A.
50 Author's interview with Lord Butler, April 1980; P. Noel-Baker to the author, 17 June 1971. See M.C. Pugh, 'British public opinion and collective security 1922–1936', unpublished PhD thesis, University of East Anglia, 1975.
51 CID Defence Requirements Sub-Committee, 21 November 1935, CAB 4/24 DRC 37, pp. 6–9.
52 *The Times*, 11 June 1936; R.A.C. Parker, 'Great Britain, France and the Ethiopian Crisis 1935–1936', *English Historical Review*, vol. 89, 1974, p. 331.
53 Chamberlain to Ida Chamberlain, 26 February 1939, NC18/1/1087.
54 F.P. Walters, *A History of the League of Nations*, London, Oxford University Press, 1960 edn, pp. 709–19, 777–84.
55 Chamberlain to Ida Chamberlain, 26 February 1939, NC18/1/1087.
56 C.M. Kimmich, *Germany and the League of Nations*, Chicago, University of Chicago Press, 1976, pp. 190–3.
57 Minutes by Cadogan and Halifax, 31 March 1938, FO371/22509, W3835/3/98; CAB24/275 CP67(38), 13 March 1938; D. Dilks (ed.) *The Diaries of Sir Alexander Cadogan 1938–1945*, London, Cassell, 1971, pp. 62–3, 67.
58 Chamberlain to Hilda Chamberlain, 13 March 1938, NC18/1/1041; Halifax, 16 March 1938 *Hansard Parliamentary Debates*, HL, vol. 108, cc. 176–84; D.C. Watt, *How War Came: The Immediate Origins of the Second World War 1938–1939*, London, Heinemann, 1989, pp. 26–7; Birn, op. cit., pp. 192–3.
59 Chamberlain, 24 March 1938, *Hansard Parliamentary Debates*, HC, 5th series, vol. 333, cc. 1404–8.
60 Chamberlain to Ida Chamberlain, 20 March 1938, NC18/1/1042.

61 Chamberlain to Hilda Chamberlain, 9 October 1937; Chamberlain to Ida Chamberlain, 26 March 1939; Chamberlain to Ida Chamberlain, 9 April 1939; Chamberlain to Hilda Chamberlain, 28 May 1939, NC18/1/1023/1091/1093/1101; Chamberlain meeting with Labour Delegation, 17 September 1938, PREM1/264, fo.14; author's interview with Lord Butler, April 1980.
62 Chamberlain to Hilda Chamberlain, 28 May 1939, NC18/1/1101.
63 Chamberlain to Hilda Chamberlain, 19 March 1939, NC18/1/1090.
64 Halifax to Foreign Office, 23 May 1939, Beck (ed.) *British Documents on Foreign Affairs*, vol. 1, pp. 291–2.
65 G. Sakwa, 'The Polish Ultimatum to Lithuania in March 1938', *Slavonic and East European Review*, vol. 55, 1977, pp. 204–26; Beck (ed.) *British Documents on Foreign Affairs*, vol. 2, pp. 327, 337–40, 345, 348–49.
66 *League of Nations Official Journal*, vol. 20, 1939, p. 386.
67 Foreign Office to the League, 9 September 1939, FO371/24040, W13402/895/98; Foreign Office to the League, 7 and 9 September 1939, *League of Nations Official Journal*, vol. 20, 1939, pp. 387, 408–9; Beck (ed.) *British Documents on Foreign Affairs*, vol. 1, pp. 295–7; Birn, op. cit., p. 202.
68 Minute by Butler, 9 September 1939, FO371/24040, W13666/895/98; Chamberlain and Attlee, 12 October 1939, *Hansard Parliamentary Debates*, HC, 5th series, vol. 352, cc. 563–71; Halifax to Campbell, 1 November 1939, Beck (ed.) *British Documents on Foreign Affairs*, vol. 1, pp. 297–8; Foreign Office to Colonial Office, 15 June 1940, FO371/24433, C2392/1596/98.
69 J. Barros, *Betrayal from Within: Joseph Avenol, Secretary-General of the League of Nations 1933–1940*, New Haven, Conn., Yale University Press, 1969, pp. 164, 189, 192.
70 Chamberlain, 24 March 1938, *Hansard Parliamentary Debates*, HC, 5th series, vol. 333, c. 1403.
71 Chamberlain to Ida Chamberlain, 26 November 1937, NC18/1/1030; Chamberlain, 21 February 1939, *Hansard Parliamentary Debates*, HC, 5th series, vol. 344, c. 228; minute by R.M. Makins, Second Secretary, 26 May 1938, FO371/22510, W6794/3/98.
72 Chamberlain to Hilda Chamberlain, 13 March 1938; Chamberlain to Hilda Chamberlain, 28 May 1939, NC18/1/1041/1101.
73 Chamberlain to Hilda Chamberlain, 4 April 1936, NC18/1/955.
74 A.J.P. Taylor, *English History 1914–1945*, Oxford, Oxford University Press, 1965, p. 379.
75 J.E. Davies, *Mission to Moscow*, London, Gollancz, 1942, p. 190.
76 Chamberlain, 7 March 1938, *Hansard Parliamentary Debates*, HC, 5th series, vol. 332, c. 1565; author's interview with Lord Butler, April 1980.
77 Memorandum by Halifax, 16 January 1939, FO371/24016, W1074/164/98; Cecil, op. cit., pp. 321–8; R. Henig (ed.) *The League of Nations*, Edinburgh, Oliver & Boyd, 1973, pp. 161–4; W.J. Hudson, *Australia and the League of Nations*, Sydney, Sydney University Press, 1980, pp. 177–80.
78 Chamberlain to Ida Chamberlain, 26 February 1939; Chamberlain to Ida Chamberlain, 26 March 1939; Chamberlain to Hilda Chamberlain, 28 May 1939, NC18/1/1087/1091/1101.
79 Chamberlain to Ida Chamberlain, 26 February 1939, NC18/1/1087;

Chamberlain, 21 February 1939, *Hansard Parliamentary Debates*, HC, 5th series, vol. 344, c. 228.
80 Chamberlain to Ida Chamberlain, 10 September 1939; Chamberlain to Hilda Chamberlain, 25 June 1938, NC18/1/1116/1057; Watt, *How War Came*, pp. 78–9.
81 Birn, op. cit., pp. 227–9; F.H. Hinsley, *Power and the Pursuit of Peace*, Cambridge, Cambridge University Press, 1963, pp. 311–20; Northedge, op. cit., pp. 278–92; Henig, op. cit., pp. 170–8; Parker, *Chamberlain and Appeasement*, pp. 307–12.
82 D. Dilks, 'Baldwin and Chamberlain', in Lord Butler (ed.) *The Conservatives: A History from their Origins to 1965*, London, Allen & Unwin, 1977, pp. 357–8, 368, 381. See also J.P. Dunbabin, 'The League of Nations' place in the international system', *History*, vol. 78, 1993, pp. 440–2.
83 *Headway*, February 1939, p. 3.

8 The atomic bomb and the Korean War, 1950–53

Callum MacDonald

Korea was the first limited war. The United States confined her response to the Korean peninsula and did not employ atomic bombs, even after the Chinese had intervened in November 1950. At the time, however, these restrictions seemed neither obvious nor inevitable. As General Matthew Ridgway, then Deputy Chief of Staff for Operations at the Pentagon, later recalled, before the North Korean attack the concept of limited warfare had 'never entered our counsels'.[1] As a result there were those, both civilian and military, who wanted to respond by a pre-emptive strike against the Soviet Union.[2] Others expected the United States to seek a decisive outcome in Korea by using the atomic bomb even at the risk of initiating World War Three. On 28 June 1950, General Dwight D. Eisenhower, who had recently retired as Chief of Staff of the US army, visited the Pentagon where he urged his former subordinates 'in most vigorous language and with great emphasis' to remove all restrictions on military action north of the 38th parallel and consider the use of one or two atomic bombs if suitable targets could be found.[3] Although the United States adopted neither course in the next three years of fighting, atomic weapons played a key role in the diplomacy of the conflict and the circumstances in which they might actually be employed were also kept under continuous review. As recent research has revealed, in this respect there was no dramatic firebreak between the Truman and Eisenhower administrations. Indeed it was under Harry S. Truman and not his successor that the United States came closest to the atomic brink.

NSC-68 AND LIMITED WAR

In September 1949 the US atomic monopoly was broken when the Soviet Union successfully tested her first bomb. The following month the communists triumphed in the Chinese civil war. These events raised doubts about the credibility of American power and led the Truman administration to embark on the fundamental re-examination of containment strategy known as NSC-68. This document assumed that by 1954 the Soviet Union would have stockpiled sufficient bombs to launch an atomic Pearl Harbor against the United States, crippling the American industrial base while the Red Army overran western Europe. It might not even be necessary for the Soviet dictator, Joseph Stalin, to take such dramatic action for as the balance of power started to tip in favour of the Soviets, western Europe might seek refuge in neutrality, cutting its ties with Washington and gradually drifting out of the American orbit. According to the Policy Planning Staff at the State Department, the Kremlin would attempt to accelerate this process by engineering a series of confrontations around the periphery of the Soviet bloc. In this respect the Truman administration was expecting a crisis somewhere in 1950, although nobody foresaw that it would occur in Korea.

In meeting the Soviet threat, NCS-68 ruled out a preventive war. Instead, American planners sought to build a position of overwhelming military strength which would not only deter but also roll back communist expansion without resort to global conflict. This meant the mobilisation of US industrial resources behind a massive rearmament drive both atomic and conventional. It also meant greater efforts by the NATO allies who were to be integrated into a militarised western bloc by US financial aid for their own rearmament programmes.[4] At the same time plans were pushed ahead for the development of an American super or hydrogen bomb, designed to forestall the Soviets at a new level of military technology.[5] Although Truman received NSC-68 in April 1950, he had taken no steps to implement its recommendations when the Korean War broke out. The programme was hugely expensive and was likely to meet opposition from an economy-minded Congress which would have to approve the large sums involved. In this situation the administration could only wait for a crisis which would illustrate the nature of the Soviet threat and provide the means of selling NSC-68 to the American people and the NATO allies. The Korean War fitted the bill. As Secretary of State Dean Acheson later remarked, Korea 'came along and saved us'.[6] With American troops committed to combat for the first time since 1945, Congress had little option but to approve a vast rearmament programme, and in September 1950 the administration adopted NSC-68 as a statement of national policy.[7]

Rearmament, however, was a long-term proposition and it would be 1952 before NSC-68 really hit its stride. As a review of the programme remarked in January 1951, 'from a military point of view, time is on our side.... The critical period, in terms of relative military strength, is... the next two or three years. If war comes during this period, though we would probably not lose it, we would have a difficult time winning it'.[8] Despite its existing atomic superiority, therefore, the United States would have to pass through a period of strategic uncertainty when the Soviets might be tempted to launch a pre-emptive strike, crippling the United States before the balance of power shifted decisively against the communist bloc.[9] According to a paper by the State Department Policy Planning Staff:

> one of the dangers in the current situation is that the Soviet rulers might decide – believing war and atomic bombardment to be an unavoidable phase of the struggle for power – to 'eat' whatever damage we can inflict [and] to push us back to the Western Hemisphere.... We believe that there are conceivable circumstances under which, from the Kremlin's point of view, this might appear to be a rational course of action.[10]

On the eve of the Korean War it was assumed that the Soviets had the capacity to overrun western Europe, with the possible exception of the Iberian peninsula, penetrate the Middle East and launch limited atomic attacks on the United States.[11] As the commander of the US Air Force, General Hoyt Vandenberg complained, American defences were so weak that 'any number of Soviet bombers could cross our borders and fly to most of the targets in the United States without a shot being fired at them'.[12] Strategic Air Command (SAC) bases in Britain, vital for an air atomic offensive against the Soviet Union, were vulnerable and it was doubtful whether SAC had sufficient bombs and aircraft to fulfil its offensive role in the US global war plan.[13] Washington had thus to seek a delicate balance, repelling the North Korean attack without provoking a conflict with the Soviet Union for which the United States was unprepared.

The inhibitions about provoking the Soviet Union increased as it became clear that Korea was more than a simple UN police action. The United States went to war in June 1950 confident of her ability to speedily defeat the North Koreans with the forces available in the Far East. Instead she found herself pitted against a skilled and determined enemy who inflicted a series of humiliating defeats on the US army in the first two months of the fighting, forcing the Americans to retreat into a narrow perimeter around Pusan.[14] The

The atomic bomb and the Korean War 177

Truman administration was forced to commit more and more resources to a war it could not afford to lose, stripping the strategic reserve and raising questions about the ability of the United States to fulfil her global war plan.[15] Even SAC found itself pressed into emergency service, sending two medium bomb groups to Japan in support of General Douglas MacArthur's beleaguered forces. Although these aircraft were not capable of carrying atomic weapons, the head of SAC, General Curtis LeMay, fretted at the loss of squadrons which were scheduled for conversion to an atomic role. He feared the precedent created and emphasised the dangers in shaving too much off the club which the United States required to deal with a more important enemy than North Korea.[16]

From the beginning therefore, Truman tried to avoid taking risks with the Soviets. In the opening days of the crisis, he withheld permission for bombing raids beyond the 38th parallel until the Soviet attitude became clear. Only when the Soviets argued on 29 June that the Korean crisis was a civil war in which the great powers should not interfere and failed to veto action by the United Nations Security Council did Truman give the head of the Far Eastern Command (FEC), General Douglas MacArthur, authority to carry the air war into the north. As the President emphasised, he was reluctant to start anything with the Soviet Union.[17] Truman's caution was shared by the British, who played a key role in US global war plans. The British Chiefs of Staff left the Attlee government in no doubt about the vulnerability of the United Kingdom in the event of war with the Soviet Union and US bomber bases in East Anglia were natural targets for a Soviet pre-emptive attack.[18] The British, therefore, emphasised the importance of avoiding a confrontation with Moscow. Faced with a draft of Truman's first public speech about Korea on 26 June, Clement Attlee suggested that he drop the phrase blaming the crisis on 'centrally directed communist imperialism', as too inflammatory.[19] Thus while nobody doubted that Stalin was behind the North Korean action, nobody wanted to say so. The risk of touching off a global war was too great.

Although Truman sometimes fantasised in the privacy of his diary about an atomic ultimatum to Moscow, such an option was never seriously considered and the advocates of preventive war received no encouragement from the White House.[20] On 25 August 1950 the Secretary of the Navy, Francis Matthews, made a speech in Boston calling for Americans to become 'aggressors for peace'. According to the *New York Times*, this was a trial balloon reflecting the opinions of his boss at the Defense Department, Louis Johnson, who had long been out of sympathy with the administration he served.[21] Although Matthews remained in office until the following year, Johnson was removed on 12 September 1950 under circumstances that remain unclear, although his willingness to risk a confrontation with Moscow by bombing North Korean targets close to the port of Vladivostock was certainly involved.[22] Simultaneously, Truman acted against the head of the Air War College, General Orville Anderson, who had publicly advocated preventive war. In a belligerent speech expressing the mood of many senior SAC officers, Anderson claimed that 'he could break up Russia's five A-Bomb nests in a week. And when I went up to Christ – I think I could explain to him that I had saved civilization'.[23] Anderson found himself compulsorily retired. According to Paul Nitze, head of the State Department Policy Planning Staff, the advocates of preventive war simply failed to grasp the real nature of the strategic balance.[24] In fact the administration reacted to the Korean crisis by accelerating bomb production and dispersing its nuclear stockpile to minimise the effects of a Soviet surprise attack on weapon stores and factories.[25] What kept the fighting in check during the critical first year was thus 'not an abstract commitment to the philosophy of limited war, but rather a sense of America's current military weakness'.[26]

ATOMIC WEAPONS AND LIMITED WAR: JUNE 1950 TO OCTOBER 1951

Despite these inhibitions, atomic weapons played an important role in US policy, for the Truman administration believed that its 'clear but qualified nuclear superiority over the Soviet Union ... ought, somehow, to be usable'.[27] This assumption was reinforced by the supposed lessons of the Berlin Blockade of 1948–49 when Truman had sent ninety SAC B-29s to Britain as a symbol of American support for European security. Although the bombers had not in fact been configured to carry atomic weapons, the deployment was believed to have deterred Stalin and exercised a vital influence on the peaceful outcome of the Berlin crisis.[28] In the summer of 1950 Truman again resorted to atomic diplomacy as a means of influencing Stalin. Since the Americans wrongly supposed that responsibility for the North Korean attack lay with Moscow rather than Pyongyang, the crisis was believed to reflect a new Soviet readiness to risk global war.[29] As US forces were sucked further into Korea, Truman looked for some way to 'let the world know we mean business' and deter the Soviet Union from exploiting the situation.[30]

On 11 July 1950, 'SAC Commander Curtis LeMay was ordered to repeat... the Berlin Blockade B-29 feint of 1948' by despatching two medium bomber groups with fighter escorts to US bases in East Anglia. The aircraft carried 'Russian target materials' and the non-nuclear components of atomic bombs.[31] The fissionable cores remained in the custody of the Atomic Energy Commission and could not be legally released without a presidential order which Truman never issued. Although the British insisted that the move should be described as a routine deployment, there was no doubt about its real purpose. The intention was 'partly to position a means of atomic retaliation if Russia suddenly attacked in Europe, but was equally meant to send a signal of deterrence to the Soviet Union'.[32] The deployment was reinforced when Truman issued a veiled public warning that further acts of aggression 'might well strain to the breaking point the fabric of world peace'.[33]

From the first days of the fighting it was assumed in Washington that if the Russians intervened in Korea, the war would become both atomic and global. At talks in Washington on the world situation in mid-July, the Americans informed the British that large-scale Soviet intervention 'would raise the immediate question of general war'. The United States 'had no intention of fighting a major war in Korea. Should war occur, it was their intention to fight in accordance with our agreed over-all strategy'.[34] To allow US forces on the peninsula to disengage and defend Japan, their assigned role under the global war plan, atomic weapons would have to be employed to retard Soviet advances and destroy important concentrations of air power. As early as 25 June 1950, at a conference with his leading advisers, Truman raised the question of Soviet airfields in the Far East. According to the Air Force Chief of Staff, General Hoyt Vandenberg, it might take some time to eliminate these bases unless atomic weapons were employed. In response the President confirmed that the 'Air Force should prepare plans to wipe out all Soviet air bases in the Far East. This was not an order for action but an order to make plans'.[35] These contingency plans involved atomic attacks on China as well as the Soviet Union for there were Soviet jets on the Liadong and Shandong peninsulas and around Shanghai. This raised interesting questions about 'the legality and propriety' of air strikes against Chinese bases if the United States found itself 'at war with the USSR for hours or days' before there was 'an official indication of the intentions of Communist China'.[36] Although it was quickly agreed that atomic weapons would be employed in the event of Soviet intervention, their value in the existing military situation was less certain.

The possibility of employing the 'winning weapon' against the North Koreans had been raised by General Eisenhower the day after the war began. It was soon taken up again as American troops fell back down the peninsula and conventional bombing seemed incapable of turning the tide of battle. On 9 July 1950, with Korean commitments already threatening American strategic reserves, the Joint Chiefs of Staff (JCS) considered 'whether or not A-bombs should be made available to MacArthur' but decided against such a move for the present.[37] The question was also under discussion at the State Department. On 15 July, as the North Koreans broke through the Kum River line, a study by the Policy Planning Staff (PPS) concluded that the bomb should be used in the event of overt Soviet and Chinese intervention or to restore the situation in Korea and assure a decisive military success, provided such employment did not 'appreciably deplete the nuclear arsenal'. The following day Paul Nitze, head of the PPS, who had served on the postwar Strategic Bombing Survey, discussed this paper with General Kenneth Nichols, described by Nitze as 'possibly the principal Pentagon military authority on the bomb'. Nichols argued that the weapon should be used even if China and the Soviet Union did not intervene 'to prevent our being pushed off the peninsula'.[38] Similar discussions were taking place at FEC headquarters in Tokyo. On 13 July General Charles Bolte, head of the Army Operations Division, suggested that the Army Chief of Staff, General J. Lawton Collins, who was visiting Tokyo, ask MacArthur for his opinion on the tactical employment of the bomb.[39] Collins apparently declined but when his companion, General Vandenberg, raised the issue of dealing with possible Chinese or Soviet intervention, MacArthur emphasised the importance of atomic weapons. According to MacArthur, Korea was a strategic cul-de-sac : 'I would cut them off in North Korea.... The only passages leading from Manchuria and Vladivostock have many tunnels and bridges. I see here a unique use for the atomic bomb – to strike a blocking blow – which would require a six month repair job. Sweeten up my B-29 force'.[40]

In a telecon conference with Washington on 24 July, MacArthur himself asked if the JCS had given any consideration to the use of the bomb. He went on to emphasise its utility even if China and the Soviet Union did not intervene. According to MacArthur, atomic attacks on enemy cities and lines of communication would reduce the flow of supplies and reinforcements from China and the Soviet

The atomic bomb and the Korean War 181

Union and destroy the capacity of the North Koreans to wage war. His suggested target list included Pyongyang, Wonsan, Hungnam and every other major city in North Korea. MacArthur's plan would have left much of North Korea a radioactive wasteland. The JCS, however, evaded the issue, preferring not to answer his enquiry 'at this time'.[41] There were technical and political problems about using the bomb in the way MacArthur envisaged. At the time the United States had no tactical atomic weapons, the first tests not taking place until January 1951. The American stockpile contained only airburst bombs, designed for a strategic bombing offensive against Russian industry but less effective against tactical targets such as railway tunnels and bridges. The destruction of North Korean cities was not considered decisive because, as MacArthur himself recognised, the real sources of enemy supply were in Manchuria. According to a study by the Army Operations Division, while the dropping of ten to twenty bombs would not jeopardise the global war plan, the current military situation seemed to offer no targets warranting their use, a situation that might change if China intervened. The study emphasised the dangers of employing atomic weapons without a decisive result, since this would undermine their deterrent effect on the Russians. It concluded that the bomb should be used in Korea only in the event of a military disaster such as a 'Dunkirk style' evacuation but recommended that the preparations be made since quick decisions would be necessary in an emergency.[42]

By the end of July 1950, the military situation in Korea had deteriorated to the point where such an emergency seemed imminent. As General Vandenberg remarked, 'things were in a hell of a mess'.[43] On 20 July the North Koreans took Taejon, shattering the US 24th Infantry Division. Nine days later the troops of the US Eighth Army retreated behind the Naktong River into a narrow perimeter around Pusan, the last defensible position on the peninsula, where they were ordered 'to stand or die'. At the same time there were growing fears of Chinese communist action, not in Korea but against Taiwan, where the USA was protecting the discredited Guomindang regime of Jiang Jieshi (Chiang Kai-shek).[44] Vandenburg had returned from Tokyo to Washington determined to fulfil MacArthur's request for more B-29s. Two SAC bomb groups were alerted for transfer to the Far East where they were to provide MacArthur with the nucleus of a Bomber Command, headed by General Emmett O'Donnell, an experienced officer who had led the first major air raid on Tokyo in November 1944. The aircraft were not configured for atomic weapons and were intended to mount a conventional bombing campaign against North Korean cities.[45] As the crisis deepened, however, it seemed that more was required and Vandenberg proposed adding ten atomic bombers. The JCS agreed on 29 July and the Defense Secretary, Louis Johnson, gained the approval of the President next day. As with the earlier deployment to Britain, the B-29s carried atomic weapons minus the nuclear cores. Unlike the conventional bombers they accompanied, these aircraft were not placed under MacArthur's operational control.[46]

Truman's new resort to atomic diplomacy had two purposes. The first was to position a SAC unit in the Far East in case the bomb was needed to prevent the destruction of the US Eighth Army, which would have left Japan defenceless and vulnerable to Soviet pressure. The second was to deter China from action either against Washington's client on Taiwan or in Korea, where Chinese intervention at that stage would certainly have meant a humiliating American defeat. It was this second aspect that appealed to Dean Acheson, who seems to have leaked the decision to the press. On 1 August 1950 the *New York Times* published 'news of the impending movement of B-29s across the Pacific for all, including the enemy, to read'.[47] This psychological warfare campaign was given an unexpected boost on 3 August 1950 when one of the aircraft crashed in California, killing the group commander and causing a huge explosion which encouraged press speculation that it had been carrying atomic weapons.[48] The crisis which had provoked the despatch of the bombers to Guam, however, soon passed. MacArthur's amphibious landing at Inchon on 12 September 1950 transformed the military situation. Seoul was recaptured and on 9 October American troops crossed the 38th parallel into North Korea in pursuit of total victory. The ten atomic bombers were no longer required and returned to the United States. It was expected that the conventional B-29s would quickly follow. The crossing of the parallel, however, proved to be not the end of one war but the beginning of another, the war with China, which raised the issue of atomic weapons in a more acute form.

THE IMPACT OF CHINESE INTERVENTION: NOVEMBER 1950 TO JUNE 1951

The Chinese People's Volunteers first appeared on the battlefield in late October, halting the American advance at the Chongchon river before withdrawing into the Korean mountains. On 4 November

1950, Nitze discussed the employment of the bomb to counter further Chinese intervention with General Herbert Loper, Assistant for Atomic Energy on the Army Logistics Staff. Nitze reported that atomic weapons would be useful against large Chinese troop concentrations but that such targets 'would probably not come about normally'. The bomb was thus 'unlikely to prove militarily decisive' and risked provoking the Soviet Union. It could also be used outside Korea against Manchurian cities like Dandong, but this would 'almost certainly bring the Soviet Union into the war'. In either case atomic attacks would alarm the allies and alienate the people of Asia.[49] Contingency planning was also initiated at the highest levels of the Pentagon. On 20 November General Collins warned the Joint Chiefs that they could be asked at short notice for their recommendations on the use of the bomb which might be the 'decisive factor' in allowing MacArthur's command to hold its position or advance to the Manchurian border.[50] The Joint Strategic Survey Committee (JSSC) was ordered to consider the use of the bomb in the event of Soviet intervention to cover the evacuation of MacArthur's troops. It was also asked to investigate the employment of conventional and atomic bombs against China with or without a previous ultimatum.[51] The JSSC reached the same conclusions as previous investigations. The bomb should be used in Korea only to prevent the destruction of MacArthur's command. In the event of Soviet intervention, it might be the sole means of averting such a disaster.[52]

At the end of November 1950 the military situation deteriorated rapidly with the open involvement of China and the humiliating retreat of MacArthur's forces from North Korea. As the extent of the reverse became clear, Truman made a statement at a press conference on 30 November which raised fears of atomic war and brought the British Prime Minister, Attlee, to Washington. In reply to questions from journalists, the President confirmed that the United States was considering every weapon, including the bomb, to deal with the threatening developments in Korea. He went on to remark that the military would decide on the objectives and that the field commander would have 'charge of the use of these weapons'.[53] This implied that a final judgement might be left up to MacArthur. Truman's statement was legally inaccurate since under the Atomic Energy Act only the President could authorise use of the bomb. It is often argued that on this occasion Truman simply blundered. Recent research, however, suggests that his words were intentional. It was assumed in Washington that China had challenged the United States at Soviet instigation and that Chinese intervention was thus a symbol of Stalin's readiness to take increased risks. Truman may have hoped to deter Moscow from exploiting the Korean crisis or encouraging Beijing to deepen its involvement by committing the Chinese air force, as yet unengaged, to the fighting.[54] A committee of the National Security Council was already working out procedures for the transfer of atomic cores to the military and the day Truman spoke SAC was ordered to prepare 'to despatch without delay medium bomb groups to the Far East' including aircraft with 'atomic capabilities'.[55] As in August 1950, this deployment would have acted as an insurance against the destruction of MacArthur's command and a symbol to the enemy of American resolve.

Truman's words triggered the alarm of the allies and showed that atomic diplomacy could be a double-edged weapon. The President assured Attlee of his hope that the bomb would never have to be used although he refused to concede the British any right to consultation about its employment.[56] General LeMay still expected his bomb groups to be despatched across the Pacific at any moment to deal with 'those well-padded boys moving down out of Manchuria', but despite the alert, the final order never came.[57] MacArthur's forces in north-east Korea were able to fight their way out of encirclement while those in the west escaped by a precipitate retreat. Although the situation remained serious, it was clear by mid-December that an immediate débâcle had been avoided. After visiting the battlefield on 8 December, General Collins commented that he had seen nothing which required the use of atomic bombs.[58] A different outcome might have forced Truman to take the kind of dramatic action implied at his press conference on 30 November. With only the 82nd Airborne Division remaining in the strategic reserve and Japan protected by little except unarmed police with nightsticks, the bomb would have been the only weapon he had left. As Bernstein remarks, if 'thousands of US troops had been confronted with annihilation or surrender, as almost happened to the marine division in December, he would have felt sorely tempted to use the weapons. For him, as for many US leaders, the major constraints were the likelihood of Soviet nuclear retaliation and the defection of NATO allies'.[59] It remained clear that Washington would retaliate against China if American forces were expelled from Korea, a danger which persisted until the spring of 1951, but short of such a catastrophe the war would remain limited.[60] As Truman emphasised in a personal letter to MacArthur on 13 January 1951:

we must act with great prudence so far as extending the area of hostilities is concerned.... In reaching a final decision about Korea, I shall have to give constant thought to the main threat from the Soviet Union and to the need for a rapid expansion of our armed forces to meet this great danger.[61]

Truman's words confirm that fear of the Soviet response was a major factor inhibiting direct US action against China by either conventional or atomic means while rearmament was still in its early stages. At a high-level meeting on 1 December, General Bradley expressed reluctance to attack Manchuria even if the Chinese air force became heavily involved in Korea. He was strongly supported by General Collins, who pointed out that retaliation might 'bring in Soviet air and even submarines. The only chance then left to save us is the use or threat of use of the A-bomb. We should therefore hold back from bombing China even if this means that our ground forces must take some punishment from the air'.[62] There was some dissent from this line. Rather than risk the destruction of MacArthur's command, which would have left Japan defenceless, Vandenberg talked on 19 December about withdrawal and a limited air and naval war with China, even at the risk of provoking the Soviets. He implied that it might be better to fight the Soviet Union in 1951, while its atomic bomb stocks were low, than to wait until later. This came close to advocating preventive war.[63] But an attack on the Soviet Union would have involved the United States in a war it could not win decisively while involvement with China would simply expend resources against what Acheson called the communist 'second team'.[64] As Vandenberg himself later admitted, the US Air Force was operating on a 'shoestring'. It could lay waste to Manchuria but only at the expense of attrition which would undermine its effectiveness against the main enemy, the Soviet Union.[65] Vandenberg was probably referring to conventional bombing but the same inhibitions applied to atomic warfare. As Nitze later emphasised, the American stockpile was 'not large enough to mount an effective attack against China and still have sufficient weapons to deal with the Soviets if they, too, decided to intervene'.[66] Washington would thus have to exercise restraint in relations with both Moscow and Beijing until a later stage.

This approach was not welcomed in Tokyo where MacArthur gave the war he was actually fighting a higher priority than preparations for a hypothetical future war against the Soviet Union. By his own account, faced with Chinese intervention, he sought new means to isolate the battlefield and cut off the enemy from Manchurian supply bases. This time he was thinking of delivering his 'blocking blow' not with atomic bombs but by sowing a radioactive cobalt belt across Korea.[67] The United States had been experimenting with this type of warfare since 1948 and field tests were conducted in February 1950 using a modified B-29. The ultimate aim was that each aircraft should contaminate twelve square miles.[68] It is unclear if MacArthur ever submitted his scheme to the Pentagon although some accounts maintain that it was considered in Washington but dismissed as impractical.[69] MacArthur's thinking about atomic weapons during the crisis is equally obscure. He certainly wanted to expand the war into Manchuria, informing Collins on 8 December that the lifting of restrictions on retaliation against China, including employment of the atomic bomb, offered the best means of holding the position in Korea.[70] According to British accounts he demanded 'commander's discretion to use atomic weapons'.[71] London viewed this prospect with horror. The British Chiefs of Staff warned that such a move would 'inevitably bring the Soviet Air Force into the war. The atom bomb is our ultimate weapon and we must keep it in reserve as a deterrent or for use in the event of the Russians launching a third world war'.[72] MacArthur did not explain how he intended to use the bomb although after the war he claimed that up to fifty should have been employed against military targets in Manchuria, particularly airfields.[73]

At the time MacArthur was more specific about his atomic requirements in the event of Soviet intervention. On 20 December the JCS informed MacArthur that they had allocated twenty bombs 'for employment ... in retardation of Soviet advances in the Far East-Pacific' under the emergency war plan and asked him to recommend suitable targets.[74] His reply listed the major cities of North China and the Soviet Far East including Beijing, Vladivostock and Khaborovsk. In addition, he asked for eight extra bombs for use against targets of opportunity such as massed invasion forces and concentrations of enemy air power.[75] Despite the allocation of twenty bombs in support of FEC, MacArthur was not given his own D-Day atomic capability. Operational control of the SAC units allocated to retardation was to remain with Washington, perhaps reflecting growing doubts amongst the Joint Chiefs about MacArthur's judgement. This decision rankled in Tokyo where MacArthur made contingency plans, codenamed CAVITY, to use O'Donnell's B-29s for night incendiary raids on Mukden and Vladivostock, utilising their experience against North Korean cities such as Sinuiju, which was destroyed in November 1950 in a bombing campaign designed to isolate the Korean battlefield.[76]

Although the JCS atomic retardation planning reflected the administration's belief that the Soviets were prepared to take greater risks in pursuit of world power, there was no encouragement for advocates of preventive war. The most outspoken was Stuart Symington, head of the National Security Resources Board, a former Secretary of the Air Force. In early January 1951 Symington called for a sustained attack on China coupled with an ultimatum to the Soviet Union warning that further aggression 'would result in the atomic bombardment of Soviet Russia itself'.[77] In a memorandum to the President, Symington criticised the fallacy of attempting to localise aggression 'while at the same time carefully avoiding the basic issue with the actual instigator of current world unrest, Soviet Russia'. This approach found no sympathy in the White House. At the end of Symington's piece Truman noted : 'My dear Stu, this is [as] big a lot of Top Secret malarkey as I've ever read. Your time is wasted on bunk such as this HST'.[78] Rejecting preventive war, the administration preferred to accelerate its rearmament programme, declaring a state of national emergency on 15 December 1950 and bringing forward the date of maximum readiness for global war from 1954 to 1952.[79] As part of this process Truman authorised atomic testing at the Las Vegas Bombing and Gunnery Range as well as in the Pacific in order to accelerate bomb research and production.[80]

Although the Chinese failed to drive the Americans out of Korea and had been pushed back over the 38th parallel by the beginning of April 1951, the most serious crisis of the war was only just beginning. It had always been assumed that Soviet involvement or anything that risked the destruction of MacArthur's command, leaving Japan defenceless, would provoke an American atomic response. At the beginning of April it seemed that the enemy was planning a dramatic escalation of the fighting. US intelligence reported preparations for a new Chinese ground offensive. At the same time a massive build-up of air power was detected in Manchuria and northeast China, including 200 Soviet bombers. Russian submarines were supposed to be massing at Vladivostock and around southern Sakhalin. The JCS feared that the Chinese intended to make a final attempt to win the war with the support of Soviet air power.[81] In a message to the Air Force commander in Tokyo, General Stratemeyer, Vandenberg speculated about a Chinese ground offensive coupled with 'a Pearl Harbor type' attack on US air bases. According to Vandenberg, such a combined operation 'might cause the loss of Korea and even possibly set up the Japanese Islands for invasion. Our ground troops, unaccustomed to hostile air attack might well be unable to become acclimated before a disaster could occur'.[82]

Faced with this danger the JCS wanted authority to strike back at Chinese airfields in the event of large-scale air attacks on MacArthur's troops and prepare for global war. It was believed that Soviet fighters would defend Manchuria even if the Soviets did not openly intervene in Korea so such counter-air-strikes were likely to escalate quickly into a wider conflict.[83] Moreover atomic planning had already revealed the difficulty of discriminating between Soviet and Chinese air bases in areas such as Liadong and Shandong. On 5 April 1951 Bradley requested the transfer of nine complete atomic weapons from the Atomic Energy Commission to the military.[84] The precise number may have been based on an earlier estimate by Stratemeyer, who had submitted a list in November 1950 'of seven Chinese and two Soviet cities considered suitable for nuclear attack in case of full-scale war with China and the Soviet Union'. These included Dandong, Shanghai, Vladivostock and Khabarovsk.[85]

On 6 April Truman approved the JCS request, ordering the head of the Atomic Energy Commission, Gordon Dean, to release the cores. According to Truman, the evidence indicated that 'not only are the Reds and the Russians ready to push us out of Korea, but may attempt to take the Japanese Islands'. He stated that 'in no event would the bombs be used in Northern Korea where he appreciated... that they would be completely ineffective and psychological 'duds' if used in Northern Korean terrain'.[86] Although Dean was concerned that the implications of the transfer had not been fully considered, he had no option but to comply. The following day the 99th Medium Bomb Wing was ordered to load the weapons, Mark IV atomic bombs, and proceed to Guam, en route for Okinawa where special bomb loading pits had already been prepared at Kadena Air Base.[87] It was intended to use these weapons against 'retardation targets', allowing American forces time to evacuate to Japan.[88]

There was a major problem, however, about sending this task force to the Far East as long as MacArthur was in command there. The general had made no secret of his opposition to limited war and had recently sabotaged the first American moves towards a ceasefire in Korea. The administration hesitated to give the field commander authority to retaliate against Manchurian airfields with conventional bombing or place SAC aircraft under his operational control for fear that he would act precipitately, plunging the United States into a global war for which it was unprepared. As Bradley noted, he might make a 'premature decision' in carrying out contingency plans.[89] The very presence of atomic bombers in the area, even if still under the command of Washington, might encourage his belligerent impulses. MacArthur was already pressing for his own 'D-day atomic capability'. On 7 February 1951, he asked for authorisation to employ SAC squadrons against Soviet air bases in the early stages of global war. He reiterated this request on 10 March.[90] With the world apparently on the brink, Truman could no longer tolerate his repeated insubordination. Unwilling to risk preemptive action by MacArthur, the President removed him on 11 April. As Bradley argued, 'if nuclear operations were pending Washington must have complete confidence in its field commander'.[91] MacArthur's successor, General Matthew Ridgway, was later given contingent authority to retaliate against Manchuria and the D-day atomic capability denied his predecessor.[92]

The despatch of atomic weapons across the Pacific was not accompanied by a presidential statement or even the kind of inspired press leak which had accompanied the earlier deployment of SAC bombers to Guam. Instead the administration opted for an indirect approach, perhaps to reassure its allies who could be relied upon to stampede at any direct mention of atomic war. In a speech justifying his removal of MacArthur, Truman emphasised his commitment to limited war but warned the enemy about the consequences of escalation. The United States and her allies did not want global conflict but their patience was not inexhaustible. At the MacArthur Hearings, administration witnesses took a similar line, stressing the advantages of a ceasefire but expressing their readiness to retaliate if the communists widened the conflict. In secret contacts with shadowy Chinese emissaries, Charles Burton Marshall of the PPS gave this message a further twist, hinting that China would face atomic destruction if Beijing chose the wrong side in a global war caused by Soviet expansion.[93] These warnings were pressed home by the despatch of more bombers, although without complete bombs, to join the 99th Bomb Wing on Guam and the arrival of 'a SAC command and control team to Tokyo ... to coordinate operational plans for possible nuclear strikes'.[94] On 11 May the Air Force authorised high-level reconnaissance of the Mukden-Changchun-Harbin area of Manchuria, 'a departure from previous practice that the enemy might interpret as a prelude to expanded fighting'.[95]

These events took place against the background of two massive

Chinese offensives in April and May 1951 and were intended to deter either Chinese or Soviet aircraft from intervening in the fighting. Since the air threat never developed and there was no attempt to interfere with the sea lanes from Japan, the B-29s were not called into action.[96] Although despatched with such haste on 7 April, they never even reached Okinawa but stopped at Guam, where they passed the next few weeks on training flights. By early June MacArthur's successor, General Matthew Ridgway, had defeated both Chinese offensives without widening the war and was again advancing across the 38th parallel. In this new atmosphere the 99th Bomb Wing was stood down and returned to the United States.[97] Shortly afterwards truce negotiations began. Its sudden flight across the Pacific in April 1951 was the only time during the war that complete atomic weapons were deployed to the Far East and revealed how seriously the Truman administration took the threat of Soviet intervention. Although the crisis passed and the war entered a new phase of negotiating while fighting, the bomb retained an important role in American policy. As during the first phase the employment of atomic weapons would be vital if the war spread. They could also play an important part in securing American objectives at the truce talks.

THE ATOMIC BOMB AND THE TRUCE NEGOTIATIONS: JUNE 1951 TO JULY 1953

Despite the armistice talks, contingency planning continued for retaliation against China in the event that negotiations failed or the enemy renewed the attempt to win the war. The role of atomic weapons in this strategy of escalation had to be decided. As early as July 1951 FEC headquarters had begun to study the possible tactical use of the bomb for both offensive and defensive purposes.[98] There was also the question of enforcing any truce agreement which finally emerged. In November 1951 Washington suggested that this could be achieved by threatening unspecified 'greater sanctions' against China if she renewed the war.[99] The proposed wording of the 'greater sanctions' statement contained an implied atomic threat, warning that 'future military aggression in Korea will result in a military reaction that would not necessarily be limited in geographic scope *or in the methods of warfare employed*'. This was eventually dropped, however, partly as a result of British objections, in favour of a blander statement that hostilities would 'in all probability' not be confined 'within the frontiers of Korea'.[100] In proposing the measure to the British in December 1951, Acheson returned to the precedent of the Berlin Blockade, implying fear of escalation had persuaded Moscow to cut its losses in Korea and propose armistice negotiations.[101] Although Acheson did not spell out the atomic implications, for fear of alarming London, General Matthew Ridgway in Tokyo was more blunt, arguing that without resort to atomic retaliation, greater sanctions would be nothing but a gigantic bluff. According to Ridgway, 'the retributive potentiality of UN military power against Red China would be noneffective unless the full results of precipitating World War 3 were to be accepted, and the use of atomic weapons authorized.'[102] Ridgway and his successor, Mark Clark, were particularly concerned about the effect of a surprise atomic attack on their supply bases and lines of communication which would render the Eighth Army helpless either to resist in Korea or to evacuate to Japan. Both pressed for the commitment of increased air atomic striking power to the Far East to counter this threat.[103]

It was against this background that atomic planning continued, encouraged by the advent of tactical weapons which were first tested successfully in the RANGER series of tests in January–February 1951.[104] The US Air Force embarked on a programme to make all its fighter bombers capable of carrying the new tactical bombs. In December 1952 a squadron of F-84Gs was withdrawn from Korea to Japan for training in the employment of these weapons, giving Clark the kind of atomic retaliatory capability he and his predecessors had long desired and shifting the burden of emergency counter-air strikes away from SAC for the first time.[105] The navy was also developing tactical atomic bombs for its attack squadrons. By 1953 at least one carrier in the Far East, the USS *Champlain*, had an atomic capability and there was also a special naval air squadron at Atsugi in Japan, although as with the air force, the fissionable cores were not deployed.[106] The army was developing a new 280 mm gun capable of firing an atomic shell, a programme which was given a high priority. The first prototype was completed in early 1952 and the Pentagon hoped for an early battlefield deployment.[107] The utility of these weapons in the Korean context was predicted by the Army Operations Division as early as July 1951. Reviewing the requests of MacArthur and Ridgway for increased atomic capability in the Far East, the report noted: 'In event of a stalemate in Korea in which the Communist forces pit manpower against our technological advantages, use of the atomic bomb to increase our efficiency of killing is desirable. In event of a general emergency including the defence of Japan, the application of the atomic bomb is essential'. It went on to complain, however, that there had been little planning for tactical use and recommended a practical study of the problems involved, including simulated strikes involving the dropping of dummy bombs packed with TNT.[108]

The JCS successfully pressed for field tests in Korea along these lines. In September/October 1951 a top secret operation, codenamed HUDSON HARBOR, investigated the employment of tactical atomic weapons in support of troops. The tests included the actual dropping of dummy bombs packed with conventional explosives on North Korean targets. According to the observation team which monitored HUDSON HARBOR, the results were disappointing. It was difficult to identify suitable targets and a system of bunker defences protected enemy troops from the effects of airburst weapons. Nevertheless, the final report recommended that as a matter of policy atomic weapons should be used in Korea to save the Eighth Army from disaster, in the event of general war or when 'developments, either military or political' forced their employment. It went on to recommend measures which addressed the technical problems revealed by HUDSON HARBOR and called for the early deployment of atomic artillery.[109] In fact the immediate significance of HUDSON HARBOR was more political than military. As Cumings notes, the operation was probably part of a wider psychological warfare plan involving 'overt exploitation in Korea by the Department of Defense and covert exploitation by the Central Intelligence Agency of the possible use of novel weapons'.[110] HUDSON HARBOR occurred in a period of tension when the communists had recessed the armistice talks at Kaesong and the United States was about to sign the Japanese peace treaty, a settlement driven through over Soviet opposition. In this respect it was intended to hold the ring in the Far East and coerce the enemy back to the conference table at Kaesong. The technical flaws in the operation, so evident to the US observer group, were less obvious to the North Koreans: 'No one knew this in Pyongyang, where leaders needed nerves of steel as their radar tracked B–29s simulating the attack patterns that had resulted in the devastation of Hiroshima and Nagasaki just five years earlier'.[111]

There were other hints at this time which may have been part of the same psychological warfare plan as HUDSON HARBOR. In August and September 1951 a number of officials and senior officers commented openly on the development of a new generation of tactical bombs. On 4 September, visiting San Francisco for the

Japanese peace treaty ceremony, Truman announced that the nation was constructing 'fantastic new weapons'. Around the same time the Secretary of the Army, Frank Pace, told reporters that the army would 'soon be equipped with tactical weapons' and Admiral Lynde D. McCormick, Commander of the US Atlantic Fleet, commented that all US carriers would eventually be equipped with 'baby A-bombs'.[112] The most dramatic remarks were contained in a speech by the head of the Atomic Energy Commission, Gordon Dean, who believed that tactical employment of the bomb was the key to victory in Korea. On 5 October 1951, in a Founder's Day address at the University of California Los Angeles, Dean claimed that recent technological advances had given the United States

> the capacity to meet a given situation with an atomic weapon tailored to meet that situation ... with each passing day, our design and production progress is steadily adding to the number of situations in which atomic weapons can be tactically employed against military targets ... we are now at the place where we should give serious consideration to the use of an atomic weapon, provided it can be used effectively from the military standpoint.[113]

Dean's address was given wide publicity which was reinforced when the BUSTER-JANGLE test series of late October and early November 1951 provoked a fresh outburst of speculation about the advent of 'baby bombs'.[114] Although the text had apparently not been cleared by the White House, Truman let Dean know that he was 'not worked up' about the speech.[115]

The Truman administration probably continued its attempts at atomic coercion until the very end. In September 1952 the State Department suggested that the Central Intelligence Agency (CIA) spread rumours about a possible widening of the war, including atomic attacks on China and North Korea, unless an armistice was rapidly concluded.[116] This whispering campaign would have exploited the escalation of conventional bombing in the spring of 1952, which included raids on the North Korean hydro-electric plants and other previously restricted targets such as Aoji near the Soviet border.[117] While there is no direct evidence that the CIA mounted a psychological warfare operation in September and October 1952, the US ambassador in New Delhi, Chester Bowles, certainly warned the Indians, who had good diplomatic links with Beijing, that the war would be expanded if an armistice was not secured.[118] Washington and Tokyo were also awash with rumours that certain elements at the Pentagon wanted escalation and total victory. These stories were picked up by the British who became alarmed that the Americans might do something dramatic, another example of the double-edged nature of atomic diplomacy.[119] There were indeed those who wanted to do more than bluff. On 23 September 1952, with truce talks stalled, the JCS asked Clark for his recommendations if negotiations failed. His reply requested authority to plan for the employment of atomic weapons against targets of opportunity and enemy air bases in Manchuria and North China. The JCS, however, deferred action until after the presidential elections.[120] If the Truman administration did mount 'a last ditch campaign to coerce the Chinese into agreeing to an armistice before the November elections', however, it failed to impress the enemy.[121] Although Washington went to the brink by unilaterally recessing the talks on 7 October 1952, China and North Korea did not yield on the outstanding issue, the repatriation of prisoners of war and in January 1953 the Korean impasse was inherited by the new Republican administration headed by Dwight D. Eisenhower.

EISENHOWER AND PEACE WITH HONOUR: JANUARY–JULY 1953

The breakthrough in the truce negotiations which followed the Republican election victory is often portrayed as a triumph for atomic brinkmanship of a type which the Truman administration hesitated to employ. The claim was first made by Eisenhower's Secretary of State, John Foster Dulles, who had a vested interest in denying that the armistice was the product of a compromise with the communists and was often repeated by later historians.[122] Eisenhower himself boasted to his aide, Sherman Adams, that peace with honour in Korea had been the result of atomic coercion: 'We told them we could not hold it to a limited war any longer if the communists welched on a treaty of truce. They didn't want a full-scale war or an atomic attack. That kept them under some control'.[123] The latest research, however, suggests that Republican rhetoric camouflaged a much more cautious approach. The new administration was certainly in a stronger position than its predecessor. When it took office the United States was moving into an era of atomic plenty as the NSC-68 programme began to produce results.[124] The hydrogen bomb decision had also come to fruition with the first successful test in October 1952. According to Trachtenberg, as the window of vulnerability changed to a window of opportunity in 1953, the United States became more willing to contemplate widening the

The atomic bomb and the Korean War 195

war, including the employment of atomic weapons on military targets in Manchuria.[125] While the changing nuclear balance may have had some influence on Moscow and Beijing, however, the Eisenhower administration was in practice notably circumspect about making overt threats. The atomic debate in the spring of 1953 took place against a background of breakthrough at the truce talks, following the death of Stalin in March 1953 and new Soviet moves towards peaceful coexistence. In this respect the atmosphere was quite different from the mood of crisis which had gripped the Truman administration during the first year of war and influenced its consideration of the atomic issue.[126]

Although Eisenhower often speculated on the tactical use of the bomb, which he considered no different from any other weapon, planning for its actual employment was neither urgent nor well integrated.[127] Bradley and Collins in particular had doubts about the effectiveness of tactical weapons in Korea itself against the deep bunker lines constructed by the Chinese although JCS planners believed that airburst weapons would knock out other types of target, most notably the jet concentrations on Manchurian airfields.[128] The National Security Council, however, did not approve military options which involved the use of atomic weapons against Manchuria until 20 May 1953. These plans would have taken a year to prepare since they involved building up conventional as well as atomic capacity in the Far East, yet Eisenhower failed to order the first steps. He simply commented that 'if circumstances arose which would force the United States to an expanded effort in Korea' the JCS plan was 'most likely to achieve the objective we sought'.[129] Shortly afterwards the United States presented her final proposals at Panmunjom and told Beijing and Moscow that she would widen the war if an armistice was not concluded. Despite Dulles's later claims, however, the American warnings represented 'an appeal for cooperation' rather than an unequivocal nuclear threat.[130] Moreover, Pandit Nehru, chosen by Dulles to inform China about the US position, later denied that he had passed anything on to Beijing.[131] Nor did Washington accompany words with action by moving SAC aircraft to the Far East or releasing fissionable cores, despite the later claims of Eisenhower's aide, Sherman Adams, that 'atomic missiles' had been sent to Okinawa in the spring of 1953.[132] Not until the very eve of the armistice in July did Eisenhower begin to hand over complete weapons to the military and this move was directly related to global war plans rather than to the demands of Korea. In fact the Korean war 'ended ... as it had begun, with not a single American nuclear weapon deployed within usable distance of the fighting'.[133]

As Dingman concludes, therefore, contrary to the traditional view, the Republicans 'did not go as far as their Democratic predecessors in using the movement of nuclear weapons to try to modify Chinese, Soviet or North Korean behavior ... the Eisenhower administration achieved an armistice in Korea without employing atomic arms for coercive diplomatic purposes'.[134] Foot suggests that Eisenhower and Dulles later exaggerated the role of nuclear threats in securing an armistice in order to justify their 'New Look' policy, which cut back on expensive military manpower in favour of an air/atomic strategy based on massive retaliation.[135] It was only after the armistice had been signed that the atomic threat was made less equivocal. The publication of the 'greater sanctions' statement in August 1953 was followed by operation BIG STICK, a flight by the 92nd SAC B–36 Heavy Bomb Wing to Japan.[136] At the same time the administration made it clear to its allies that a renewal of the fighting would involve the automatic use of nuclear weapons against China. As Eisenhower informed Churchill in December 1953, 'if war came or there was a serious breach of the armistice in Korea the people of the United States would never understand it if the weapon were not used'.[137] This soon grew into a strategy designed to exploit the new American strategic superiority and divide Beijing from Moscow by threatening China while moving towards detente with the Soviet Union.[138] The fact remains, however, that this strategy of brinkmanship towards Beijing, so obvious in the later crises over the offshore islands, did not precede the conclusion of a Korean armistice, an armistice which was actually reached by a process of mutual compromise, rather than a unilateral communist surrender to American atomic threats.[139]

The effectiveness of American atomic diplomacy is difficult to assess. The Soviets certainly pursued a cautious line throughout the war, failing to veto American resolutions at the UN in June 1950 and reneging on a promise of air support to China in October when the People's Volunteers entered the fighting. Apparently Stalin was prepared at that stage to see the Democratic Peoples' Republic of [North] Korea eliminated and suggested that Kim Il Sung establish an exile government in Manchuria.[140] When Soviet aircraft were finally deployed in Manchuria in November 1950, they were allowed to fly over North Korea only under strict guidelines designed to avoid a public confrontation with the United States.[141] The following year, with the Chinese offensives defeated and US forces again crossing the 38th parallel, it was Moscow which proposed a ceasefire amongst the belligerents and a return to the status quo. There is little doubt that a sense of strategic vulnerability influenced Soviet policy. According to Nikita Krushchev, Stalin feared a pre-emptive strike and avoided direct challenges to the United States: 'He knew that we were weaker than the United States. We only had a handful of nuclear weapons while America had a large arsenal of nuclear arms.... Stalin never did anything that might provoke a war with the United States. He knew his weakness'.[142] After Stalin's death in March 1953, his successors were equally anxious to avoid provocation and pursued a policy of detente designed to slow down western rearmament and delay the integration of West Germany into NATO.[143] There is no direct evidence, however, that either Truman or Eisenhower deterred the Soviets from specific actions at any stage in the Korean fighting by resort to atomic diplomacy. As for the Chinese, the latest research suggests that they entered the war conscious of the risks of atomic retaliation but aware of the limitations on American policy. As Ryan emphasises, Beijing was well informed about the main lines of debate in Washington and the problems, both political and technical, of employing the bomb in Korea or Manchuria.[144] While the shifting strategic balance may have led both Moscow and Beijing to wind down the war for fear of American retaliation in the spring of 1953, the main concessions were made before Eisenhower's supposed atomic brinkmanship.[145]

CONCLUSION

As Dingman argues, it proved difficult for US policy-makers to convert their sense that the bomb ought to be useful into any meaningful advantage: 'Nuclear weapons were not easily usable tools of statecraft that produced predictable results'. The Korean War offered the first example of 'the paradox of nuclear weapons: They confer upon those who possess them more responsibility for restraint than disposable power'.[146] The evidence suggests that, like the Americans, the Soviets and the Chinese kept the war limited rather than risk a wider global conflict which even at that early stage of nuclear development would have been hugely destructive. But it had been a close run thing. An American military disaster in the period December 1950 to April 1951 would inevitably have led to retaliation against China and perhaps a confrontation with the Soviet Union involving atomic weapons. Truman's determination to avoid a humiliating defeat was graphically demonstrated in April

1951 when complete bombs were deployed to the Far East. This was undoubtedly the most dangerous period in the Cold War before the Cuban Missile Crisis of October 1962. Britain, excluded from atomic planning, remained in fear of escalation until the armistice. As Acheson remarked in January 1951, the British were fixed to the tail of the American kite and concerned about 'where the kite is going'.[147] Despite British fears the fighting never spread, but the Korean experience of war was far from limited. If atomic weapons were not employed, three years of conventional bombing with high explosives and napalm had much the same effect. As the head of FEAF Intelligence, General Zimmerman, boasted in 1954, 'the degree of destruction suffered by North Korea, in relation to its resources, was greater than that which the Japanese islands suffered in World War II'.[148] What this actually meant was the death of over 2 million civilians, around a quarter of the population in a bombing campaign 'that went far beyond anything done in Vietnam in a conscious program of using air power to destroy a society'.[149] In this respect Korea was the first victim of mutual deterrence in the Cold War era which displaced great power conflict into Third World areas, ensuring that most of the suffering and dying would be experienced by others in what the United States chose to define as 'limited war'.

NOTES

1 M. Ridgway, *The Korean War*, New York, Doubleday, 1967, p. 11.
2 M. Trachtenberg, *History and Strategy*, Princeton, NJ, Princeton University Press, 1991, pp. 103–7.
3 M. Ridgway, Papers, Historical Record June/July 1950, File 16, US Army War College, Carlisle, Pennsylvania.
4 Trachtenberg, op. cit., pp. 107–11; B. Cumings, *The Origins of the Korean War, vol. 2, The Roaring of the Cataract*, Princeton, NJ, Princeton University Press, 1990, pp. 177–82; S. Wells, 'Sounding the Tocsin: NSC 68 and the Soviet Threat', *International Security*, Fall 1979, pp. 116–58. J.L. Gaddis, *Strategies of Containment*, New York, Oxford University Press, 1982, pp. 89–126, underestimates the rollback element in the new policy.
5 R. Pollard, 'The national security state reconsidered', in M.J. Lacey (ed.) *The Truman Presidency*, Cambridge, Cambridge University Press, 1989, pp. 227–32.
6 B. Cumings (ed.) *Child of Conflict*, Seattle, Wash., University of Washington Press, 1983, p. 49.
7 D. Acheson, *Present at the Creation*, London, Hamilton, 1970, pp. 420–2; C. MacDonald, *Korea: The War before Vietnam*, London, Macmillan, 1984, p. 38.
8 'Memorandum for the Record of State – Joint Chiefs of Staff Meeting',

24 January 1951, *Foreign Relations of the United States* 1951, vol. I, p. 35. Hereafter *FRUS*.
9 Trachtenberg, op. cit., pp. 111–15.
10 Paper drafted by the Policy Planning Staff, undated 1951, *FRUS*, 1951, vol. I, p. 67.
11 J.L. Gaddis, *Russia: The Soviet Union and the United States*, New York, Wiley, 1978, p. 199.
12 H.R. Borowski, *A Hollow Threat: Strategic Air Power and Containment Before Korea*, Westport, Conn., 1982, p. 191. See also W.S. Poole, *History of the Joint Chiefs of Staff, vol. IV, The Joint Chiefs of Staff and National Policy*, Washington, DC, 1979, pp. 10–12.
13 Trachtenberg, op. cit., pp. 120–1; Poole, op. cit., pp. 161–77.
14 MacDonald, op. cit., pp. 204–6.
15 Ridgway, *The Korean War*, pp. 34–6.
16 McKinley Kantor Papers, Notes for the Tame Blue Yonder, Miscellaneous Manuscripts, Package 32, Item 4, Box 70, Manuscripts Division, Library of Congress. Hereafter Kantor Papers. Kantor was the unofficial public relations man for SAC in Korea.
17 B. Kaufmann, *The Korean War Challenges in Crisis, Credibility and Command*, New York, 1986, pp. 37–8; R.J. Donovan, *Tumultuous Years: The Presidency of Harry S. Truman 1949–1953*, New York, Norton, 1982, p. 212.
18 C. MacDonald, *Britain and the Korean War*, Oxford, Oxford University Press, 1990, pp. 19–26.
19 ibid.
20 R.H. Ferrell (ed.) *Off the Record: The Private Papers of Harry S. Truman*, London, 1980, pp. 250–1; B. Bernstein, 'New light on the Korean War', *International History Review*, vol. 3, 1989, p. 272.
21 Trachtenberg, op. cit., pp. 117–18.
22 Cumings, op. cit., p. 711. Johnson had also wanted to allow Jiang Jieshi to bomb Chinese troop concentrations opposite Taiwan, raising the risk of Chinese intervention in Korea. See J.F. Schnabel and R.J. Watson, *History of the Joint Chiefs of Staff, vol. 3, pt 1*, Washington, DC, 1979, p. 511.
23 Trachtenberg, op. cit., p. 106.
24 P.H. Nitze, *From Hiroshima to Glasnost*, London, 1989, p. 110.
25 R.M. Anders, *Forging the Atomic Shield*, Chapel Hill, NC, 1987, pp. 22–4.
26 Trachtenberg, op. cit., p. 118. On this point see also R. Foot, *The Wrong War: American Policy and the Dimensions of the Korean Conflict*, Ithaca, NY, Cornell University Press, 1985, p. 37.
27 R. Dingman, 'Atomic diplomacy during the Korean War', *International Security*, vol. 13, p. 53.
28 ibid., pp. 51–2.
29 Recent research has emphasised the North Korean rather than the Soviet role in initiating the fighting in June 1950 and placed the event in the context of a Korean civil war which began in 1945. See C. MacDonald, 'Rediscovering history: new light on the unknown war', *Bulletin of Concerned Asian Scholars*, vol. 24, 1992, pp. 62–71.

30 A. Farrar-Hockley, *The British Part in the Korean War, vol. 1, A Distant Obligation*, London, HMSO, 1990, p. 354.
31 Dingman, op. cit., pp. 57–8. See also Poole, op. cit., pp. 150–1. According to this account Vandenberg emphasised that having the bombs in place would reduce by half the time required to mount a strategic air offensive. He was worried that the increasing diversion of transport aircraft to the Far East caused by the Korean fighting would create a bottleneck in supplying bombs to SAC squadrons in Britain in the event of a sudden outbreak of global war. He also wanted to disperse bomb stocks as a precaution against a new 'Pearl Harbor'.
32 Farrar-Hockley, op. cit., p. 354.
33 Trachtenberg, op. cit., p. 116.
34 Memorandum of Conversation, 25 June 1950, *FRUS*, 1950, vol. VII, pp. 158–9.
35 Summary of United States-United Kingdom Discussions on the Present World Situation, 20–4 July 1950, ibid., pp. 462–65.
36 CINCFE to Department of the Army, 18 September 1950, RG6: FECOM, General Orders, Folder 9, Korea, June-October 1950, Douglas MacArthur Papers, MacArthur Library, Norfolk, Virginia. Hereafter MacArthur Papers.
37 Cumings, op. cit., p. 749; Bernstein, op. cit., p. 261.
38 Bernstein, op. cit., p. 262.
39 Dingman, op. cit., p. 62.
40 M.A. Ryan, *Chinese Attitudes towards Nuclear Weapons: China and the United States during the Korean War*, New York, Sharpe, 1989, pp. 25–6.
41 Telecon Conference, 24 July 1950, RG9: Messages – Telecons, Box 113, MacArthur Papers.
42 Memorandum by Army Operations Division, 5 July 1950, RG319, Army Operations 091 Korea, Box 34A, Modern Military Records, US National Archives, Washington, DC. Hereafter USNA.
43 Dingman, op. cit., p. 62.
44 MacDonald, *Korea*, p. 206.
45 ibid., p. 229.
46 Dingman, op. cit., pp. 62–3.
47 ibid., pp. 63–4.
48 ibid., pp. 63–4.
49 Ryan, op. cit., pp. 32–3.
50 ibid., p. 34.
51 ibid., p. 35.
52 ibid., p. 35.
53 Schnabel and Watson, op. cit., pp. 348–9.
54 See B. Cumings and J. Halliday, *Korea: The Unknown War*, New York, Viking, 1988, p. 123; B. Kaufmann, *The Korean War: Challenges in Crisis, Credibility and Command*, New York, 1986; J.C. Goulden, *Korea: The Untold Story of the War*, New York, 1982, pp. 396–7. It is perhaps significant that the 'clarification' of Truman's remarks issued a few hours later stated all weapons 'were always considered for use' whenever US forces were in combat: Schnabel and Watson, op. cit., p. 349.
55 Anders, op. cit., pp. 89–90; Cumings and Halliday, op. cit., p. 123.
56 MacDonald, *Britain and the Korean War*, pp. 43–4.

The atomic bomb and the Korean War 201

57 Colonel Kalberer (SAC) to Kantor, 28 November 1950, Kantor Papers.
58 Dingman, op. cit., p. 67.
59 B. Bernstein, 'The Truman Administration and the Korean War', in M.J. Lacey (ed.), op. cit., p. 433.
60 For a discussion on this point see Foot, op. cit., pp. 113–30; Bernstein 'New Light', pp. 266–8; J.E. Wilz, 'The MacArthur Hearings of 1951: the secret testimony', *Military Affairs*, vol. 39, 1975, pp. 167-72.
61 H.S. Truman, *Memoirs, vol. 2, Years of Trial and Hope*, New York, 1956, pp. 435–6.
62 Memorandum of Conversation, 1 December 1950, *FRUS*, 1950, vol. VII, pp. 278–80.
63 Memorandum of Conversation, 19 December 1950, ibid., pp. 1,572–3.
64 MacDonald, *Korea*, pp. 69–70.
65 R.F. Futrell, *The United States Air Force in Korea 1950–1953*, New York, 1961, pp. 227–8.
66 Nitze, op. cit., p. 110.
67 D. MacArthur, *Reminiscences*, New York, 1964, pp. 437–8. He envisaged this as the preliminary to amphibious landings on both coasts of North Korea leading to final victory. According to Cumings he also wanted to support a Chinese Nationalist invasion of South China to overthrow the communist regime, op. cit., p. 748.
68 Memorandum by Colonel Creasey, Chief of Research and Experimentation, US Army Chemical Corps to Ad Hoc Committee on CEBAR, 24 February 1950, Recently Declassified Documents, Modern Military Records, USNA. According to Creasy one use considered was 'special interdiction', defined as the 'neutralization' of personnel and material without destroying infrastructure.
69 M. Schaller, *Douglas MacArthur: The Far Eastern General*, New York, Oxford University Press, 1989, p. 30, and D. Clayton James, *The Years of MacArthur, vol. 3, Triumph and Disaster*, Boston, Mass., 1985, pp. 578–9, doubt if the plans were ever formally submitted. W. Manchester, *American Caesar: Douglas MacArthur 1880–1964*, Boston, Mass., Little Brown, 1978, p. 627, suggests the plan was rejected by the JCS.
70 Schaller, op. cit., p. 221.
71 Cumings, op. cit., p. 750.
72 J.L. Gaddis, *The Long Peace: Inquiries into the History of the Cold War*, New York, Oxford University Press, 1987, p. 119.
73 Ryan, op. cit., p. 218.
74 Major General Bolte to General MacArthur, 21 December 1950, RG9: Messages – Personal July 1946–March 1951, Box 112, MacArthur Papers.
75 CINCFE to Department of the Army, undated December 1950, ibid.
76 CG FEAF to CG Fifth Air Force, 23 December 1950, RG9: Airforce – December 1950, Box 7, MacArthur Papers.
77 Trachtenberg, op. cit., pp. 123–4.
78 Memorandum by the Chairman of the National Security Resources Board (Symington) to the President, undated, *FRUS*, 1951, vol. I, pp. 21–33.
79 Kaufmann, op. cit., pp. 116–17.

80 Anders, op. cit., pp. 68–9.
81 Dingman, op. cit., pp. 69–71.
82 HQ USAF Washington to CG FEAF Tokyo, undated, RG9: Messages – Personal for Various People April 1948–April 1951, Box 112, MacArthur Papers.
83 The JCS had discussed this on 1 December and accepted that if Russian planes became involved it would be difficult to avoid use of the bomb. See note 62.
84 Dingman, op. cit., p. 72.
85 Ryan, op. cit., p. 220.
86 Anders, op. cit., p. 137.
87 Dingman, op. cit., p. 73; Cumings, op. cit., p. 731.
88 Schaller, op. cit., pp. 235–6.
89 Schnabel and Watson, op. cit., pp. 534–5. At this point MacArthur was pressing to widen the war in other ways including bombing Najin near the Soviet border and the North Korean hydro-electric plants which supplied power to Manchuria and Soviet Siberia as well as to North Korea.
90 CINCFE to Department of the Army, 7 February 1951, RG9: Messages – Outgoing July 1950-April 1951, Box 43, MacArthur Papers; Cumings, op. cit., p. 750.
91 Ryan, op. cit., p. 220.
92 Dingman, op. cit., pp. 75–6.
93 ibid., pp. 75–6. Memorandum by Charles Burton Marshall of the PPS, 7 May 1951, *FRUS*, 1951, vol. VII, pt 2, pp. 1,476–503.
94 Dingman, op. cit., pp. 75–6.
95 ibid., p. 76; Hickey to Stratemeyer, 11 May 1951, Ridgway Papers, Correspondence CINCFE T-Z, Box 19. Truman banned flights over Soviet installations at Dalian in Manchuria and Vladivostock in June 1950 for fear of provoking Russia. See Truman, p. 346 and Memorandum by Dean Rusk, 6 July 1950, *FRUS*, 1951, vol. VII, pp. 316–18.
96 Ryan, op. cit., pp. 51–2.
97 Dingman, op. cit., pp. 78–9.
98 P. Hayes, L. Zarasky and W. Bello, *American Lake*, Harmondsworth, Penguin, 1987, pp. 50–1.
99 Foot, op. cit., p. 154.
100 Ryan, op. cit., p. 223. The final wording is in R.J. O'Neill, *Australia in the Korean War, vol. 1, Strategy and Diplomacy*, Canberra, 1981, p. 465.
101 Dingman, op. cit., p. 79.
102 MacDonald, *Korea*, p. 131.
103 Ryan, op. cit., pp. 54–5.
104 Anders, op. cit., pp. 105–6.
105 Ryan, op. cit., p. 139.
106 JSPC Report, 12 June 1953, RG218, CCS383.21 Korea (3–19–45) Sec. 130, Box 44, Modern Military records, USNA. The navy had three carriers with an atomic capability by the autumn of 1950. See Poole, op. cit., p. 151.
107 Ryan, op. cit., pp. 141–2.
108 Memorandum by Army Operations Division, 5 July 1951, RG319 Korea 091 Army Operations, Box 38A, Modern Military Records, USNA.

109 Memorandum for Chief of Staff, 20 November 1951, ibid; Cumings, op. cit., p. 752.
110 Cumings, op. cit., p. 752.
111 ibid.
112 Ryan, op. cit., pp. 142–3.
113 Anders, op. cit., pp. 276–85.
114 Ryan, op. cit., pp. 14–45.
115 Anders, op. cit., p. 174.
116 Ryan, op. cit., p. 56.
117 MacDonald, *Korea*, pp. 240–4.
118 Ryan, op. cit., p. 56.
119 MacDonald, *Britain and the Korean War*, pp. 77–83.
120 Schnabel and Watson, op. cit., pp. 930–3.
121 Ryan, op. cit., pp. 56–7.
122 The tradition was established in David Rees, *Korea: The Limited War*, London, Macmillan, 1964, pp. 418–20. This was for long the standard account of the war.
123 S. Sherman, *First Hand Report*, New York, 1961, pp. 48–9.
124 S.F. Wells, jr, 'The origins of massive retaliation', *Political Science Quarterly*, vol. 96, 1981, pp. 47–51.
125 Trachtenberg, op. cit., pp. 128–31.
126 R. Foot, *A Substitute for Victory*, Ithaca, NY, Cornell University Press, 1990, pp. 166–83. The JCS History also notes that planning took place in a more optimistic atmosphere. See Schnabel and Watson, op. cit., p. 956.
127 Dingman, op. cit., pp. 80–6.
128 Foot, *Substitute*, pp. 161–4; Ryan, op. cit., pp. 62–5; Schnabel and Watson, op. cit., pp. 949–62.
129 Dingman, op. cit., p. 85.
130 ibid., p. 87.
131 Foot, *Substitute*, p. 178.
132 Adams, op. cit., p. 48.
133 Dingman, op. cit., p. 88. For other views of the atomic threat in this period see E.C. Keefer, 'President Dwight D. Eisenhower and the end of the Korean War', *Diplomatic History*, vol. 10, 1986, pp. 267–89; E. Friedman, 'Nuclear blackmail and the end of the Korean War', *Modern China*, vol. 1, 1975, pp. 75–91. There is a full discussion of the academic debate in Ryan, op. cit., pp. 152–6.
134 Dingman, op. cit., pp. 88–9.
135 R. Foot, 'Nuclear coercion and the ending of the Korean conflict', *International Security*, vol. 13, p. 112.
136 D.A. Anderton, *Strategic Air Command*, London, 1975, p. 45.
137 Foreign Office Minute, 5 December 1953, FO371/105574, FR1241/G. On US military planning for atomic attacks on China in the event of an armistice violation, see Ryan, op. cit., pp. 69–72. These plans accepted what Ridgway and Clark had always argued – that without atomic weapons the greater sanctions statement was nothing but bluff.
138 D.A. Mayers, *Cracking the Monolith*, Baton Rouge, Louisiana State University Press, 1986, pp. 97–150; C. MacDonald, 'The paradox of

power : Eisenhower and the New Look', in D. Carter (ed.) *Cracking the Ike Age*, Aarhus, 1993, pp. 11–34.
139 Foot, 'Nuclear coercion', pp. 102–4.
140 M. Hunt, 'Beijing and the Korean crisis', *Political Science Quarterly*, vol. 107, 1992, pp. 458–63.
141 The pilots were forbidden to fly over the sea or within 60 miles of the battlefront in case they were shot down and captured. They were even banned from speaking Russian on the radio, a restriction often ignored in the heat of battle. The Americans colluded by avoiding public discussion of Soviet participation. As Paul Nitze remarked, 'if we publicised the facts, the public would expect us to do something about it and the last thing we wanted was for the war to spread to more serious conflict with the Soviets': J. Halliday, 'A secret war', *Far Eastern Economic Review*, 22 April 1993, pp. 32–6.
142 J.L. Schecter (ed.) *Krushchev Remembers: The Glasnost Tapes*, Boston, Mass., Little Brown, 1990, p. 101.
143 Trachtenberg, op. cit., pp. 150–2.
144 Ryan, op. cit., pp. 165–90. For a supporting view of the technical difficulties of using the bomb against Chinese positions in Korea see D. Calingaert, 'Nuclear weapons and the Korean War', *Journal of Strategic Studies*, vol. 2, 1988, pp. 177–202.
145 Foot, 'Nuclear coercion', pp. 111–12.
146 Dingman, op. cit., p. 91.
147 Gaddis, *The Long Peace*, p. 121.
148 Futrell, op. cit., p. 644.
149 B. Cumings, *War and Television*, London, 1992, p. 158.

9 Restoring the 'special relationship'
The Bermuda and Washington conferences, 1957

Michael Dockrill

The Suez crisis left a bitter legacy of anti-American feeling in Britain, particularly in the ruling Conservative Party.[1] However, leading Conservative politicians were anxious to repair the breach with the United States as soon as possible, and with the final withdrawal of British and French troops from Egypt in December 1956 and the US Treasury's agreement to ease Britain's financial difficulties on 21 December, a restoration of the relationship seemed possible.[2] The Chancellor of the Exchequer, Harold Macmillan, and the Deputy Prime Minister, R.A. Butler, both contenders for the ailing Anthony Eden's position should the latter be forced to resign as Prime Minister, were strong advocates of repairing the 'special relationship' with the United States.[3] Macmillan had already suggested to the Cabinet on 22 November 1956 that 'we might hope to re-establish close political relations with the United States and secure a satisfactory and lasting settlement in the Middle East'.[4] On 10 January 1957 Macmillan became Prime Minister.

The recently appointed British ambassador to Washington, Sir Harold Caccia, had already reported, on 28 December 1956, that Eisenhower was anxious to restore the Anglo-American 'alliance'. The ambassador advised Whitehall that Britain 'should not run after' the Americans by seeking a summit meeting but should try to repair relations by cautious diplomacy at lower official levels. He concluded that 'if we thrust ourselves into the Councils of the Administration for reasons of prestige, we shall merely produce the same pitiful impression the French have so often made'.[5] In January he urged London to act quickly to restore the Anglo-American relationship while Eisenhower's prestige after his election victory was at its height.[6]

However, as eager as the British government was for reconciliation, it had no intention of appearing as a supplicant for American favour. If the Americans were anxious for improved relations with Britain, they would have to make the first approach to London. Moreover, the United States must fully accept Britain's straitened circumstances and should be prepared to take over some of the global commitments which the British could no longer afford to maintain. This should be accompanied by a major American effort to help Britain recover her prestige after the Suez humiliation, for which the United States was perceived in London as being largely responsible. Britain would be forced to make major cuts in her conventional forces, but Macmillan was determined that Britain should retain her great power status.[7] In this respect, Sir Ivone Kirkpatrick, the Permanent Under-Secretary at the Foreign Office, addressed a meeting of US State Department and British officials at the Foreign Office on 15 January 1957, the first low-level contacts between the two sides since Suez, making it clear

> that in the fight against Communism Britain was the only country which was really making a substantial contribution whether in Germany or in the Middle East or in Hong Kong. [Kirkpatrick] said that in the race with Germany for the world's markets, the German runner was running in shorts and running shoes, while [Britain was] carrying a rifle and a pack and running in army boots. We were prepared to continue carrying the rifle but the time had come to discard the boots.[8]

The first official ministerial contacts between Britain and the United States since Suez followed an invitation from Charles Wilson, the US Secretary of Defense, to Duncan Sandys, the newly appointed British Minister of Defence in the Macmillan government, to visit Washington at the end of January to discuss defence and nuclear issues. Sandys had been charged by Macmillan with the task of pruning Britain's inflated defence expenditures and had produced a draft defence White Paper which demanded drastic cuts in Britain's conventional forces and a greater reliance on nuclear deterrence as the mainstay of Britain's future defence posture.[9] The US Joint Chiefs of Staff demanded that Britain discuss her proposed cuts with the United States before she finalised them, particularly the proposed reductions in the British Army of the Rhine (BAOR), which the Joint Chiefs feared would encourage other NATO allies to follow her example.[10] For his part Sandys wanted greater British access to American nuclear know-how to enable Britain to sustain her nuclear programme.[11] As Caccia commented on 3 January, our acceptance as a great power now rests to a large extent on our having a military nuclear programme ... it would be difficult to overestimate at this juncture the importance of our having megaton as well as kiloton weapons.... Apart from these considerations our recent experience over Suez also brings out the danger if we were ever to leave our nuclear protection to the United States alone.... It is a sad but inescapable fact that our best chance of a satisfactory cooperation with the United States on the military side will depend on our proven capacity to produce the whole range of nuclear weapons.[12]

The Joint Chiefs, in a memorandum for Wilson on Britain's defence problems, insisted that

the national security interests of the United States must be paramount ... but a sympathetic understanding of the United Kingdom's economic problems is necessary.... Any United States support of the British defence establishment should be contingent upon (1) the United Kingdom honouring its present NATO commitments within its financial capability and (2) the determination that the United Kingdom continue to make the maximum effort in the field of defence.[13]

Sandys held a series of meetings with Wilson and American officials at the Pentagon on 28 and 29 January 1957. The British Minister of Defence welcomed a Pentagon offer of four squadrons (sixty missiles) of American Intermediate Range Ballistic Missiles (IRBMs), which would be deployed in Britain under a dual key arrangement and which would give Britain temporary security against the Soviet Union while she was building up her own Blue Streak missile force. The Americans also promised more rapid progress on the issue of exchanging information with Britain on nuclear research and development. Sandys gave the Americans a general outline of his draft Defence White Paper and told them that Britain intended to reduce BAOR from 80,000 to 50,000 men. 'The first duty of an ally', he told Wilson on 28 February, 'was to be solvent'.[14] That evening, invited to drinks with John Foster Dulles, Sandys, carefully primed before he left London by the Foreign Secretary, Selwyn Lloyd, to 'avoid giving the appearance of running after the Americans, but at the same time ... not to appear resentful' over Suez, took the opportunity, as he put it, to give Dulles 'the works', telling the Secretary of State that 'we all felt badly let down and it would require a big effort by the Americans to restore British confidence in them'.[15]

The Foreign Office's preference for a low-key approach towards mending fences and 'not to give [the] impression that we are in a hurry for [a] top level meeting',[16] was overtaken by Eisenhower's offer of 22 January to meet Macmillan in March in Bermuda, an invitation Macmillan readily accepted. He informed the Cabinet on 29 January that 'the invitation was a welcome sign that the United States government were now prepared to resume friendly relations with this country'.[17]

The Foreign Office was determined that the British delegation to Bermuda should be fully prepared for the meeting. T.W. Garvey was appointed secretary-general of the British delegation with instructions to assemble a team of officials from the various government departments to draw up briefs for the Prime Minister and to organise preliminary discussions between the US Embassy in London and the State Department in Washington to isolate 'the big issues' on which the leaders would concentrate at Bermuda. A ministerial group consisting of Macmillan, Selwyn Lloyd, Lord Salisbury, the Lord President of the Council, R.A. Butler, the Lord Privy Seal and Sandys was set up to review the briefs.[18]

A memorandum drawn up by Sir Patrick Dean, a Deputy Foreign Office Under-Secretary of State, entitled 'What we want to get out of the Bermuda Conference' listed the extensive demands to be made of the United States at Bermuda. These were, in Europe, American acquiescence in British force reductions in West Germany, help in settling the question of support costs for British troops in West Germany, endorsement of the Sandys–Wilson agreements, agreement over Britain's future defence and economic relations with Europe, agreement on policy towards German reunification and European security and agreement on policy towards the Soviet satellites, particularly Poland. In the Middle East, Britain wanted support for British policy towards Cyprus, agreement on at least a short-term regime for the Suez Canal which did not leave President Nasser with a potential stranglehold over Canal users, agreement on plans for the economic development of the Middle East countries, agreement on the means for securing Middle East oil supplies for the free world, and agreement on policy towards the Baghdad Pact. The British wanted a clear understanding of United States policies and intentions under the so-called Eisenhower Doctrine[19] and agreement on policy towards Egypt and Syria. Elsewhere there should be agreement on the need to keep Soviet influence out of Africa, co-ordination of intelligence activities, agreement over Kashmir, elucidation of America's attitude towards Communist China, agreement on east–west trade and, finally, agreement on the future of the United Nations and on disarmament.[20]

After reading this long shopping list, the Prime Minister felt that 'if we were to secure what we ourselves want, we are bound to make some concessions towards the American point of view', for example over Saudi Arabia, or Cyprus, or Libya or over troop reductions in Europe. 'Is there any way', he asked, 'in which we could be more forthcoming to King Saud, without prejudicing our position in the oil Sheikdoms? Equally can we make any reassuring noises to the Americans about their strategic shield in the Far East?'[21] However, the State Department accepted the British agenda for the conference, although Dulles added the future of British defence commitments and atomic energy to the list.[22]

On the issue of colonialism, on which Anglo-American relations had come to grief in 1956, the Colonial Secretary, Alan Lennox-Boyd, advised the Prime Minister that

> it is our reluctance to take a positive line about our colonial policy which gets us the reputation for being on the defensive and which encourages the Americans in their unsatisfactory beliefs... the Americans are still reluctant to accept the thesis that out Colonial policy is the best means of keeping the Communists out of Africa. This seems a good example of the traditional unconstructive American attitude to 'colonialism' which is one of the stumbling blocks to a fruitful understanding between our two countries... over the whole field of international politics. We must surely attack their attitude frontally and I hope you will find the opening you want when you discuss the item with the President.[23]

The Foreign Office suggested that Britain emphasise the need to keep the Soviet influence out of Africa, arguing that 'This is the right context in which to put any such problem to the Americans who regard their foreign policy as essentially a struggle against the Communist bloc'.[24]

British resentment at her treatment by the United Nations organisation during the Suez crisis was also reflected in the demand that Britain and the United States co-operate to reduce the increasing influence of the Afro-Asian group in the United Nations General Assembly which had made the Assembly 'irresponsible and incapable of international justice and fair dealing'.[25] As a result of this Afro-Asian pressure the General Assembly was no longer an instrument of western policy.

On defence issues, the Ministry of Defence urged that Britain should obtain a firm offer of the IRBMs promised to Sandys in January.[26] The Chancellor of the Exchequer, Peter Thorneycroft, and Sir Frederick Hoyar Millar, who replaced Kirkpatrick as Permanent Under-Secretary at the Foreign Office on 4 February, persuaded the Ministry of Defence not to publish the defence White Paper until 4 April 1957, since, in Hoyar Millar's words, its immediate effect 'will be, however wrongly, to create the impression abroad that we no longer regard ourselves as a first-class power, that we are pulling out of Europe and that we are completely dependent on the United States'. He added that early publication 'will forfeit a great deal of American sympathy and support which will be so necessary for us if we are to maintain our position in international affairs in the future'.[27] In the United States, the State Department's bureau of economic affairs urged Dulles not to object to Britain's proposed defence cuts since 'such representations would not be welcomed by the British, and more important.... it would not be in our interest to press them to maintain commitments beyond their means'.[28]

As the conference approached, Britain's economic decline preoccupied the State Department, which prepared a lengthy paper on the subject based on a series of meetings between various officials. The Americans were convinced that Britain possessed few of the attributes which had in the past enabled her to assume the role of front-rank world power and found little evidence that her decline could be arrested. However, American officials were prepared to concede that she still retained 'certain elements of strength and influence of vital importance to the United States' – a stable political and social system, her trading, banking, investment and technological skills and the high quality of her military forces. Her leadership of western Europe was important for United States' interests, and the dominions still remained a source of power to the United Kingdom. Moreover, there was now little Anglo-American conflict over Britain's diminishing colonial empire and she would, despite Suez, retain some influence in the Persian Gulf and with the Baghdad Pact countries. In conclusion, the State Department insisted that, for all these reasons, it was essential for the United States to maintain the alliance with Britain. It recommended that the United States should endeavour to strengthen Britain by developing mutually consistent policies in areas of the world where their interests coincided, by encouraging regular Anglo-American consultation, by helping

Britain to fulfil her responsibilities for the maintenance of world peace and stability and by urging the United Kingdom to participate in moves towards European integration.[29]

The State Department also produced a number of position papers on specific Anglo-American issues. One, on the Middle East, stated that 'we believe that the maintenance of the British position in the Middle East, to the extent feasible, is in the interests of the Free World.... We recognise that the British problem in the Middle East has been adversely affected by recent developments in the area' and by her 'straitened circumstances'. This meant that the United States 'is called on to play a larger role' in the area than hitherto. Despite Britain's hostility towards Colonel Nasser – believing 'it is virtually impossible to do business with' him – the USA's long-term policy in the Middle East was to restore close American–Egyptian relations. This would provide Washington with the necessary influence over Nasser to persuade him to agree to a satisfactory settlement of the Suez issue and to draw him away from his close relationship with the Soviet Union. 'The United States would be happy to deal with a more reasonable Egyptian Government than the one headed by Nasser', but 'it would be unrealistic ... to believe that the time had come when the Nasser regime could be toppled easily and with any prospect of replacement by a stable, friendly successor government.... The United States will not become involved in attempts to unseat the Nasser regime'.[30]

The Americans were prepared to join the military committee of the Baghdad Pact, although not the pact itself, to seek guarantees for the maintenance of the flow of Middle East oil through new pipelines, to keep British needs in mind in dealing with 'the limitation and eventual elimination of nuclear test explosions' and to approve the deployment of four squadrons of IRBMs to the United Kingdom by 1960. They would also inform the British that 'we are sympathetic to their efforts to bring their military and economic commitments into balance with their resources'. The Americans were not prepared, however, to support any British initiative in Europe which would prejudice 'the integrity of the six-nation basis for European unity' (i.e. the Common Market), and would resist any attempt by Britain 'to curtail the General Assembly's role in the peace and security field and restore it to the Security Council'. They also insisted that Britain should continue her moratorium on Communist China's admission to the United Nations.[31]

Eisenhower, Macmillan, Selwyn Lloyd and Dulles arrived in Bermuda on 20 March 1957 and met at an informal dinner in

Macmillan's suite at the Mid-Ocean Club that evening. Both sides agreed on the need to secure 'an acceptable Suez Canal settlement'. There was a certain amount of desultory conversation: Macmillan wondered whether it was worth Britain's while to continue to hold Cyprus given the increasing range of aircraft and he complained about American and world pressure on the Europeans to embark on hasty decolonisation, reminding Eisenhower of the importance to Europe of Africa, Malaya and Singapore. For his part the President wondered whether the populations of colonial territories might be persuaded to accept autonomy instead of independence if the former was made attractive to them. Dulles insisted that the United States would remain in Okinawa while Macmillan told the Americans that Britain was considering abandoning Hong Kong, which had brought Britain needless expense while benefiting only Chinese traders. Dulles dwelt on the importance of that colony to the west, complained about Britain's policy towards Communist China and urged Britain to join with the United States in holding on to insular and peninsular positions around the communist land mass in Asia. He added that if Britain would agree to align her policy with the United States by abandoning both its recognition of Beijing and its support for China's admission to the United Nations, the United States might 'be able to help it [Britain] hold it [Hong Kong]'. According to Dulles, 'the P.M. said that this might be considered' while 'Lloyd said that he had come to feel that American policy [towards Communist China] was more right [sic] than ours'.[32]

The first plenary session of the conference took place on Thursday 21 March at 10.30 p.m. Macmillan's carefully prepared opening statement declared that 'the meeting was taking place at a critical moment in world history', when 'immediate problems of great difficulty' needed to be solved. In the intense struggle between the forces of good and evil – between Communism and freedom – Britain 'intended to stay in the game and to play her part in defending freedom, though it might be necessary for her to reorganise her resources so as to make her strength more effective'. Unless Britain and the United States were associates in this effort 'the game might be lost'. Macmillan admitted that 'it may be that both the United Kingdom and the United States had made mistakes in the handling of the [Suez] situation last autumn', while of Nasser he said, 'It's like Mussolini – he started as an Italian patriot. He ended up as Hitler's stooge.... Let's make it clear that we'll get him sooner or later.... Well, that's over-spilt milk. Don't let's cry over it – still less wallow in it'. He exhorted the Americans: 'you need us: for ourselves; for the Commonwealth; and as leaders of Europe'. He appealed to the United States to help Britain secure a fair settlement of the Suez Canal issue since if not 'it would then take much longer to repair the rift which had opened between the two countries'.

In reply Eisenhower stated that it was essential 'to continue the old and well tried wartime association. It must never be forgotten that the fundamental struggle was between atheistic Communism and civilisation based on moral law'. He was 'anxious that there should not later be any repetition of recrimination' between the two countries and promised that the United States would work to ensure a satisfactory solution of the Canal issue and work out how to help the United Kingdom sustain some of her responsibilities.[33]

In the afternoon of 21 March 1957 the conference proper began with a long discussion of Middle East issues such as the internationalisation of the Gulf of Aqaba, the payment of Canal dues and the compensation payable to the Suez Canal Company for the loss of its ownership of the Canal.[34] Selwyn Lloyd believed that if the problems of Aqaba and the Gaza Strip could be solved, the Middle East situation as a whole would improve: the Israelis no longer felt hemmed in, the United Nations Emergency Force (UNEF) had been established and the extent of Soviet penetration of the Middle East had been revealed to the world. Moreover 'the bubble' of Egyptian military power had been 'pricked': 'the other Arab countries could see this and there was no chance of Nasser's becoming a new Saladin'. He continued that 'it was said that these events had undermined British influence in the area, but it was easy to exaggerate this. Little had happened that would not have happened in any case'. Britain would now concentrate on consolidating her position in the Gulf and above all in Kuwait, with its enormous oil reserves, where Britain would take 'prompt action' if Nasser tried to organise a coup against the sheikh.

Eisenhower failed to persuade the British to help the United States build up King Saud of Saudi Arabia as a counterweight to Nasser by finding a solution to the Buraimi Oasis dispute. Macmillan insisted that Britain could not accept any settlement of this dispute which betrayed her friends in the Gulf. He added that 'despite recent events, he felt that the United Kingdom still had an important role to play in the Middle East'. Eisenhower proposed the setting up of a standing group of Anglo-American officials to consider common problems in the Middle East. Dulles thought it particularly important to get agreement on aims and methods as the United States would have to play a more active role in the area in future.

It was agreed that the two foreign ministers should organise 'close US and UK liaison in this field'.

The two delegations could not reach agreement over Cyprus, where Eisenhower wanted the British to allow Archbishop Makarios to return to the island from exile. Selwyn Lloyd doubted that this would be a sensible move given that Makarios 'had shown himself to be a ruthless political leader and was largely responsible for the build-up of terrorism on the Island'.[35]

On the Suez Canal the United States agreed to press on Egypt an interim settlement about the payment of the Suez Canal dues. A meeting of Anglo-American officials during the morning on this subject had proposed that if Cairo rejected a reasonable settlement, all economic aid to Egypt should be withheld, and Britain and the United States should introduce measures in the Security Council against Egypt and go to the International Court to seek its opinion about the rights of passage of Israeli shipping through the Canal.[36]

The plenary on 22 March dealt with Anglo-European relations, with German reunification, with relations with the Soviet Union and with the Far East. There was little meeting of minds on many of these issues. While Dulles told the British that 'in the economic field he would like to see Europe itself draw close together' since 'weakness in Europe tends to create dependence on the U.S.', Selwyn Lloyd dwelt on the incompatibility of the European Economic Community's high tariff policy with Britain's free trade philosophy. Dulles rejected a British plea for a meeting on German reunification with the Soviets during the summer. While the British Foreign Secretary wanted the United States 'to give ground on the trade side' with Communist China, on Chinese admission to the United Nations he admitted that 'the change in composition of UN membership has changed many UK views. He said now that we have no Western working majority, the Chinese capacity for making mischief would be even greater'.[37]

In the afternoon Eisenhower confirmed the Sandys–Wilson agreement on the deployment of American IRBMs to Britain, but the details still had to be worked out and this was to prove a long and contentious process. He also promised that Washington would not put forward any proposals on nuclear test suspension without consulting Britain first and proposed an Anglo-American declaration that both countries would limit their testing of nuclear weapons 'to a level not exceeding the point of radioactive safety'. Macmillan gave an outline of Britain's forthcoming Defence White Paper and would give no undertaking not to reduce BAOR although he agreed to leave the strategic reserve of 5,000 men in West Germany.[38]

At the final meeting on Saturday 23 March it was clear that Britain would not get her way over United Nations reform. The Prime Minister 'felt that the U.N. should be downgraded and perhaps regional associations upgraded'. Dulles complained of Macmillan's 'negative attitude' towards the organisation and pointed out that 'the American people were a moralistic, and perhaps sentimental people, but they had a real faith and belief in the U.N., and U.S. policy remained faithful to it'. The British side finally agreed to an American proposition that the United Nations was not to be written off as 'a hopeless failure' and 'their broad conclusion was that, so long as British and American policies were aligned and [they] tried to think out the issues which were arising before the crisis came, we ought to be able to keep a good working majority in the Assembly'.[39]

With the end of the conference on 24 March, Macmillan informed the Australian Prime Minister, Sir Robert Menzies, of his satisfaction with the outcome:

> To sum up, I think there is no doubt that as far as the President is concerned things are back on the old footing. Dulles, who by temperament and conviction is a sort of Gladstonian Liberal, who dislikes the nakedness of facts, has also come a long way, but I think he lags a little behind the Head of State.[40]

He telegraphed Butler:

> I don't know whether I am being too optimistic, but I feel two things have been achieved. First, we have not been in the dock. On the contrary the Americans have been rather apologetic about their position. Second the personal relations between myself and the President have been established on a level of confidence which is very gratifying.[41]

Earlier Eisenhower thought that 'the meeting was by far the most successful international meeting I have attended since World War II'. 'We got some definite answers for once' and 'the atmosphere' had been one 'of frankness and confidence'.[42]

While the atmosphere between the two countries had certainly improved considerably, Bermuda had not resulted in many major substantive agreements: indeed the two governments had differed over a number of issues in the Middle and Far East, and these continued to divide the two during the summer. Nor had the conference created any permanent mechanism which bound the two countries more closely together. It is clear, however, from his subsequent actions, that Macmillan was seeking an opportunity to build on the good feelings engendered at Bermuda to convert the relationship into something more than occasional meetings between the two heads of government and between Anglo-American officials. This opportunity presented itself with the successful orbit of the Soviet Sputnik around the globe on 4 October 1957, which greatly shook American confidence in their technological superiority over the Soviet Union.

Even before Sputnik, Macmillan had sent his principal private secretary, Frederick Bishop, to Washington between 2 and 7 September to see Dulles and to try to inject a new momentum into the alliance. 'It was', the Prime Minister wrote to the US Secretary of State, 'as near as we could get together ourselves'. Bishop, later described by the State Department as 'a nice guy and a friend',[43] commented that 'he [Dulles] was really very friendly and very outspoken and I must confess I came away with an immense regard for his ability and grasp'. Dulles now appeared to have become converted to Macmillan's view about the importance of the United Nations and even talked about setting up a new organisation which would genuinely work towards disarmament. However, the real motive for Bishop's visit was revealed when both men discussed the possibility of another Anglo-American summit meeting to review outstanding issues.[44]

In October, shortly after the Sputnik orbit, Macmillan followed up Bishop's initiative by writing to Eisenhower to ask 'what are we going to do about these Russians?' The Prime Minister suggested that if the two countries 'join together and direct the efforts of the free world we can build up something that... will wear them [the Soviets] out and force them to defeat themselves'. Eisenhower responded enthusiastically and Macmillan suggested an immediate meeting to 'talk over the general situation and see whether we cannot together initiate some new approach to all international problems – military, economic and political'.[45]

Dulles told a meeting of State Department officials in mid-October (at which Selwyn Lloyd, who was visiting the United States on United Nations business, was present) that he felt that the UK was beginning to feel 'dissatisfied with our recent alliance' and was

> seeking to improve it.... We are in a psychological crisis in the world and P.M. Macmillan's offer and suggestions give us an opportunity and a peg for constructive action.

Livingston T. Merchant, the US ambassador to Canada, was recalled to Washington to act as co-ordinator of the American position at the forthcoming conference. In a memorandum of 19 October he wrote that 'the request by Mr Macmillan for the meeting constitutes a supreme effort by the British to regain their wartime position of exclusive and equal partnership with the United States'. Merchant continued that, as a result of Sputnik,

> Mr Macmillan has found himself, quite possibly unexpectedly, dealt a reasonably good hand.... I believe and feel strongly that it is in our interest to readmit the British to a far closer and more responsible partnership with us. They have more to contribute to our survival than any other nation, with the possible exception of Canada.[46]

A pre-conference briefing paper for the President prepared by Dulles called for the attainment of 'a true sense of community' so that 'our joint efforts... revive confidence in the determination of the United States and the United Kingdom to provide coordinated leadership for the free countries'. Dulles wanted machinery to be set up for 'ensuring closer collaboration with the United Kingdom' with Dulles and Selwyn Lloyd acting as

> agents for monitoring the execution of decisions taken, supervising the progress of collaboration between the heads of other Departments and Agencies in the country concerned, and deciding for reference to you and the Prime Minister in future any subjects or problems which you and the Prime Minister should discuss and decide'.[47]

Macmillan arrived in Washington on 23 October and, together with Selwyn Lloyd, met Eisenhower and Dulles and their respective advisers three times in plenary sessions at the White House between 23 and 25 October. Dulles and Selwyn Lloyd also met separately and discussed a wide range of global issues.[48] At the first plenary at the White House on the morning of 24 March, Eisenhower declared that 'we should develop ourselves as better partners almost to the point of operating together under one policy' and wanted the two countries to exalt 'the spiritual and ethical values which support our type of society'. Dulles said that 'for centuries past Christian civilisation had dominated the world. It now seemed possible that unless present trends could be reversed, the world would be submerged by Communism', while Macmillan thought that 'free nations have large assets and if they could hold out long enough there was hope that Marxist doctrine would eventually cease to dominate the minds of the Russian people and their threat to the Free World would fade'.[49]

The outcome of all this rhetoric was 'The Memorandum of Understanding' and 'A Declaration of Common Purpose' which Eisenhower and Macmillan initialled on 25 October. Macmillan informed the Cabinet on 14 November that the latter was

> a declaration of interdependence, recognising that the old concept of national self-sufficiency is out of date and that the countries of the Free World can maintain their security only by combining their resources and sharing their tasks. The United Kingdom and the United States Governments have agreed to act henceforward in accordance with this principle.[50]

The memorandum called for the maximum practical co-ordination of policies in political, economic and defence issues and in psychological warfare. To this end it was agreed that there should be consultations between the two foreign ministers from time to time, and that working groups of officials should be set up to co-ordinate policy at all levels. There should be greater Anglo-American cooperation than hitherto in weapons research and development, and in the direction of resources to specific projects to ensure effective utilisation of funds, facilities and skilled labour. American legislative restrictions which were blocking vital research and development in missiles and submarines and preventing the transfer and exchange of nuclear materials for military purposes and exchanges of weapons information would be removed. Specific weapons design and development should be allocated between the two countries and, to save British talent, the United States should supply complete weapons systems to the United Kingdom under dual key arrangements, which would enable Britain to modify or terminate the production of such weapons in the United Kingdom.[51]

Altogether nine working groups of officials were set up in Washington 'to achieve', in Eisenhower's words, 'the maximum political co-ordination of the policies of our two Governments in the political, economic, defence, scientific and psychological warfare fields', with the foreign policy teams dealing with specific areas such as the Middle East, Africa, Algeria and Saudi Arabia. Both leaders emphasised the need for the re-invigoration of confidence in NATO, the South East Asia Security Organisation (SEATO) and the Baghdad Pact, by greater Anglo-American leadership in these organisations. The British and Americans were also to examine the pooling of resources and the provision of a more balanced collective force structure in NATO.[52]

Macmillan believed that the Washington Conference had been a resounding success in building on the foundations laid at Bermuda and in creating an intricate machinery for future close co-operation between the two. All the arrangements made for joint working groups and officials remained confidential lest 'sensitive Americans' (and presumably the French) objected that the United States was giving Britain 'special treatment'.[53]

The Bermuda and Washington conferences appeared to have successfully re-established the so-called Anglo-American 'special relationship', which had been so badly dented during the Suez crisis. Indeed the Washington conference placed the alliance on a new footing, with Britain having achieved much of what had eluded her during the early 1950s – almost wholehearted American support for her nuclear and thermo-nuclear programmes and close collaboration at working levels between Whitehall and Washington on joint policies across the globe. It seemed that the close wartime partnership, now greatly mythologised, had been completely re-established.[54] From the American perspective, as Walworth Barbour, the Chargé d'Affaires at the US Embassy in London, put it at the end of December, while 'in recent years the United Kingdom has obviously been a declining power', she 'is still a dependable and "natural ally" and likely to remain so in the foreseeable future'.[55] Indeed given the firm convictions of both Eisenhower and Dulles about the evils of communism, and given that Britain was the United States' most loyal Cold War supporter, neither was likely to allow Britain to retreat into embittered neutralism after Suez without making strenuous efforts to re-establish the alliance. Macmillan and his Cabinet were more than ready to respond to American advances.

Thus by the end of 1957, aided by the shock of Sputnik to the American psyche and Eisenhower's basic Anglophilism, Britain had forged a new Anglo-American partnership which, on the surface at least, appeared to be one based on equality and not on subordination. But in the long run, despite Eisenhower's fine words after Bermuda, and as many American observers suspected, the revitalised Anglo-American relationship did not help Britain to escape from her predicament. Her continued failure to stabilise her economy made her usefulness as an American ally increasingly tenuous since this failure impacted on her overseas and defence policies. She had been forced, by the events of 1956 and 1957, to accept American leadership in the Middle and Far East.

By 1970 Britain had retreated from the bulk of her overseas positions, and had become a supplicant for membership of the European Economic Community, an option she had spurned in the late 1950s. Her nuclear deterrent was scarcely 'independent' at all, given that during the 1960s she became more or less totally dependent on American technology and hardware to sustain it and, in any case, would never have used it without prior American assent.[56] Indeed it was Macmillan's deal with Kennedy over Polaris in 1962 – much acclaimed at the time as a major British success – which set the seal on Britain's role as a United States' nuclear satellite. Britain's subordinate status, which had become glaringly apparent by the events of 1956, was, in the end, and despite Macmillan's optimism, confirmed by the Bermuda and Washington conferences.

NOTES

1 For instance, see Walter P. Hoffman, American consul, Birmingham, to the State Department (despatch), 1 November 1956, on the bitter feelings of Midlands Conservatives towards the United States, State Department decimal files, Box 2477, 611.41/3-156. On the Suez crisis see K. Kyle, *Suez*, London, Weidenfeld & Nicolson, 1991.
2 D.B. Kunz, *The Economic Diplomacy of the Suez Crisis*, Chapel Hill, NC, University of North Carolina Press, 1991, pp. 153ff.
3 W. Scott Lucas, 'Divided we stand: the Suez Crisis of 1956 and the Anglo-American Alliance', Unpublished PhD thesis, University of London, 1990, p. 419.
4 Quoted in ibid., p. 424.
5 Caccia, desp 411, 28 December 1956, PREM11/2189.
6 Caccia, desp 23, Guard, 22 January 1957, FO371/126083.
7 Dulles to American Embassy, London, 18 January 1957, State Department, Box 2477, 611.41/3–156; J.H.A. Watson minute, 29 December 1956 and minute by Selwyn Lloyd for Prime Minister, 1 January 1957, FO371/126042; Caccia, 1 January 1957, FO371/126682.
8 Kirkpatrick to Caccia, 18 January 1957, FO371/126042.
9 For details of the Defence White Paper of 1957, see S. Navias, *Nuclear Weapons and British Strategic Planning, 1955–1958*, Oxford, Clarendon Press, 1991, pp. 134ff. For Eisenhower's 'New Look' defence policy, on which Sandys's reforms were modelled, see S. Dockrill, 'Eisenhower's "New Look": a maximum deterrence at a bearable cost', in M. Handel (ed.) *Economic and Non-rational Dimensions in Strategy*, US Army War College, forthcoming.
10 Memorandum for Secretary of Defense by Admiral Radford, 19 January 1957, Defense Department Papers, Washington, DC.
11 For full details of Anglo-American nuclear relations during this period, see T.J. Botti, *The Long Wait: The Forging of the Anglo-American Nuclear Alliance, 1945–1958*, Westport, Conn., Greenwood Press, 1987, pp. 137ff.

12 Caccia, 1 January 1957, FO371/126082.
13 Memorandum for Secretary of Defense by Joint Chiefs of Staff, 19 January 1957, Joint Chiefs of Staff Papers, Washington, Box 31.
14 Record of Anglo-American meeting at the Pentagon, 28 January 1957. For details of other meetings see FO371/129306. See also Botti, op. cit., p. 176.
15 Minister of Defence to Prime Minister and Foreign Secretary, 28 January 1957, FO371/126683.
16 Kirkpatrick to Caccia, 18 January 1957, FO371/126683.
17 Quoted in Navias, op. cit., p. 193; A. Horne, *Macmillan, 1957–1986, vol. II*, London, Macmillan, 1989, pp. 21–2. The French Prime Minister, Guy Mollet, and the French Foreign Minister, Pineau, were invited to visit Washington on 26 February, thus providing Eisenhower and Macmillan with a welcome excuse not to invite the French to Bermuda, ibid.
18 Macmillan to Eisenhower, 7 February 1957; Foreign Office to Washington, 12 and 13 February 1957; FO371/128328.
19 For the Eisenhower Doctrine, which the President announced to Congress on 5 January 1947, see S.E. Ambrose, *Eisenhower the President, 1952–1968*, London, Allen & Unwin, 1984, pp. 381–3.
20 Dean memorandum, undated (?21 February 1957), FO371/129328. See also Dulles to Barbour, London, 1 February 1957, State Department decimal files, Box 2477, 611.41/3-156. Many of these issues were already under discussion between Caccia and the State Department, whose agreed recommendations would be presented to the Bermuda Conference. Garvey minute, 8 March 1957, FO371/129329.
21 Garvey minute, 5 March 1957, FO371/129328.
22 Garvey minute, 21 February 1957, FO371/129328.
23 Alan Lennox-Boyd to Macmillan, March 1957, FO371/129329
24 J.H.A. Watson minute, 15 February 1957, FO371/129307.
25 Selwyn Lloyd 'expressed certain reservations about the line taken' in this proposal. Garvey minute, 8 March 1957, and minute by Lloyd, FO371/129329.
26 Powell to Caccia, 8 March 1957, FO371/129329. Eisenhower ordered that the United States should conclude no agreement with Britain on the transfer of the IRBMs before the Bermuda conference, *Foreign Relations of the United States*, 1955–57, vol. XXVII, pp. 690–4. Hereafter *FRUS*.
27 Hoyar Miller to Selwyn Lloyd, 15 March 1957; R.W.S. Hooper minute, 20 March 1957, FO371/129307; Caccia, 14 March 1957, FO371/129399. On his return from Bermuda, Macmillan, Norman Brook and his Cabinet Office staff revised the White Paper to reduce 'alarm and despondency abroad', or as Macmillan put it to Sandys, 'I hope you will feel that the bits we have put in with an eye on the foreigner do not spoil your main theme': R.W.J. Hooper minute, 20 March 1957, FO371/129307; Prime Minister to Duncan Sandys, 29 March 1957, FO371/129308. Both before and during the Bermuda Conference the Americans pressed Britain to delay the publication of the White Paper to enable its contents to be discussed with the United States and the other NATO allies.
28 Thorsten V. Kalijarvi, Bureau of Economic Affairs, State Department

222 *Michael Dockrill*

to Under Secretary, 11 February 1957, State Department decimal files, Box 2477, 611.41/3-156.
29 M.C. Parsons jr. to Reinhardt, 13 March 1957, enclosing memorandum, 'Current Appraisal of the U.K.–U.S. Relationship', State Department decimal files, Box 2478, 6111.41/3-157.
30 Bermuda conference position papers, undated (early March 1957), Eisenhower Papers, Abilene, Box 9.
31 'Summary Briefing Paper: Bermuda: Folder for the President', undated (March 1957), Eisenhower Papers, Box 9; 'Folder for the President, Reduction of British Overseas Commitments', Eisenhower Papers, Box 9.
32 Memorandum of a dinner conversation at the Mid-Ocean Club, Bermuda, Dulles Papers, Box 113; *FRUS*, 1955–57, vol. XXVII, pp. 707–8.
33 Horne, op. cit., p. 24; 'British Record of the First Plenary Session of the Bermuda Conference', 21 March 1957; PREM 11/1838. 'Notes' by the Prime Minister of opening statement at Bermuda, 29 March 1957, CAB 129/86; *FRUS*, 1955–57, vol. XXVII, pp. 709–11. The American version does not contain Macmillan's more dramatic language.
34 'British Record of the First Plenary Session', 21 March 1957, PREM 11/1838.
35 The Cabinet eventually agreed to release Makarios from his internment in the Seychelles.
36 'British Minutes of the Second Plenary Meeting at Bermuda', 21 March 1957, PREM11/1838; *FRUS*, 1955–57, vol. XXVII, pp. 712–18.
37 *FRUS*, 1955–57, vol. XXVII, pp. 722–33.
38 R.W.J. Hooper minute, 26 March 1957, FO371/12933; *FRUS*, 1955–57, vol. XXVII, pp. 736–42, 748–52. At a NATO meeting in December 1957 the Allies agreed to a reduction in BAOR to 63,000–64,000 to be reached by 1 April 1958. Navias, op. cit., p. 184.
39 *FRUS*, 1955–57, vol. XXVII, pp. 753–7; Prime Minister to the Lord Privy Seal, 25 March 1957, FO371/129330.
40 Macmillan to the Australian Prime Minister, 25 March 1957, PREM 11/1789.
41 Prime Minister to the Lord Privy Seal, London, 25 March 1957, FO371/129330.
42 Diary entry by the President, 21 March 1957, *FRUS*, 1955–57, vol. XXVII, pp. 718–21.
43 'International Meetings: President Eisenhower's visit to London Briefing 27 August–2 September 1959', Eisenhower Papers, Box J.
44 Bishop, Washington, to Prime Minister, 10 September 1957; Bishop to Caccia 11 September 1957, PREM 11/2190.
45 *FRUS*, 1955–57, vol. XXVII, pp. 785–9.
46 *FRUS*, 1955–57, vol. XXVII, pp. 789–96.
47 'Summary Briefing Paper... The Macmillan Conference', by Dulles, 21 October 1957, Eisenhower Papers, Box 7.
48 Horne, op. cit., pp. 55–6. For details of the Dulles–Lloyd talks see *FRUS*, 1955–57, vol. XXVII, pp. 835–9.
49 'White House Meeting, United States Record, 10.30 a.m., 24 October 1957', Eisenhower Papers, Box 20; Commonwealth Relations Office to

The Bermuda and Washington conferences, 1957 223

British High Commissioners, 6 and 8 November 1957; PREM 11/1725. See also *FRUS*, 1955–57, vol. XXVII, pp. 816–21.
50 'Anglo-American Cooperation', note by the Prime Minister, 14 November 1957, CAB129/90.
51 'Memorandum of Understanding between the President and the Prime Minister of 25 October 1957', FO371/129326.
52 C. Burke Elbrick, State Department, to Dulles, 29 October 1957. State Department decimal files, Box 2478, 611.41/5-157; Eisenhower to Strauss, 5 November 1957, Eisenhower Papers, Box 5; Eisenhower to James H. Douglas, 5 November 1957, Eisenhower Papers, Box 1.
53 Sir Gilbert Laithwaite, CRO, to Sir Savile Garner, UK High Commissioner, Ottawa, 12 November 1957, FO371/129326.
54 G. Warner, 'The Anglo-American Special Relationship', *Diplomatic History*, vol. 13, 1989, pp. 479–99.
55 Walworth Barbour, London to State Department, 30 December 1957. State Department decimal files, Box 2478, 611.41/5-157.
56 See Navias, op. cit., p. 142.

Index

Abyssinian crisis 4, 83–104, 116, 158, 161–2, 166
Acheson, Dean 175, 182, 185, 191, 198
Adams, Sherman 194, 195
Adamthwaite, Anthony 129
Aden 87–8
air disarmament 74–5
Albania 115–16
Aldrovandi, Count 48
Alexander, King of Yugoslavia 5, 109–12, 124
Anderson, General Orville 178
Anglo-American special relationship 205–20
Anglo-Italian Agreement 140
Anschluss 23, 140, 163–6
Anti-Comintern Pact 143
appeasement 6, 9–10, 129, 153–68
Astor, William Waldorf 3, 44, 45, 49
atomic weapons 7, 174–98
Attlee, Clement 104, 156, 177, 183, 184
Auer, Lujevit 108, 113
Austria 164
Austro-German customs union scheme 23
Avenol, Joseph 160, 166

B29 bombers 178–9, 182, 186
Backhouse, Admiral Sir Roger 94
Badham-Thornhill, Colonel 46
Badoglio, Marshal 95, 96
Baghdad Pact 208, 210, 211, 218
Baker, Philip Noel 24–5

Balbo, Air Marshal 96
Baldwin, Stanley 4, 84–5, 88, 91, 101–2
Balfour, Arthur James, 1st Earl 13
Bank of England 15, 16–17, 19–20
Bank for International Settlements 19
Barbour, Walworth 219
Bauer, Monsignor Ante 110, 111
Beck, Peter J. 6
Belgium 161
Beneš, Eduard 117, 153–4
Bérard-Jordana Agreement (1939) 143–4
Berlin Blockade 191
Bermuda Conference (1957) 7–8, 208–16, 219–20
Bernstein, B. 184
Bishop, Frederick 216
Blum, Léon 130, 131, 139, 140
Board of Trade 11–14, 20–21, 26
Bolivia 62
Bolte, General Charles 180
Bonnet, Georges 141, 144, 153
Bowles, Chester 193
Boyce, Robert 2
Bradley, General 185, 188, 189, 195
Briand, Aristide 20–21, 22
British Army of the Rhine (BAOR) 206, 207, 215
British disarmament policy 67–9, 73–6
British foreign policy management and co-ordination 2, 9–35
Brüning, Heinrich 63, 67, 70–72

Index

Bulgaria 160
BUSTER-JANGLE tests 193
Butler, Richard Austen 153, 154, 157, 165–6, 205, 208

Caccia, Sir Harold 205, 206
Cadogan, Sir Alexander 131, 137, 143, 154, 164
Cambon, Roger 139
Campbell, Ronald 100
Canada 91
Carr, E.H. 19
Cavagnari, Admiral 99
Cave Committee 14
Cecil of Chelwood, Lord Robert 90, 157–8
Central Intelligence Agency (CIA) 193
Chamberlain, Sir Austen 17, 161
Chamberlain, Neville: Abyssinian crisis 85, 98–9, 103; appeasement 6, 155, 158–60, 162–8; British foreign policy management 33–4; Czech problem 153; Spanish Civil War 129, 135, 137, 138, 140, 141, 142–3, 144
Chang Hsueh-liang 44
Channon, Sir Henry 154
Chatfield, Lord 89–90, 92–3
China: Korean War 182–90; Manchurian crisis 2–3, 42–57, 63; relations with Italy 96; and United Nations 212, 214; United States policy 212
Church of England 118–19, 121
Churchill, Winston 6, 84, 156, 157, 166, 196
Ciano, Galeazzo 138, 142
civil aviation, internationalisation 64, 71, 75
Clark, Mark 191, 194
Clemenceau Letter 61
Collins, General J. Lawton 180, 183–6, 195
colonialism 209
Commercial Attaché Service 11–12, 13, 15
commercial intelligence 12–15, 33
Committee of Imperial Defence: Defence Requirements Sub-committee 162; Sub-Committee on Abyssinia 86
Condor Legion 133
Conservative Party: and League of Nations 6, 156–8, 162; special relationship with US 205
Constantinople Convention (1888) 86
Consular Service 10–11, 12, 15
Cooper, Alfred Duff 140
Corbin, Charles 132, 138, 142
Corfu Declaration (1918) 109
Croat Peasant Party 109, 110, 114, 120
Crowe, Sir Eyre 11, 12, 13, 14, 17, 21, 25
Cumings, B. 192
Cunningham, Viscount 103
Curzon, Lord George Nathaniel 14, 15–16
Cyprus 208, 209, 214
Czechoslovakia 117–18, 153–4, 164–5

Daladier, Edouard 129, 131, 140, 141, 144, 153
Dalton, Hugh 103, 156
Dean, Gordon 188, 193
Dean, Sir Patrick 208
Declaration of Common Purpose 218
Delbos, Yvon 131, 132, 133
Department of Overseas Trade (DOT) 13–15, 17, 23, 30
Deutschland (battleship) 134, 136
Dilks, David 167–8
Dingman, R. 196, 197
disarmament 3, 24, 60–79
Dockrill, Michael 7–8
Dollfuss, Engelbert 116
Dominions Office 24, 26
Drummond, Sir Eric 23
Dulles, John Foster 7, 194–6, 207, 209–17
Duncan Committee (1969) 34

Eastes, A.E. 47
Economic Advisory Council (EAC) 27, 32

Index

Eden, Anthony: Abyssinian crisis 87, 97, 98, 103; Foreign Office reforms 9, 33–4; and League of Nations 156–7; Spanish Civil War 131, 132, 133–4, 137–8, 139
Egypt 90–92, 94, 96, 97, 100, 208, 214
Eisenhower, Dwight D. 7, 174, 180, 194–7, 205, 208, 211–19
Eisenhower Doctrine 208
Ethiopia *see* Abyssinian crisis
European trade preferences 20–21, 23–4

Far Eastern Command 177, 180, 186
fascism 62–3
Finland 154–5
Fisher, H.A.L. 94
Fisher, Sir Warren 9–10, 16–18, 25, 29, 31–3, 35
Fisher, Admiral Sir William 89, 91, 94–5, 103
foreign loans 16–17, 19–20
Foreign Office: economic affairs 9–35; Eden reforms 9, 33–4; politico-economic intelligence section 21–3, 29–33
Four Power Conference on Danubian reconstruction (London, 1932) 28
France: Abyssinian crisis 88–9; alliances with Italy/Soviet Union (1935) 65; appeasement 129; Disarmament Conference 63–6; European trade proposals 23–4; Franco-German customs union 63–4; possible invasion by Italy 99; Spanish Civil War 129–46; tank disarmament 73
Franco, General Francisco 132, 133, 136, 137, 139–44
Francqui, Emile 23
free trade 20–21
Front Populaire 130, 132

Gamelin, General Maurice 131, 140
Garstin, C.E. 48
Garvey, T.W. 208
Gaselee, Steven 30
Geddes, Sir Auckland 14

Geneva Disarmament Conference (1932–34) 3, 24, 60–79
Geneva Gas Protocol (1925) 63, 98
Germany: Abyssinian crisis 90–91; Austro-German customs union 23; disarmament 60–61; Disarmament Conference 63, 66–7, 70–73, 78; economic affairs 12; Franco-German customs union 63–4; National Socialists 62–3, 70; rearmament aspirations 65–7; reparations levied by Britain 15–16, 17–19; Spanish Civil War 133–5; withdrawal from League of Nations 78, 161
Gibson, Hugh 69
gold standard, abandoned 25–6
Graeco-Bulgarian dispute 160
Graham, William 20–21, 24
Grandi, Dino 71, 139
Greece 137, 160
Grey, Sir Edward (Grey of Fallodon) 11, 13
Gröner, General 66
Grün, George 1
Guam 180, 190
Gulf crisis 83
Gwatkin, Frank Ashton 28, 29, 30–33

Haas, Robert 50, 52
Haile Selassie, Emperor 95, 161
Halifax, Edward Lord 131, 140, 142–3, 154, 160, 164–5, 167
Hamilton, Sir Horace 31
Hardinge, Lord 11
Headlam, Arthur Cayley, Bishop of Gloucester 111–12, 121
Hemming, Francis 133, 138, 141
Henderson, Arthur 18–19, 22, 24–5
Herriot, Edouard 63, 71
Hitler, Adolf 78–9, 112, 161, 164
Hlond, Cardinal 115
Hoare, Sir Samuel 88, 90, 102
Hoare-Laval Pact (1935) 85, 95, 102, 104
Hoeven, L. Van der 56
Hong Kong 212
Hoover, Herbert Clark 69, 70
Hopkins, Sir Richard 18

Index 227

Horne, Sir Robert 16
Howard Smith, Charles 27, 31, 137
Hoyar Millar, Sir Frederick 210
HUDSON HARBOR 192
Hutzinger, General 91

Intermediate Range Ballistic Missiles (IRBMs) 207, 210, 211, 214
Ireney, Bishop of Dalmatia 121
Italo-Yugoslav Agreement (1937) 120
Italy: Abyssinian crisis 4, 83–104, 116, 158, 161–2, 166; alliance with France (1935) 65; and China 96; Disarmament Conference 70; Nyon Conference 136–7; possible invasion of France 99; relations with Yugoslavia 119; sanctions against 84–8; Spanish Civil War 133–5, 138–9, 142; withdrawal from League of Nations 161; *see also* Mussolini, Benito

Japan: Abyssinian crisis 90; air/tank disarmament 73; Disarmament Conference 63, 73, 76; Manchurian crisis 42–57, 63; withdrawal from League of Nations 161
Jeftic, Yugoslavian Prime Minister 112–13
Jiang Jieshi (Chiang Kai-shek) 181
Johnson, Louis 177–8, 182
Johnston, Sir Reginald 48
Jordan, Nicole 130

Kellogg Pact 65, 165
Kennedy, John F. 8, 220
Kent, Peter C. 5
Kim Il Sung 196
Kirkpatrick, Sir Ivone 206
Koo, Wellington 44–5, 51–2
Korean War 6–7, 174–98
Korosec, Father 117
Krushchev, Nikita 197
Kuwait 213

Labour Party 156, 159
laissez faire 11, 15, 16, 26

Lampson, Sir Miles 45–6, 51
Lausanne Conference (1932) 28, 63
Laval, Pierre 89, 96
League of Nations: anti-appeasement 6, 153–68; Czechoslovakia 153–4; Finland 154–5; Geneva Disarmament Conference (1932–34) 3, 24, 60–79; as inter-governmental organisation 160–63; Manchurian crisis 42–57; Preparatory Commission for the Disarmament Conference 61–2; reform 163; sanctions 84–8, 158, 162–3; tariff truce 20–21
League of Nations Union (LNU) 155, 156, 158–9, 168
Leeper, Rex 137
Léger, Alexis 131, 139, 140, 144
Leipzig (cruiser) 134
Leith Ross, Sir Frederick 18, 26, 27, 28, 32
LeMay, General Curtis 177, 179, 184
Lennox-Boyd, Alan 209
Lessona, Alessandro 96
Lester, Sean 153
Libya 93, 95–6, 100, 209
Lindt, Dr August 50
Lithuania 165
Litvinov, Maxim 164, 166
Lloyd, Selwyn 207–8, 211, 213, 214, 216–17
Locarno Treaty 61, 65, 66
Loiseau, Charles 109
London Naval Treaty 70
Loper, General Herbert 183
Loveday, Alexander 23
Lytton, Lord 3, 43–4
Lytton Commission 2, 42–57

Ma Chanshan 48–50
MacArthur, General Douglas 177, 180–90
McCormick, Admiral Lynde D. 193
McCoy, General 48
MacDonald Plan (1933) 69, 76–9
MacDonald, Callum 6–7
MacDonald, Ramsay: British foreign policy 19, 22–5; disarmament 63–4, 69–72, 76–9

Index

Macek, Vladko 110, 114, 120–21, 122
Macmillan, Harold: Anglo-American relations 7–8, 205–6, 208–9, 211–20; appeasement 157
Madariaga, Salvador de 61–2
Maffey Report 96
Makarios, Archbishop 214
Malta 89, 91, 94, 102
Manchurian crisis 2–3, 42–57, 63
Marshall, Charles Burton 189
Massigli, René 139
Matignon Agreements 130
Matthews, Francis 177–8
Memorandum of Understanding 218
Menzies, Sir Robert 215
Merchant, Livingston T. 217
Middle East 211, 213, 218
militarism 62–3
Ministry of Agriculture and Fisheries 26–7
Mongols 53
Monteiro, Armindo 139
Montgomery-Massingberd, Field-Marshal Sir Archibald 97
Morewood, Steven 4
Moscatello, Monsignor 110–11
Moss, George 3, 46–8, 49, 51–7
Mounsey, Sir George 29, 131, 137
Müller, Hermann 66
Munich Conference 153–4
Murray, Gilbert 155
Mussolini, Benito: Abyssinian crisis 83–5, 87, 93, 95, 96, 99–102; Albania 115; disarmament 70, 79; on League of Nations 161; Spanish Civil War 129, 137–42

Nasser, Gamal Abdel 208, 211, 212, 213
nationalism 62–3
NATO 175, 197, 207, 218–19
Nehru, Pandit (Jawaharlal) 195
Neurath, Baron Constantin von 161
Nichols, General Kenneth 180
Nish, Ian 2
Nitze, Paul 178, 180, 183, 185

Non-Intervention Agreement (Spain) 131
Non-Intervention Committee (Spain) 132, 133–41
non-intervention (Spain) 129–46
Norman, Montagu 17, 23
NSC-68 174–8, 194
Nyon Conference (1937) 136–7

O'Donnell, General Emmett 181, 186
Okinawa 188, 190
O'Malley, Owen 29–30
Operation BIG STICK 196
Oppenheimer, Sir Francis 11
Ormsby-Gore 100
Ottawa Imperial Conference (1932) 28

Pace, Frank 193
Pacelli, Cardinal Eugenio 108, 115, 117
Palestine 90
Papen, Franz von 63, 71
Paraguay 62
Paul, Prince of Yugoslavia 112, 113, 117, 120, 123
Paul-Boncour, Joseph 153
Paul-Boncour Plan 65
Peace Ballot (1935) 158–9
Pelligrinetti, Cardinal 108, 123
Pelt, Adrianus 56
Perth, Lord 142
Pétain, Marshal Philippe 144
Peter of Yugoslavia 112
Phipps, Sir Eric 103, 141
Pius XI 4, 108, 111, 112
Plymouth, Lord 133, 137
Poland 165, 208
Portugal 131, 133, 134–5, 140, 144, 145
Pu Yi 48
Puzzo, Dante 130

Quai d'Orsay 130, 131, 133, 139
Quartararo, Rosario 4, 92–4

Radic, Stephen 109
Rae, Sir James 31–2
RANGER tests 191

Reading, Lord Rufus 26
Regia Aeronautica 89, 93, 94, 95, 102
reparations 15–16, 17–19, 26–7; Lausanne Conference (1932) 28, 63
Reynaud, Paul 144
Richardson, Dick 3
Ridgway, General Matthew 174, 189, 190, 191
Robertson, Esmonde 1
Romania 130
Royal Navy: Abyssinian crisis 85–8, 92–3, 94–5, 103; Spanish Civil War 134
Runciman, Walter 13
Ryan, M.A. 197

Salisbury, Lord 208
Sandys, Duncan 206–7, 208, 210
Sargent, Sir Orme 131, 137, 139
Saric, Archbishop of Sarajevo 122
Saud, Abdul Aziz Ibn 209, 213
Saudi Arabia 209, 218
Schuschnigg, Kurt von 116–17
Selby, Sir Walford 25, 31
Serb Orthodox 109, 111, 112, 118–23
Shorrock, William 129
Siege of Bilbao 136
Simon, Sir John 28, 29, 31–2, 159
Sinclair, Sir Archibald 104
Singapore 101, 212
Snowden, Philip 18–19
South East Asia Treaty Organisation (SEATO) 218
Soviet Union: alliance with France (1935) 65; atomic weapons 174–8; Disarmament Conference 63, 70; Gulf War 83; invasion of Finland 154–5; Korean War 178–81; Sputnik 216–17, 219
Spanish Civil War 5–6, 129–46
Sputnik 216–17, 219
Stalin, Joseph 175, 177, 178, 195, 196, 197
Stamp, Sir Josiah 18
Steel-Maitland, Sir Arthur 14
Steele, Archibald 50
Stepinac, Bishop 120–21, 122
Stimson, Henry L. 71

Stone, Glyn 5
Stoyadinovich, Milan 113, 119–24
Strategic Air Command (SAC) 176–8, 184
Stresa Conference 29
Suez Canal: Abyssinian crisis 85, 86, 90, 91, 98; Suez crisis 7, 205–9, 212–13, 214
Sugimura Yotaro 42
Swinton, Lord 135
Symington, Stuart 187
Syria 90, 208

Taiwan 181–2
tank disarmament 73–4
Tardieu, André 71, 72
Tardieu Plan (1932) 64, 71
Taylor, A.J.P. 103, 166
Temperley, A.C. 71
Thomas, J.H. 24
Thomas, Sir Shenton 101
Thorneycroft, Peter 210
Trachtenberg, Marc 194–5
Trades Union Congress 101
Treasury: financial attachés 28; and Foreign Office 9, 15–20
Treaty of Mutual Assistance (1923) 67
Treaty of Versailles (1919) 60–61, 66, 71, 72–3
Truman, Harry S. 174–5, 177–9, 182–90, 193, 197
Turkey 99, 137
Tyrrell, Lord 18

United Nations: Afro-Asian group in General Assembly 209–10; Emergency Force (UNEF) 213; reform proposals 215
United States: Anglo-American special relationship 205–20; Chinese policy 212; Disarmament Conference 69–70; economy 21; Gulf War 83; Korean War 6–7, 174–98
USS *Champlain* 191

Vaïsse, Maurice 3, 60, 79

230 *Index*

Vandenberg, General Hoyt 176, 179, 180, 181–2, 185, 187–8
Vansittart, Sir Robert: British foreign policy management 24, 29, 32; Spanish Civil War 131, 137, 139, 143
Varnava, Serb Orthodox Patriarch 121, 122
Vatican 108–24
Venezia Giulia 114–15

Wall Street crash 62
Walters, Frank 160
Wark, Wesley 100
Warner, G.R. 30
Washington Conference (1922) 62, 63, 70
Washington Conference (1957) 7–8, 217–20
Wauchope, Sir Arthur 91

Weir, Major-General George 89, 95–6
Wellesley, Victor 2, 12–16, 21–2, 24–5, 27, 29–30, 32, 35
Wheeler-Bennett, John 71
Wilson, Charles 206, 207
Wilson, Sir Horace 32, 33–4
Winter War 154–5, 160
Woo Sao-fong 52, 54, 55
World Economic Conference (1932) 29
World recession 62

Yoshida Isaburo 45
Young, Owen 18
Yugoslavia: concordat (1935–37) 4–5, 108–24; invasion by Italy 99; relations with Italy 119; Spanish Civil War 130

Zimmerman, General 198
Zog, King of Albania 115

For Product Safety Concerns and Information please contact our EU representative GPSR@taylorandfrancis.com
Taylor & Francis Verlag GmbH, Kaufingerstraße 24, 80331 München, Germany

www.ingramcontent.com/pod-product-compliance
Lightning Source LLC
Chambersburg PA
CBHW062141300426
44115CB00012BA/1998